VYGOTSKY'S LEGACY

VYGOTSKY'S LEGACY

A Foundation for Research and Practice

MARGARET E. GREDLER
CAROLYN CLAYTOR SHIELDS

THE GUILFORD PRESS
New York   London

Printed in the United States of America

This book is printed on acid-free paper.

Last digit is print number: 9 8 7 6 5 4 3 2 1

Library of Congress Cataloging-in-Publication Data

Gredler, Margaret E.
Vygotsky's legacy : a foundation for research and practice / by Margaret E.
   Gredler and Carolyn Claytor Shields.
      p. cm.
   Includes bibliographical references and index.
   ISBN-13: 978-1-59385-491-1 (hardcover : alk. paper)
   ISBN-10: 1-59385-491-9 (hardcover : alk. paper)
   1. Educational psychology. 2. Learning, Psychology of. 3. Vygotskii, L. S.
(Lev Semenovich), 1896–1934. I. Shields, Carolyn Claytor. II. Title.
   LB1060.G734 2007
   370.15—dc22
                                                        2007016140

#1237766967

About the Authors

Margaret E. Gredler, PhD, is Professor of Educational Psychology and Research at the University of South Carolina. Dr. Gredler's articles and presented papers address applications of learning theory and self-directed learning. *Learning and Instruction: Theory into Practice*, her book on learning theories and related instructional strategies, is in its fifth edition.

Carolyn Claytor Shields, PhD, is Associate Professor in the Richard W. Riley College of Education at Winthrop University in Rock Hill, South Carolina. Dr. Shields teaches courses at the undergraduate and graduate levels in educational psychology, human growth and development, and research. Her research interests include learning theories and their educational applications and methods for developing conceptual thinking.

Preface

Lev Semenovich Vygotsky, in his brief 10-year career, constructed an elegant and detailed description of the development of human consciousness. However, only a few of his ideas have reached present-day theorists and practitioners in psychology and education. Therefore, the purpose of this text is twofold. First is to explicate Vygotsky's thinking, illustrating both his process orientation and the logical coherence of his ideas. Second is to discuss the implications of this thinking for current research and practice, including relevant examples.

The book begins with the sociohistorical context in which Vygotsky worked (Chapter 1). Then the discussion of Vygotsky's ideas is organized into four parts. The first part, "General Principles," discusses Vygotsky's views on research and his research method, the mastery of one's thinking through the appropriation of cultural signs and symbols, and the outcomes of cognitive development and the role of education (Chapters 2, 3, and 4). Part II, "Major Cultural Signs," includes speech and thinking (Chapter 5) and the formation of concepts (Chapter 6). Part III, "The Cycle of Development," describes Vygotsky's view of the structure and dynamics of human development (Chapter 7) and an overview of his stable and critical periods of development (Chapter 8). Part IV, "Some Implications of Vygotsky's Theory," describes pervasive themes in Vygotsky's work and implications for society (Chapter 9). In addition to these discussions, examples are presented throughout the

chapters, and each chapter concludes with a discussion of the implications for educational practice.

   Implicit in the narration are the insightfulness of Vygotsky's thinking
as he addressed the flaws he found in the thinking of others, his belief in
the ability of humans to master their thinking and emotions, and his
focus on the ways that the individual child develops the meanings of cultural signs and symbols.

   This book is intended for all who are interested in Vygotsky's ideas,
including teachers and students who are involved in teacher education,
educational psychology and research, and cognitive development.

Contents

PART II. MAJOR CULTURAL SIGNS

PART III. THE CYCLE OF DEVELOPMENT

PART IV. SOME IMPLICATIONS OF VYGOTSKY'S THEORY

VYGOTSKY'S LEGACY

1

Introduction

> Every inventor, even a genius, is always the outgrowth of his
> time and environment. His creativity stems from those needs
> that were created before him, and rests upon those
> possibilities that, again, exist outside of him.
> —VYGOTSKY (1930, in van der Veer & Valsiner, 1991, p. xi)

Lev S. Vygotsky—literary scholar, theorist, clinician, and researcher—lived
and worked in a time very different than our own. The Soviet Socialist
Republic had undergone both a revolutionary change in government and
a civil war and faced major economic and social problems. Moreover,
Vygotsky himself experienced recurring bouts of tuberculosis as he
worked to develop a comprehensive understanding of human development and the role of society in that process. Factors that influenced his
work include the sociohistorical context, his talents, and the methods
and analyses through which he developed his cultural–historical theory.

THE SOCIOHISTORICAL CONTEXT

In any society, the influence of social and political actions on the discipline of psychology and education may be either indirect or direct. In
most societies, the psychologist, usually unconsciously, subscribes to the
assumptions of his or her culture as "natural" and "self-evident" (Bauer,
1952, p. 10). In such situations, the influence of society's values is indi-

1

rect. For example, the United States views performance on paper-and-pencil tests as an important measure of the effectiveness of schooling. Studies of teaching and instruction typically include such tests to determine learning outcomes.

In a totalitarian state, persons acting with either an implicit or an explicit theory make policy decisions that intervene in psychological theory and research (Bauer, 1952). The tsars of Imperial Russia implemented various measures in an effort to limit the autonomy of science and thereby restrict the scientific spirit. The problem for the tsars was that the scientific spirit includes a critical attitude toward authority, a relativist (not absolute) interpretation of nature and society, and an individualistic approach to solving problems. Particularly troubling for the authoritarian government was the belief in the ultimate wisdom of the rational capabilities of humans (Vucinich, 1970, p. xi). For the tsars, permitting the expression of rational thinking was to risk serious questioning of the doctrine that supported tsardom and the mysticism of the Russian Orthodox Church.

Although the tsar was forced to abdicate in 1917, scientific freedom remained an elusive goal. The Bolsheviks, a small revolutionary cadre led by Lenin (Vladimir Ulyanov), took control of the government in October of that year. Discussed in this section are the postrevolutionary beliefs that influenced psychology, Vygotsky's entry into psychology, and the triumph of *partiinost*.

Postrevolutionary Beliefs

During the decade of the 1920s, three different beliefs influenced Russian psychology. They are the spontaneous belief in the automatic creation of a new society, the concept of *partiinost* introduced by Lenin, and Marxist–Leninist ideology.

Belief in the Creation of the "New Man"

The fall of the tsar in 1917 unleashed widespread euphoria and visionary hope about the transformation of human nature (Hosking, 2001, pp. 434–435; McLeish, 1975, p. 3). The basis of this utopian speculation was the assumption that human nature was basically good and that bad institutions and evil political systems had prevented the expression of the good (Stites, 1989, p. 226). Therefore, removal of the bad institutions plus the spontaneous action of the people acting on the good within themselves could transform society (p. 226).

Elimination of the nobility, therefore, was believed to "*guarantee* the appearance of a new kind of person: the liberated proletarian [worker] with new morals, culture, and rules of conduct" (McLeish, 1975, p. 15, italics added). People would be more harmonious and socially conscious than people trapped in a society scarred by social conflict (Hosking, 2001, p. 434). In addition, many had faith in the natural sciences to assist in this effort. The belief was that humans could create miracles by the free play of rational intellect (Bauer, 1952, p. 49).

The first generation of Soviet (postrevolutionary) scholars shared this belief (Kozulin, 1984, p. 15). For them, the revolution was "a cosmic event that would change everything from technology to the very nature of people, their conduct, and [their] culture" (p. 15). Alexander Luria, Vygotsky's colleague and a world-renowned neurologist, noted in his memoirs that "my entire generation was infused with the energy of revolutionary change . . . the Revolution freed us to discuss new ideas, new philosophies, new social systems" (Luria, 1979, pp. 17–18).

The theoretical intensity and sense of mission in Vygotsky's work is one example (Bakhurst, 1991, p. 60). He was passionately devoted to his cause, which was to develop a science of man. In a letter to one of his students, he stated, "What can shake a person looking for truth? How much inner light, warmth, support there is in this question itself!" (Vygotsky, cited in van der Veer & Valsiner, 1991, p. 16).

Vygotsky's textbook on psychology (completed in 1924) also expressed an almost unlimited faith in the plasticity of humans that can be developed by organizing the social environment in a particular way (see van der Veer & Valsiner, 1991, pp. 54–56). In a later essay, he prophesied that "the new society will create the new man" [and] "in the future society, psychology will indeed be the science of the new man" (Vygotsky, 1982–1984/1997l, pp. 342–343).

Years later, Alexander Luria (1979) noted that it was very difficult, after so long a time, to recapture the enormous enthusiasm of the research group (Vygotsky, Luria, Leont'ev, and five student-collaborators) in their weekly discussions and research projects. However, the group did devote "almost all of its waking hours to our grand plan for the reconstruction of psychology" (p. 52).

The Concept of Partiinost

A major aspect of the Russian cultural heritage from the time of the tsars stemmed from the concept of total loyalty to the government. Included in the concept were placing the common good above one's personal welfare and engaging in active obedience by willingly relinquishing one's abilities and possessions in service to the state (Black, 1979, cited in Valsiner, 1988, p. 29).

One influence of this credo on psychology was an emphasis on the study of collective and interindividual psychological events (p. 21). An example is the Russian interpretation of Darwin's theory of evolution. The central Darwinian principle is that new species appear and either adjust to the environment or die out. It is sometimes expressed as "survival of the fittest." However, "the law of tooth and nail in the animal kingdom at large" ran counter to the Russian view of mutual cooperation in the collective (Joravsky, 1961, p. 22). Disagreeing with interindividual competition as the engine of evolution, the Russian view identified mutual aid and the cooperation of organisms as essential in adapting to the environment. The Russians maintained that only those animals that acquire habits of mutual assistance would undoubtedly be the fittest (Valsiner, 1988, p. 33).

The concept of *partiinost* built on the foundation of cooperation and the importance of the welfare of the group. The term, which means "partyness" or partisanship, was "Lenin's strange new word for the influence of collective interests on cognition" (Joravsky, 1989, p. 193).

However, Lenin's concept of *partiinost* went beyond simply respecting collective interests. One is the obligation, when analyzing or estimating any event, to directly adopt the viewpoint of a definite social group (McLeish, 1975, p. 187). Lenin defined it as an enthusiastic acceptance of the view provided by the party in power (Valsiner, 1988, p. 75). That is, *partiinost* is an organizing concept that certifies any perspective, once the party approves it (p. 76).

The Bolshevik leadership asserted that *partiinost* was not a fixed set of principles but an interpretation based on reason and science. Nevertheless, history indicates that the decisions about acceptable theories were capricious. A perspective or theoretical system may win official Party approval today, only to be labeled the opposite tomorrow (p. 76). The result in psychology in the late 1920s was intense competition among various perspectives for the symbolic approval of the Party. Each attempted to demonstrate ways in which it was truly Marxist, while portraying other views as "non-Marxist" (p. 76).

Marxist–Leninist Ideology

Karl Marx and Frederick Engels proposed fundamental principles of economics, politics, and history that they also applied to science (Graham, 1987, p. 26). Their principles, known as Marxism, are important in Russian psychology because Lenin and the Bolsheviks used them to make judgments about acceptable and unacceptable forms of research and scholarly inquiry.

The Marxist social commentary depicted a class struggle between capitalists (exploiters) and workers (the exploited). It also predicted that the dynamics of capitalism would lead to its downfall (Bauer, 1952; Cole, 1952–1956; Joravsky, 1961). Lenin, however, developed a more militant version of Marxism. He maintained that "revolutions do not simply come, they have to be made" (Tucker, 1985, p. 6), and he demonstrated this belief in the October 1917 takeover of the government.

Marxism also described the world as consisting of matter that is a combination of processes. Examples are light and the movement of positive and negative particles in an atom. In other words, everything is in flux; there are no autonomous static entities (McLeish, 1975, p. 264).

In addition to explaining the nature of the world, Marxism includes three other principles adopted by Lenin. One is that human knowledge flows from the objective world, which determines the categories by which people think. Moreover, because reality is defined as the material world, Lenin also asserted that science (not other disciplines) must discover facts about that reality. He labeled the use of ideas or other mental approaches to describing reality as subjective and, therefore, untrustworthy. Consistent with that view, Lenin supported the use of objective research methods and quantitative rather than qualitative methods (Bauer, 1952, p. 49). In the 1920s, for example, a Party leader described Ivan Pavlov's laboratory research on conditioned reflexes as "a weapon from the arsenal of materialism" (Joravsky, 1989, p. 259).

Second, consistent with the belief that knowledge flows from the objective world is the belief that thinking is influenced primarily by the social environment (Graham, 1987). In other words, society, appropriately structured, could create "the new man." A corollary of the role of the social environment is that individuals raised in different cultural environments will differ in both the content of their thinking and the ways that they think. This view became a foundational principle of Vygotsky's cultural–historical theory.

A third Marxist principle that became prominent in Soviet social science research is that practice is the criterion of theory. Researchers must confirm or validate their theoretical principles through implementation. In the Soviet Union, this principle meant that researchers should establish a clear social purpose for their work by linking it to social needs (Graham, 1987, p. 57). Vygotsky, for example, worked with children with mental or physical disabilities, and his analyses of their difficulties informed his work on his cultural–historical theory. In addition, he referred to applied psychology as the stone, formerly rejected by the builders, that was becoming "the head stone of the corner" (Vygotsky, 1982–1984/1997l, p. 305). Practice, in other words, "reforms the whole methodology of the science" (p. 306). Practice both establishes the tasks to be implemented and informs psychology on the formulation of its laws.

Marx and Engels referred to their philosophy as materialism, which reflected the focus on the material world as the source of knowledge. Lenin referred to the Bolshevik adaptation as "dialectical materialism" to reflect the emphasis on both the objective world and the process of change (Graham, 1987). Lenin also applied this philosophy to discredit and remove scholars whom the Party identified as using ideas, not experimental data, as the basis for understanding the world. In other words, the Bolsheviks used Marxism as both "a political control and intellectual organizer" (McLeish, 1975, p. 2). Bauer (1952) noted that fighting the battles of everyday politics and economics in a scholarly arena may seem out of place to anyone who is not familiar with the history of Bolshevism. However, "standard procedure in the Bolshevik manual of tactics [was] to use every weapon available, from the prosaic to the most esoteric" (p. 32).

Vygotsky's Entry into Psychology

Vygotsky's entry into an academic career in psychology was, in several ways, an accident of history. First, upon graduation from a private Jewish gymnasium, he had earned a gold medal for the highest grades in all his subjects. That should have guaranteed him university admission, given that the tsarist government only permitted 3 to 5% of university admissions to be Jewish (Vucinich, 1970). However, the year that Vygotsky applied, the selection method was changed to a lottery system. Fortunately, he was selected and pursued a law degree at the University of Moscow. Law was one of the few professions that allowed a Jewish graduate to live and work outside of the Pale of Settlement (the area assigned to the Jewish population) (van der Veer & Valsiner, 1991).

While enrolled at the University of Moscow, Vygotsky also completed studies in history and philosophy as well as courses in psychology and education at the Shanyavsky People's University. These studies provided an important foundation for his then unknown later career. After graduation, Vygotsky returned to his native province, Gomel, in southwestern Russia. He eventually began teaching literature and history at various new schools opened by the Bolshevik government. While teaching at Gomel Teacher College, he set up a small laboratory for simple experiments on reactions (van der Veer & Valsiner, 1991).

Three subsequent events opened the door to an academic career for Vygotsky. They were the changing nature of psychology, changes in the program of a national psychoneurology conference, and one of Vygotsky's presentations at that conference.

A Changing Discipline

Prior to the revolution, "psychology had eked out a meager existence" (Leont'ev, cited in Levitin, 1982, p. 113). There were few university classes and only one center of learning in psychology: the Institute of Experimental Psychology in Moscow. Two well-known researchers at other institutions, Ivan Pavlov and Vladimir Bekheterev, studied reflexes. They did not consider themselves psychologists, and most psychologists viewed them only as physiologists (Joravsky, 1989).

The Soviet government officially entered the academic sphere with an essay by Lenin in March 1922 (Valsiner, 1988, p. 72). Lenin wrote that "no natural science . . . can hold out in the struggle against the on-slaught of bourgeois ideas . . . without a solid philosophic basis" (McLeish, 1975, p. 104). The term "bourgeois ideas" included any beliefs that were not sanctioned by the Party, and the "solid philosophic basis" was dialectical materialism.

Ten months later, Konstanin Kornilov, one of the key presenters at the First All-Russian Congress of Psychoneurology, proposed that psychological research should be "reconciled" with Marxist ideology. Kornilov's research, which included references to materialism and dialectics, held out the promise of developing an original Marxist psychology (Kozulin, 1984, p. 14). In late 1923, the government replaced the founder and director of the Institute of Experimental Psychology with Kornilov. As director, Kornilov supported various perspectives within the Institute provided that they address how they might fit within "the future system of Marxist psychology" (Joravsky, 1989, p. 229). Kornilov began to hire new staff, and one of his later hires, Lev S. Vygotsky, joined the Institute in 1924.

Vygotsky's Conference Presentation

One of the three papers that Vygotsky presented at the second congress on psychoneurology in January 1924 attracted Kornilov's attention and led to his appointment at the Institute. However, the presentation also was, in part, an accident of history. Prior conferences had limited attendance to university and medical personnel, excluding teachers and others from the provinces. In contrast, the conference that Vygotsky attended was staged as a triumph for Marxism. Participation from a broad sector was encouraged, and attendance was expanded to 900 participants instead of the prior limit of 500 (Joravsky, 1989, p. 224).

Vygotsky's (1926/1997m) paper on research methods discussed the importance of psychology becoming a unified science. His presentation also focused on the importance of the mind in studying behavior. Although he advocated addressing mental events, he avoided censure from Party authorities in four ways. First, he cited the statements of Pavlov and Bekheterev, the two prominent Russian physiologists, on the importance of the mind. Pavlov, for example, stated that mental events could not be ignored because they are closely connected with physiological events (Vygotsky, 1926/1997m, p. 45).

Second, Vygotsky avoided both flag waving and stereotypical labels (such as "mentalism" or "materialist"). Third was the literary flair of his persuasiveness (Joravsky, 1989, p. 260). For example, he noted that "it is as impossible for a concrete science of human behavior to be restricted to classic reflexology as it is for concrete physics to be restricted to the principle of gravity" (p. 35). Fourth, he made everyone see the need for assuming that a mental structure guides behavior: We have to either (a) accept the biological absurdity that the mind is completely unnecessary in the behavioral system, (b) deny the existence of the mind, or (c) find a way to research it (Vygotsky, 1926/1997m, p. 44). Through his matter-of-fact argument, Vygotsky substantiated the need to supplement neurophysiology with an objective psychology that "analyzes the structure of our [conscious] behavior" (Joravsky, 1989, p. 260). In other words, "mind without behavior is as impossible as behavior without mind" (Vygotsky, 1926/1997m, p. 46).

Vygotsky's focus on developing psychology as a unified science and his rationale attracted the attention of Kornilov (Leont'ev, 1997; Yaroshevsky, 1989). He hired Vygotsky as a "scientific co-worker of the second rank" in the General Experimental Psychology Section in the Institute (van der Veer & Valsiner, 1991, p. 128).

Kornilov's interest in Vygotsky's paper would, in normal times, have been insufficient for an invitation to join the Institute. However, in the reorganization of society after the revolution, old professional hierarchies had broken down. Moreover, psychology faced the directive to develop a discipline compatible with the Marxist–Leninist perspective. Vygotsky's humanist education had the potential to assist in that task. Valsiner (1988) noted that, 10 years earlier, psychology would not have been interested in Vygotsky, and 10 years later, because of his humanist background, psychology would not have interested him.

The Triumph of *Partiinost*

For Russian psychology the decade of the 1920s was a brief period characterized by "a fundamental faith in free scientific debate" (Bauer, 1952, p. 50). This decade contrasts sharply with the years that followed. First, mentioned earlier, was the enthusiasm of some younger psychologists for the task of building new systems of psychological science (Valsiner,

1988, p. 77). Second, in the 1920s, Marxist ideology functioned as both a relatively loose framework for conducting psychological research and as a screening device to identify some schools as clearly unacceptable (Bauer, 1952, p. 52). For example, Sigmund Freud's psychodynamic theory viewed the inner self as the servant of early biological drives. However, this view conflicted with the Marxist belief that the social environment is the major influence on behavior. Therefore, the mid-1920s official version of Freud sanctioned only his therapeutic method for treating abnormal personalities, not his psychodynamic theory of normal development (Joravsky, 1989, p. 236).

As the decade progressed, disputes among competing psychological perspectives became increasingly negative, and scientific substance was easily lost (Valsiner, 1988, p. 78). The competition among psychological views may have continued for a time except for the ascendancy of Joseph Stalin as the leader of Soviet Russia. By the end of the 1920s, Stalin had won the power struggle among prominent Party leaders that had followed Lenin's death in 1924, and he began to remake the social fabric of Soviet Russia. In addition to initiating a crash effort to industrialize the country and forcing the peasants into farming collectives, Stalin's repression included the professions, literature, and the social sciences. Economists, engineers, professors, and others were accused of conspiring with foreign enemies. They were removed from their positions, and some were imprisoned.

These events closed down the "golden age," relatively speaking, of fairly open discussion in Soviet psychology (Joravsky, 1989, p. 109). Theoretical views in various academic disciplines were closely examined for congruence with Marxism as interpreted by the Bolsheviks (who now referred to themselves as Communists). Open discussions of the scientific model ceased, and pronouncements from the Kremlin established the legitimacy of ideas. The "very principle of professional autonomy was rejected in favor of partiinost" (Joravsky, 1989, p. 420).

In 1931, the Institute in Moscow came under attack and Vygotsky's cultural–historical theory received its first criticisms (Valsiner & van der Veer, 2000). These criticisms coincided with the beginning of a two-summer cross-cultural study planned by Vygotsky and Alexander Luria. Conducted by Luria in two remote provinces of Soviet Russia, the study investigated the levels of thinking in different cultures (see Appendix A). The 600 protocols obtained in the study indicated differences in categorization and abstract thinking between groups who had received some education and illiterate peasants. The government maintained that the study defied Communist reality in which everyone was equal. Communist officials charged that the study had insulted the national minorities of Soviet Asia, who were "depicted as an inferior race unable to behave reasonably" (Kozulin, 1984, p. 110). The study was not published until 40 years later (Luria, 1976).

The initial criticisms of Vygotsky's theory had faulted him for ignoring the role of labor in discussing the history of man. Criticisms then accelerated, stating that Vygotsky included idealist, subjectivist concepts and uncritically incorporated Western bourgeois (i.e., anti-Marxist) theories in his work (van der Veer & Valsiner, 1991). One young Party boss in mathematics and science, for example, declared that to even think of any theory or scholarly discipline as autonomous or independent of Party doctrine signaled opposition to the [Communist] Party (Joravsky, 1989, p. 312).

The criticisms of Vygotsky's theory escalated, and he was subjected to several interrogations in 1933 (Valsiner & van der Veer, 2000, p. 338). These events suggest that severe punishment was soon to follow. However, Vygotsky, who had tuberculosis, suffered a serious hemorrhage in May 1934 and died several days later.

In the next few years, child study (paedology in the Soviet Union) came under attack. One aspect of child study was the use of IQ tests. The prevailing belief was that such tests could aid in the discovery of hidden talents in lower-class individuals (Joravsky, 1989, p. 347). However, the tests were much more effective in detecting deficits than talents, and large numbers of the children of workers and peasants were identified as needing special classes. The Central Committee accused psychologists of "willful bias" (p. 348), and a 1936 decree of the committee banned all psychological testing, publications, and journals. Vygotsky's writing, which included his work with children with mental and physical problems, was effectively banned for 20 years.

VYGOTSKY'S PERSPECTIVE

Vygotsky, during his brief academic career, worked under extremely difficult conditions. Soviet society faced many problems after the devastation of two wars and the 1920–1921 famine. Infrastructure and civil services had been swept away, and major shortages continued through the 1920s. Academics in the 1920s typically held multiple professional positions, and Vygotsky was no exception (Knox & Stephens, 1993, p. 5). He was a consultant for the various specialists who were working with "defective children" in different institutes (van der Veer & Valsiner, 1991, p. 60), taught psychology courses at the First Moscow State University, developed papers on various issues, clinically diagnosed children with mental and physical defects, and began editing translations for publishing houses. He undertook the work for publishers to supplement his nominal salary from the Institute.

In addition to Vygotsky's passion for developing a scientific psychology, three other factors contributed to his thinking on cognitive development. They were his talents, early influences on his thinking (Hegel, Spinoza, and Protebnya), and his view of Marxism. These factors played an important role in his identification of major issues in psychology.

Vygotsky's Talents

Two personal traits contributed to Vygotsky's productivity during his physical and, later, political difficulties. They were his intellectual mastery of new material and his personality.

Intellectual Mastery

Vygotsky's mastery of psychological issues is evident in the range of topics he addressed early in his career. His papers in 1924 ranged from the education of physically handicapped children to the theories of psychoanalysis and behaviorism and the nature of consciousness (Valsiner & van der Veer, 2000, p. 335). He also edited and wrote the introduction to a reader on defectology (study of disabilities) in 1924 (van der Veer & Valsiner, 1991, p. 45). By 1926, Vygotsky had acquired sufficient knowledge of psychology to analyze the state of the discipline (Valsiner & van der Veer, 2000, p. 344). His lengthy essay (Vygotsky, 1982–1984/1997l) on needed research methods and the fragmentation of views in psychology illustrates Vygotsky's exceptional breadth as well as his seriousness of purpose (Joravsky, 1989, p. 262).

Yaroshevsky (1989) credited Vygotsky's ability to be in touch with the details of work in diverse fields to his skill in rapid reading and his ability to shed light on the problems latent in any aspect of scientific knowledge (p. 121). Luria reported that Vygotsky was a speed reader and had a photographic memory. He was able to recall verbatim book passages that had particularly interested him (Knox & Stevens, 1993, p. 8). His daughter Gita also commented on his exceptional memory. She and her childhood friends would put together lists of 100 words for her father to master. After reading the words, he would recite the whole list, both forward and in reverse. Also, when asked, he would name, for example, the fourth, 23rd, and 61st words without error (Vygodskaia, 1995).

Vygotsky's Personality

Two major characteristics of Vygotsky's personality were his rare charm and warmth and his exceptional verbal gifts. Joravsky (1989) noted that the few photographs of Vygotsky show "large dark eyes lit with gentle intensity rather than arrogance, reinforcing disciples' talk of an 'enchanting personality' " (p. 254). Kurt Lewin, a prominent Gestalt psychologist, although having had personal contact with Vygotsky for only 2 weeks, described him as "an absolutely extraordinary person full of inner gentleness and at the same time effective strength, and also a scholar of an exceptional rank" (Yaroshevsky, 1989, p. 26). Kolbanovsky (1934, cited in van der Veer & Valsiner, 1991, p. 14) indicated that Vygotsky's sensitivity, responsiveness, and tactfulness enabled him to attract students to his task of building psychology.

Nevertheless, Vygotsky did not hesitate to critique flaws or errors in the thinking of other psychologists. For example, he wrote penetrating criticisms of Luria's effort to link the concepts of Freud with Marxism while keeping Luria's admiring friendship, and he criticized his immediate chief Kornilov while remaining in his favor (Joravsky, 1989, p. 261).

In addition, Vygotsky's verbal gifts attracted large numbers to his lectures. "Tall and slender, with an unhealthy blush on his cheeks, his features sharpened by his grave disease . . . he would pace the auditorium for hours, the overcoat thrown over his shoulders against the inner chill, his hands behind his back, discussing problems of psychology" (Yaroshevsky, 1989, p. 25).

Early Influences on Vygotsky's Thinking

Two philosophers whose work Vygotsky had read as an adolescent influenced his basic beliefs about cognition and cognitive change. They were Benedict Spinoza and G. W. F. Hegel. Spinoza, Vygotsky's favorite philosopher (Yaroshevsky, 1989; van der Veer & Valsiner, 1991), emphasized the importance of the reasoning process in developing knowledge about the world. Often referred to as the supreme rationalist philosopher, he believed that, in principle, everything can be known through reasoning. Moreover, the reasoning process provides enough practice in deductive thinking to keep opinion, passion, and prejudice under control (Gullan-Whurr, 1998, p. xiii). Finally, emotions can benefit us only when they are understood through reason.

Vygotsky (1982–1984/1997g) noted Spinoza's (1677/1955, p. 187) words that "thinking is at first, the servant of passions, but that man who has reason is the master of his passions" (Vygotsky, 1982–1984/1997g, p. 97). This view is reflected in Vygotsky's concept that an essential component of cognitive development is self-mastery. Specifically, individuals, from childhood through adolescence, eventually develop complex cognitive processes by gaining ever greater mastery of their thinking.

Concepts in Hegel's thinking that influenced Vygotsky were his belief that reality consists of the processes of change and the complex nature of change. (See Chapter 2.) Vygotsky (1960/1997d), chastising psychologists for not detecting the "true uniqueness of child behavior" (p. 98), noted that they had failed to recognize the ever-changing nature of cognitive development.

A third influence on Vygotsky's thinking was the work of Alexander A. Potebnya, a Ukrainian and Russian philologist. Potebnya studied such problems as the interrelationship of language and thinking and the origin of language. Two of his views accepted by Vygotsky are that speech is "a means to understand oneself" (Potebnya, 1913/1993, p. 102; Vygotsky, 1982–1984/1997g, p. 95) and "language is not a means to express a ready-made thought, but to create it" (Potebnya, 1913/1933, p. 120). Potebnya's view of language as a tool of thinking became a major component of Vygotsky's theory of cognitive development.

Vygotsky and Marxism

In Soviet psychology, Marxism influenced the work of psychologists in two ways. One was their response to Lenin's 1922 directive to adopt dialectical materialism as the guiding framework for developing knowledge. The other influence on their work was the judgments levied on particular theories and psychological developments by the Soviet power structure. This role was complicated by differing governmental pronouncements on Marxism at different times.

In response to the call for a Marxist psychology, some academics identified occasional connecting points between their work and Marxism. For example, early advocates of Freud's theory noted that, like Marxism, it was atheistic. Others attempted to find phrases in Marxism that could be included in their work. Vygotsky (1982–1984/1997l), in his 1926 analysis of the state of psychology, criticized these efforts. The major problem was that these psychologists expected to find principles "ready-made in the haphazard psychological statements of the founders of Marxism" (p. 312). These efforts were misplaced because psychologists were "looking, firstly, *in the wrong place*; . . . secondly, *for the wrong thing*; . . . thirdly, *in the wrong manner*" (p. 313). They were looking in the wrong place because none of the Marxist philosophers had developed a methodology of psychology. Second, Russian psychologists were seeking a pompous formula that is "as empty and cautious as possible" (p. 313). Third, the searchers were focusing on dogma, not methods. Vygotsky (1982–1984/1997l) further noted that psychology needed a theory that would provide an understanding of the mind, not a formula that seemed to provide ultimate truth. In other words, psychology did not need "fortuitous utterances" (p. 331).

In his work, Vygotsky accepted the statements of Karl Marx and Friedrich Engels that (a) the two periods in the development of the human race are biological evolution and human history, (b) the social environment is a key influence on human behavior, (c) practice is the standard for testing theory, and (d) humans consciously plan their actions. In an early essay on the importance of studying human thinking, Vygotsky (1925/1997c) drew on Marx's comparison of the actions of bees and spiders with the planning undertaken by humans. The spider constructs complex webs, and the bee puts many architects to shame with its construction of cells. Nevertheless, even the worst architect plans his structure in his imagination before actually constructing it (Marx, 1890/1981, Vol. I, Part 3, p. 193, cited in Vygotsky, 1925/1997c, p. 63). This differentiation between animals and humans was important at the time because Edward Thorndike and the Gestalt psychologists were making inferences about human cognition from their research on animals.

In other words, Vygotsky took the writings of Marxism seriously as a philosophy but "gave no sign of submission to Marxism as an ideology" (Kozulin, 1984, p. 116). Joravsky (1989) noted that "Vygotsky had studied 'the classics of Marxism' for deeper reasons than political convenience or ideological fashion . . . he was seeking unified understanding of human beings as natural objects with conscious minds" (p. 261).

Other Issues

When Vygotsky joined the Institute of Experimental Psychology, he identified understanding the human intellect as the most critical and central problem for the whole system of psychology (Vygotsky, 1930/1997i, p. 190; Vygotsky, 1960/1997n, p. 13). To adequately address this problem, psychology should study not only internal mental processes (such as mastering one's attention [Vygotsky, 1982–1984/1997e]), but the whole of human consciousness (Vygotsky, 1925/1997c, 1930/1997f). Vygotsky's rationale for this broad focus was to study basic problems such as the process of developing an understanding of oneself and the areas of thinking, feeling, and will. To reflect this broad view of the necessary focus for psychology, Vygotsky (1930/1997f) maintained that the appropriate designation should be *psychological* processes. They include, but are not limited to, mental processes (p. 120). Psychological processes include the content the individual has learned, mental processes, attitudes and feelings, and the individual's awareness of himself, his thoughts, and his feelings.

Moreover, to neglect the study of consciousness is to omit any reactions that are not visible to the naked eye (Vygotsky, 1925/1997c, p. 64). It also denies researchers access to the most important problem facing psychology—determining the structure of human behavior (p. 66).

Related to the need to study human consciousness was the need for appropriate research methods. Vygotsky's (1960/1997k) goal of developing an objective system of research methods became a major theme in his work (van der Veer, 1997). His recommendations and examples are discussed in Chapter 2.

Vygotsky began his work by reading and critiquing the ideas and thinking of other scholars. Weaknesses or flaws that he detected in their reasoning fueled his identification of important questions for psychology to address. His review of the two major learning theories indicated, from his perspective, that psychology had failed to address both the complex nature of the human intellect and human development. Edward Thorndike (1913), for example, described cognition as simply establishing connections between stimuli and the learner's responses. An example is the equation 9 x 5 (stimulus) = 45 (response). This mechanistic description, according to Vygotsky (1934/1997h), addressed only the formation of specific habits. Also, the stimulus–response paradigm does not capture the specific quality of higher forms of behavior (Vygotsky, 1960/1997k, p. 60). Moreover, Thorndike's psychology text for teachers portrayed the teacher as "a perfect rickshaw-puller who drags [along] the educational process" (Vygotsky, 1926/1997j, p. 160). The teacher is simply regulating stimuli in order to get pupils' reactions.

In contrast, Gestalt psychology, also referred to as structural psychology (Vygotsky, 1926/1997b, p. 82), focused on the role of perception in problem-solving situations. The Gestaltists maintained that mentally restructuring a visual situation was the key to cognition (Vygotsky, 1930/1997i). For example, when a chimpanzee perceives that a nearby stick can be used as a tool to pull bananas into his cage, learning has occurred (Köhler, 1929; Vygotsky, 1930/1997i, p. 179). However, Gestalt psychology had made two major errors (Vygotsky, 1934/1997h, 1960/1997n). One is that mental restructuring is not the same for the chimpanzee and the child because a structured action is not necessarily an intellectual act (p. 205). The ape's goal-directed action is meaningless beyond a particular situation (Vygotsky, 1934/1997h, p. 209). The child, in contrast, can develop the general concept of the role of tools in solving problems, and this inference is not dependent on any particular situation (p. 214). Although Gestalt psychology sought commonalities in the cognition of animals and humans, it left no room for the unique forms of human behavior (Vygotsky, 1960/1997n, p. 8).

Second, the principle of mental restructuring could not explain why the constellations in the heavens perceived by an astronomer and an ordinary person are entirely different (Vygotsky, 1934/1997h). The error in Gestalt psychology, according to Vygotsky (1960/1997n, p. 10), was that one link (perception of structure) was taken as the whole chain (development).

In seeking to achieve his goal of developing a psychology that explained the complexities of cognitive development, Vygotsky also drew on the writings of European and Russian scholars in fields other than psychology. Included were anthropology, ethnopsychology, linguistics, and sociology (see van der Veer, 1991; van der Veer & Valsiner, 1991). Although writings in these fields addressed a variety of topics, Vygotsky read them with an eye for clues to the unique characteristics of human thinking and the ways that it develops. Among the scholars he reviewed are the well known (e.g., Alfred Binet and Jean Piaget) and the now forgotten (e.g., Karl Bühler, Lucien Lévy-Bruhl, Ernst Meuman, Théophile Ribot). Vygotsky rejected some ideas and modified others, combining and integrating them with other ideas into a theoretical perspective that went beyond the disciplinary boundaries of the social sciences, humanities, and psychology (Wertsch, 1985).

ORGANIZATION OF THE TEXT

Two strengths of Vygotsky's cultural–historical theory are the extensive relationships and connections among major ideas and the richly detailed descriptions of cognitive processes. They are the result of his examining the issue of cognitive development in its complexity. Included in his discussions are the role of cultural signs and symbols, the outcomes of cognitive development, the role of speech, and so on. As a result, there is no inherent linear sequence of ideas in his theory. Nevertheless, his ideas form a logical, comprehensive framework for understanding cognitive development. This book has organized the discussion of his ideas into four general categories. The first category, "General Principles," comprises Chapters 2, 3, and 4. Chapter 2 presents Vygotsky's research method, key experiments using the method, and implications for action research and research in educational psychology. This chapter reflects one of Vygotsky's major goals, which was to develop a research method adequate for the task of studying cognitive development from its early stages.

The research of Vygotsky and his colleagues indicated qualitative differences between different age groups in learning to use cultural signs and symbols in the development of thinking. Chapter 3 is a discussion of the role of these signs in cognitive development, which he equated with self-mastery, and the formal stages of sign use suggested by the experiments. Chapter 4 discusses the outcomes of cognitive development, known as the higher mental functions, characteristics of their development, and the role of education.

Part II, "Major Cultural Signs," includes two chapters. Chapter 5 discusses the critical role of speech as the primary tool of thinking and the stages of development in learning to use speech for thinking. Chapter 6 addresses the nature of preconceptual and conceptual thinking, the stages in concept development, and the importance of subject matter or academic concepts in developing thinking. Both Chapters 5 and 6 illustrate the stages of speech development for thinking and the stages of concept formation as examples of the stages of sign use introduced in Chapter 3.

Part III, "The Cycle of Development," addresses one of Vygotsky's efforts in the last 2 years of his life. Chapter 7 addresses the structure and dynamics of age-related periods of development. It discusses Vygotsky's schematic of stable and critical periods in development from birth through adolescence. Chapter 8 presents an overview of each of these periods and illustrates the role of the child's changing social relations with adults as a major catalyst in development.

Chapter 9 comprises Part IV, "Some Implications of Vygotsky's Theory." The chapter identifies implicit yet pervasive themes in Vygotsky's work and the implications of these themes for society and education.

REFERENCES

Bakhurst, D. (1991). *Consciousness and revolution in Soviet philosophy.* New York: Cambridge University Press.

Bauer, R. A. (1952). *The new man in Soviet psychology.* Cambridge, MA: Harvard University Press.

Cole, G. D. H. (1952–1956). *A history of socialist thought* (3 vols.). New York: St. Martin's Press.

Graham, L. R. (1987). *Science, philosophy, and human behavior in the Soviet Union.* New York: Columbia University Press.

Gullan-Whurr, M. (1998). *Within reason: A life of Spinoza.* New York: St. Martin's Press.

Hosking, G. (2001). *Russia and the Russians: A history.* Cambridge, MA: Harvard University Press.

Joravsky, D. (1961). *Soviet Marxism and natural science.* London: Routledge & Kegan Paul.

Joravsky, D. (1989). *Russian psychology: A critical history.* Cambridge, MA: Blackwell.

Knox, J., & Stevens, C. B. (1993). Translators' introduction. In R. W. Rieber & A. S. Carton (Eds.), *Collected works of L. S. Vygotsky: Vol. 2. The fundamentals of defectology* (pp. 1–35). New York: Plenum.

Köhler, W. (1929). *Gestalt psychology.* New York: Horace Liveright.

Kozulin, A. (1984). *Psychology in utopia.* Cambridge, MA: MIT Press.

Leont'ev, A. N. (1997). On Vygotsky's creative development. In R. W. Rieber & J. Wollock (Eds.), *Collected works of L. S. Vygotsky: Vol. 3. Problems of the theory and history of psychology* (pp. 9–32). New York: Plenum.

Levitin, K. (1982). *One is not born a personality.* Moscow: Progress Publishers.

Luria, A. (1976). *Cognitive development: Its cultural and social foundations.* Cambridge, MA: Harvard University Press.

Luria, A. (1979). *The making of mind.* Cambridge, MA: Harvard University Press.

McLeish, J. (1975). *Soviet psychology: History, theory, content.* London: Methuen.

Potebnya, A. A. (1993). *Mysl' I yazyk.* Kiev: SINTO. (Original work published 1913)

Spinoza, B. (1955). *On the improvement of the understanding: The ethics. Correspondence.* New York: Dover. (Original work published 1677)

Stites, R. (1989). *Revolutionary dreams: Utopian vision and experimental life in the Russian Revolution.* New York: Oxford University Press.

Thorndike, E. L. (1913). *Educational psychology: Vol. II. The psychology of learning.* New York: Teachers College Press.

Tucker, R. C. (1985). Lenin's Bolshevism as a culture in the making. In A. Gleason, P. Keniz, & R. Stites (Eds.), *Bolshevik culture* (pp. 25–38). Bloomington: Indiana University Press.

Valsiner, J. (1988). *Developmental psychology in the Soviet Union.* Bloomington: Indiana University Press.

Valsiner, J., & van der Veer, R. (2000). *The social mind: Construction of the idea.* New York: Cambridge University Press.

van der Veer, R. (1991). The anthropological underpinnings of Vygotsky's thinking. *Studies in Soviet Thought, 42,* 73–91.

van der Veer, R. (1997). Some major themes in Vygotsky's theoretical work: An introduction. In R. W. Rieber & J. Wollock (Eds.), Collected works of L. S. Vygotsky: Vol. 3. Problems of the theory and history of psychology (pp. 1–7). New York: Plenum.

van der Veer, R., & Valsiner, J. (1991). *Understanding Vygotsky: A quest for synthesis.*

Vucinich, A. (1970). *Science in Russian cultures, 1961–1917.* Stanford, CA: Stanford University Press.

Vygodskaia, G. L. (1995). Remembering father. *Educational Psychologist, 30*(3), 57–59.

Vygotsky, L. S. (1997a). Analysis of higher mental functions. In R. W. Rieber (Ed.), *Collected works of L. S. Vygotsky: Vol. 4. The history of the development of higher mental functions* (pp. 65–82). New York: Plenum. (Original work published 1960)

Vygotsky, L. S. (1997b). Apropos Koffka's article on self-observation. In R. W.

Rieber & J. Wollock (Eds), *Collected works of L. S. Vygotsky: Vol 3. Problems of the theory and history of psychology* (pp. 81–83). New York: Plenum. (Original work published 1926)

Vygotsky, L. S. (1997c). Consciousness as a problem for the psychology of behavior. In R. W. Rieber & J. Wollock (Eds.), *Collected works of L. S. Vygotsky: Vol. 3. Problems of the theory and history of psychology* (pp. 63–79). New York: Plenum. (Original work published 1925)

Vygotsky, L. S. (1997d). Genesis of higher mental functions. In R. W. Rieber (Ed.), *Collected works of L. S. Vygotsky: Vol. 4. The history of the development of the higher mental functions* (pp. 97–119). New York: Plenum. (Original work published 1960)

Vygotsky, L. S. (1997e). Mastering attention. In R. W. Rieber (Ed.), *Collected works of L. S. Vygtosky: Vol. 4. The history of the development of higher mental functions* (pp. 153–177). New York: Plenum. (Original work published 1982–1984)

Vygotsky, L. S. (1997f). Mind, consciousness, the unconscious. In R. W. Rieber & J. Wollock (Eds.), *Collected works of L. S. Vygotsky: Vol. 3. Problems of the theory and history of psychology* (pp. 109–121). New York: Plenum. (Original work published 1930)

Vygotsky, L. S. (1997g). On psychological systems. In R. W. Rieber & J. Wollock (Eds.), *Collected works of L. S. Vygotsky: Vol. 3. Problems of the theory and history of psychology* (pp. 91–107). New York: Plenum. (Original work published 1982–1984)

Vygotsky, L. S. (1997h). Preface to Koffka. In R. W. Rieber & J. Wollock (Eds.), *Collected works of L. S. Vygotsky: Vol. 3. Problems of the theory and history of psychology* (pp. 195–232). New York: Plenum. (Original work published 1934)

Vygotsky, L. S. (1997i). Preface to Köhler. In R. W. Rieber & J. Wollock (Eds.), *Collected works of L. S. Vygotsky: Vol. 3. Problems of the theory and history of psychology* (pp. 175–194). New York: Plenum. (Original work published 1930)

Vygotsky, L. S. (1997j). Preface to Thorndike. In R. W. Rieber & J. Wollock (Eds.), *Collected works of L. S. Vygotsky: Vol. 3. Problems of the theory and history of psychology* (pp. 147–161). New York: Plenum. (Original work published 1926)

Vygotsky, L. S. (1997k). Research method. In R. W. Rieber (Ed.), *Collected works of L. S. Vygotsky: Vol. 4. The history of the development of higher mental functions* (pp. 27–63). New York: Plenum. (Original work published 1960)

Vygotsky, L. S. (1997l). The historical meaning of the crisis in psychology: A methodological investigation. In R. W. Rieber & J. Wollock (Eds.), *Collected works of L. S. Vygtosky: Vol. 3. Problems of the theory and history of psychology* (pp. 233–343). New York: Plenum. (Original work published 1982–1984)

Vygotsky, L. S. (1997m). The methods of reflexological and psychological investigation. In R. W. Rieber & J. Wollock (Eds.), *Collected works of L. S. Vygotsky: Vol. 3. Problems of the theory and history of psychology* (pp. 35–49). New York: Plenum. (Original work published 1926)

Vygotsky, L. S. (1997n). The problem of the development of higher mental functions. In R. W. Rieber (Ed.), *Collected works of L. S. Vygotsky: Vol. 4. The history of the development of higher mental functions* (pp. 1–26). (Original work published 1960)

Wertsch, J. V. (Ed.) (1985). *Culture, communication, and cognition: Vygotskian perspectives*. Cambridge, UK: Cambridge University Press.

Yaroshevsky, M. G. (1989). *Lev Vygotsky*. Moscow: Progress Publishers.

Part I

GENERAL PRINCIPLES

2

Research Methods

In studying any new area, it is necessary to begin by seeking
and developing a method ... every basically new approach to
scientific problems leads inevitably to new methods and ways
of research.

—VYGOTSKY (1960/1997e, p. 27)

A major theme in Vygotsky's work was research methodology, and he
addressed this topic throughout his brief career (van der Veer, 1997). He
set a goal for himself of developing a plan for the construction of "a *unified* objective system of methods for interpreting and experimenting with
human behavior" (Vygotsky, 1960/1997e, p. 44).

In the course of his work, Vygotsky introduced two developments
that are relevant for contemporary research in educational psychology,
educational practice, and action research conducted by teachers in their
classrooms. First, instead of attempting to interpret behavior *after* an experiment, researchers should analyze and interpret the events they are
studying *before* the experiment, and Vygotsky outlined the steps in this
task. (Vygotsky's focus is reflected in the word sequence in his phrase
"interpreting and experimenting with human behavior" [Vygotsky, 1960/
1997e, p. 44]). Second, he developed a particular approach for research
on cognitive behavior. Named the experimental–genetic method, this
single-subject method combines research tasks designed to reveal the
participant's thinking with a clinical approach. Discussed in this chapter

are Vygotsky's recommendations for research and his pivotal experiments on memory and attention and the child's development of concepts.

A FRAMEWORK FOR RESEARCH

Vygotsky believed that new research methods were needed because psychology had produced primarily descriptive information. To correct this situation, psychology should follow the example set by the so-called hard sciences. As those sciences matured, they moved beyond descriptive information to the development of causal–dynamic explanations of events (Vygotsky, 1960/1997a, p. 69). This shift is important because the task for research in any discipline is to understand complex events, and this focus requires developing causal explanations (Vygotsky, 1982–1984/1997g). For example, observing that a particular cognitive activity, such as conceptual thinking, occurs at a particular age is insufficient. Research should be able to demonstrate how and why such an activity occurs.

Essential to designing research studies that can lead to causal explanations is to first develop a sound conceptual framework. Discussed in this section are Vygotsky's general requirements for this planning step and the framework he developed for his research.

General Requirements

Two general requirements for research that seeks causal explanations are to (a) clarify a conceptual–theoretical basis for research questions and (b) conduct a detailed analysis of the events to be studied.

Rationale for a Conceptual–Theoretical Foundation

In planning for research, investigators should first state their basic beliefs about the events or processes to be studied. Making this information explicit is important because these beliefs influence decisions about both the research focus and acceptable methods for the study. For example, a researcher may believe that the subconscious mind consists of events absent from thinking. Or, instead, he may believe that the major characteristic of the subconscious is the suppression of the sex drive. Whichever description the researcher selects "fundamentally changes the character, quantity, composition, nature, and properties of the material we will study" (Vygotsky, 1982–1984/1997g, p. 259). For example, a basic belief about complex thinking articulated by Vygotsky was that higher forms of thinking began with early humans. This belief required that he develop information about cognitive development in early cultures.

Vygotsky also suggested that research questions should be based on theory because this step provides a rational approach to the development of hypotheses. However, researchers should not attempt to combine material from different systems, doctrines, or sources. This practice, eclecticism, typically introduces "monstrous distortions" in the basic ideas of each theory in order to achieve a fit (Vygotsky, 1982–1984/1997g, p. 261). The situation would be somewhat like attempting to deal with Christianity without Christ.

Eclecticism also leads to inappropriate questions and unreliable answers because the theoretical concepts are taken out of context. This problem sometimes occurs in teacher education programs. Preservice teachers, for example, are presented with typical classroom challenges and asked to identify concepts from two or more theories that may be related to each challenge. This task, however, typically results in errors of application because the basic theoretical foundation is missing.

The Role of Analysis

The next step in planning is to conduct an analysis of the events to be studied. However, Vygotsky did not accept the traditional definition of the term. Analysis typically means to separate or break down any whole into particular elements (Vygotsky, 1934/1987c, 1935/1994b, 1934/1997d). For example, water decomposes into two elements: hydrogen and oxygen. Vygotsky pointed out that, in this analysis, the properties of the whole are lost, and research on the elements will yield inaccurate answers. The capacity of water to put out a fire cannot be determined by studying hydrogen, which burns, and oxygen, which supports combustion (Vygotsky, 1934/1987c, p. 45).

Applied to psychological research, the "decomposition" form of analysis led to two major errors. One is that only the external appearance of events is studied (Vygotsky, 1982–1984/1997g). For example, researchers often focus on student responses to particular tasks or problems, but the responses do not indicate the details of the student's thinking. The second error is that the identification of elements led to the study of mental processes as though they were stable things. Thorndike, for example, studied learning as sequences of stimuli and responses. Similarly, a contemporary perspective on information processing subdivides the process of memory into the categories of working memory, long-term memory, episodic memory, and so on, each with stable and unchanging characteristics.

In contrast, Vygotsky (1960/1997a) maintained that mental events are complex processes that "change before our eyes" (p. 68). For example, the young child's memory is a natural process that simply records concrete perceptions and experiences. Yet, by school age, the child begins to develop the capability to direct and manage memory; this process leads to the construction of new internal connections between objects and events.

Given these issues, Vygotsky (1960/1997a, 1982–1984/1997g) maintained that the meaning of analysis should be "radically changed" (Vygotsky, 1960/1997a, p. 69). Instead of breaking down processes into elements, analysis should identify only the characteristics and instances that retain the properties of the whole (Vygotsky, 1934/1987c, p. 45; 1934/1997d, p. 143; 1960/1997a, p. 67). That is, analysis must identify the "essence" of the whole that is under study.

To accomplish this purpose, Vygotsky (1960/1997a) advocated "conditional–genetic analysis" (p. 69). This process should reveal the real connections that are hidden behind the surface appearance of cognitive processes. Included in the analysis are questions about the origin, conditions, and all the relations that form the basis of any psychological process (p. 69). In this role, analysis is a scientific explanation, not simply a description of the phenomenon to be studied.

Vygotsky's Research Framework

Vygotsky's conceptual framework included (a) his beliefs (i.e., basic assumptions) about the nature of cognitive development, and (b) his analysis of complex thinking. Also, his analysis of the literature on culture and thinking led to his identification of the origin of complex thinking and the essence or central characteristics of higher mental capabilities.

Basic Assumptions about the Nature of Cognitive Development

The central assumption that supported and influenced Vygotsky's work was Hegel's belief that reality is a complex process of ongoing change. Consistent with this view, Vygotsky (1960/1997b) characterized cognitive development as constantly undergoing change. (See Table 2.1.) In other words, the nature of cognitive development in its early stages differs from the process at a later age. Included are a disproportionate development of separate intellectual processes, transformation of some forms of thinking into others, and complex interactions of external and internal factors that influence thinking (p. 99).

TABLE 2.1. Vygotsky's Analysis of the Nature of Cognitive Development

Component	Content
Major assumptions	1. Cognitive development progresses through a variety of complex changes; the process does not consist of unchanging elements. 2. Higher forms of cognitive behavior emerged in the historical development of humans.
Origin	The complex thinking of an adult originated in the rudimentary forms of cognition of early humans.
Essence	The essence of higher cognitive capabilities consists of creating or appropriating auxiliary stimuli to determine one's behavior. The auxiliary stimuli have no natural connection to the task. They function as aids for the individual to master his or her behavior in relation to the task. An example is cutting notches into wood to represent the words in a missionary's sermon.

Origin of Complex Thinking

Vygotsky did not agree with the view that the mind simply perfected itself on its own (Vygotsky, 1960/1997i, p. 17). Instead, he accepted the belief of Marx and Engels that the human race developed higher forms of thinking in the process of historical development. In analyzing cognitive development, Vygotsky believed that information about early humans could be helpful in two ways. First, studying the cognition of early humans should provide clues about the events that influence the development of abstract thinking. Second, this focus also could help explain the ways in which human cognition had changed (Vygotsky & Luria, 1930/1993, p. 81). Vygotsky (1960/1997e) emphasized that he was "not at all interested in rudimentary, dead psychological forms in themselves" (p. 53). Instead, "we are looking for the key to higher behavior" (p. 53).

A problem with undertaking the historical study of early humans was that only traces of their lives remained. However, Vygotsky concluded that the existing, yet relatively primitive, cultures studied by anthropologists and ethnographers could provide the needed information. These cultures, which often maintained ancient customs and traditions, represented the beginning of the historical development of humans (Vygotsky & Luria, 1930/1993, p. 83).

Vygotsky disagreed with the views that considered the differences between primitive and contemporary humans to be too great to develop a unified theory of cognition. For example, one view maintained that early humans had developed a primitive knowledge of their surroundings but could not accomplish even simple calculations. Others viewed primitive thinking as mystical or prelogical; only contemporary thinking was logical (Vygotsky & Luria, 1930/1993, pp. 86–88). However, Vygotsky and Luria concluded that the knowledge differences were cultural, not biological. Moreover, primitive humans displayed logical thinking in the invention and use of tools, hunting, farming, and cattle raising (p. 88).

Essence of Higher Cognitive Processes

Vygotsky did believe that thinking changes historically, and this belief became a fundamental concept in his cultural–historical theory (van der Veer, 1991, p. 78). Nevertheless, such changes did not rule out the presence of a common thread of cognitive activity from primitive to more advanced cultures. On the basis of his reading of anthropological writings, Vygotsky identified the first use of artificial symbols to guide one's thinking as the root of complex cognition. Specifically, primitive humans, at a certain phase of their development, shifted from reliance on natural memory to an entirely new process. They began to dominate their memory through created artificial symbols, which he referred to as signs (Vygotsky, 1960/1997e; Vygotsky & Luria, 1930/1993, p. 101). An example is a Kaffir man who remembered the sermons of a missionary by cutting notches in a piece of wood (Lévy-Bruhl 1926, cited in Vygotsky, 1960/1997e, p. 51).

Another example, from Thurnwald (1922) and Clodd (1905), was an early forerunner of writing known as *quipu*. Used in ancient Peru, it was a method of tying long strings of knots to send messages, and to record ownership of property and other economic events (Clodd, 1905, cited in Vygotsky & Luria, 1930/1993).

Cutting notches in wood and the knot tying of the Peruvians are forerunners of the current automatic practice of jotting down brief notes to remember important tasks. This simple behavior does not currently play a pivotal role in cognition. However, Vygotsky maintained that the early methods of mastering one's memory were the beginning of the thread that led to contemporary thinking (Vygotsky, 1960/1997e, p. 41).

The essential characteristics of the rudimentary cognitive actions of early humans that are the key to higher cognitive processes are as follows. First, humans actively intervened in their primitive or elementary mental processes (such as natural memory). Second, they created a new situation in order to master their behavior. They accomplished this purpose by creating artificial stimuli as aids. Third, the artificial stimuli altered their behavior by establishing new connections in the brain. Also, in these and other examples, the created stimuli were very different from the stimuli that were the object of the task. The notches cut into the piece of wood, for example, had no inherent relationship to the words being spoken by the missionary. Similarly, current alphabets and their configurations have no inherent relationships to the words they represent. (They have replaced early picture-writing systems, such as hieroglyphics.) Through the creation of more advanced artificial stimuli, such as written language and number systems, humans began to transform their thinking.

Summary

A major theme in Vygotsky's work was the issue of research methodology. This issue was important for his goal of developing an objective system to interpret and experiment with human behavior and to develop causal explanations for behavior. Two of his recommendations that are relevant for contemporary psychological research are the necessity of analyzing and interpreting events to be studied before conducting research and his experimental–genetic method.

Analysis and interpretation should be based on a framework that makes explicit the investigator's basic beliefs about the process to be studied, because these beliefs influence the selection of methods. The research framework also should base research questions on theory, but not material from different theories, because this orientation provides a rational approach to developing hypotheses. Then the researcher should conduct an analysis that identifies the properties of the whole, the real connections that are hidden behind surface appearances. In this role, analysis is a scientific explanation, not simply a description.

The conceptual framework that supported Vygotsky's research was derived from his assumptions that (a) higher forms of thinking had their origins in early history and (b) cognitive development in the human race and the child is an ever-changing process. The essence of higher forms of thinking is the individual's intervention in the processes of his or her thinking through the creation and use of an auxiliary stimulus or stimuli. This intervention establishes new connections in the brain and enables the individual to master his or her behavior at a higher level.

THE EXPERIMENTAL–GENETIC METHOD

Vygotsky's primary goal was to explain the whole of cognitive development. He maintained that the methodological significance of his analyses was the structural principle that explains higher cognitive behavior (Vygotsky, 1960/1997e). This principle is the transformation of primitive or elementary cognitive processes into higher forms of thinking.

This transformation occurs through the incorporation of signs and symbols into one's thinking. In other words, the child in today's society masters the use of cultural symbols as integral components of cognitive tasks. The importance of this process is that it raises the learner's thinking to higher levels.

However, through a lengthy historical period of development, simple methods for controlling one's memory and attention have become mechanical and automatic (Vygotsky, 1960/1997a, p. 71). Such processes, "perfected by the millionth repetition," have lost their initial appearance. Therefore, one purpose of his research was to document children's first use of cultural symbols for thinking. The youngest groups in the studies consisted of 4- to 6-year-olds. A second purpose was to determine the structure and development of the variety of concrete forms of behavior organized and directed by auxiliary stimuli (cultural signs and symbols; Vygotsky, 1960/1997a). Discussed in this section are the basic research design, the experiments on memory and attention, and the experiments on concept formation.

The Basic Experimental Design

The task for research is to develop causal explanations of complex processes and events (Vygotsky, 1982–1984/1997g). Therefore, researchers should avoid data collection methods that yield only superficial information. In addition, experiments on cognition should be designed to reveal the thinking of the research participants.

Methods to Avoid

Vygotsky (1982–1984/1997g) equated causal explanations with scientific knowledge, and he identified three types of information that are not scientific knowledge. First, research intended to generate causal explanations of complex processes does not simply document external events. An example is the difference between observing that a plant has put out two new leaves in a week and the related internal process. Internally, the plant turns sunlight, carbon dioxide, and water into sugars and other organic substances. Information about external events is descriptive, but it does not indicate the essential characteristics of internal processes.

Second, research oriented toward explanations of events should not rely on self-reports by individuals about the nature of their thinking. Self-observations and self-reports of one's thoughts and feelings are not reliable indicators of those processes. If they were, *"then everybody would be a scientist-psychologist"* (Vygotsky, 1982–1984/1997g, p. 325).

Explanatory research then would simply consist of everyone recording their perceptions of events.

Vygotsky (1926/1997h) compared self-reports of one's thinking with the utility of the testimonies of the victim and the culprit in an inquest. Any use of such information must include verification and comparison with other sources (p. 49). A contemporary example of this problem is the use of questionnaires that ask students how well or how often they implement particular learning strategies. Students often overestimate the extent to which they carry out actions such as outlining their study notes, finding a quiet place to study, and so on.

Vygotsky also identified another very serious problem with using reports from individuals about the nature of their thinking. The self-reports provide information only about students' opinions of their thinking, not thinking itself. It is similar to studying the reflection of a table in the mirror rather than the table itself (Vygotsky, 1982–1984/ 1997g, p. 337).

A third practice to avoid is a reliance on simply registering facts (Vygotsky, 1982–1984/1997g, p. 251). Instead, research should extend the boundaries of knowledge by relating new facts to new concepts. An example is Pavlov's research. He did not merely document that dogs salivate at the sight of meat powder. Observations in Pavlov's laboratory indicated that a particular reaction, salivating, can be trained to respond to previously neutral events (e.g., a bell ring, a bright light). He had discovered a new concept, which he named the conditional reflex. Further research led to knowledge about the development of emotional reactions in people, such as fear and avoidance.

Experimental Tasks

Vygotsky (1960/1997e) maintained that every basically new approach to scientific problems requires the development of new methods of research (p. 27). In Vygotsky's case, a necessity in the experiments was to externalize the participants' thinking. This requirement was necessary to observe the various ways that the research participants used auxiliary stimuli to accomplish particular cognitive tasks.

The selected experimental tasks were above the participants' natural ability, such as remembering a long list of words (Vygotsky, 1929). Objects were placed nearby, such as paper, pictures, or colored cards. In other words, the tasks consisted of object stimuli (focus of the task) and other materials (potential auxiliary stimuli). The researchers observed whether the additional materials ceased to be neutral stimuli and became part of the child's efforts to be successful in the task, thereby changing the nature of the cognitive processing.

This design is a type of single-subject research, in which one participant at a time is studied. Vygotsky (1960/1997a) referred to the approach as the experimental–genetic method because "it artificially elicits
and creates a genetic [developmental] process of mental development"
(p. 68). Also, given the structure of the tasks (two sets of stimuli), the
method is referred to as the functional method of double stimulation
(Vygotsky, 1929, p. 430; 1982–1984/1999, p. 59; Vygotsky & Luria,
1994, p. 154).

Experiments on Memory and Attention

The cognitive processes originally researched were memory and attention (Vygotsky, 1982–1984/1997f, 1982–1984/1997c). In some of the
memory experiments, the objective was to remember a list of 15 words
in order or a series of numbers. The potential auxiliary stimuli for the
word list consisted of a set of 30 pictures (Berg, 1970). The experimenter
also informed each participant of the impossibility of directly remembering the set of words in the correct order (Vygotsky, 1982–1984/1997f,
p. 180). In some cases, the experimenter chose the pictures for the
words; in other cases, the children selected a picture to help them recall
each word.

The experimenter instructed the individual to select a picture after
each word is read aloud. He also recorded the chosen pictures (Berg,
1970). He collected the pictures after the individual had selected the last
one. Arranging them in their original order, the experimenter then asked
the individual for the word associated with each picture.

In the experiments on attention, one child at a time participated in
an activity that required lengthy and focused attention (Vygotsky, 1982–
1984/1997c, p. 154). The format, in the form of play, was based on a familiar children's game, referred to as the "forbidden colors" game. Interspersed among rapid-fire questions such as "Did you ever go on a
train?" were queries such as "What color is the floor?" As indicated in
Table 2.2, the experimenter familiarized the child with the format of the
task (phase 1). Then the child's performance was determined without the
auxiliary stimuli (colored cards) and with their availability (phases two
and three).

Results

The findings in the experiments on memory and attention indicated
qualitative differences in cognitive behavior across the age groups. In the
memory experiments, the young children relied on their natural memory
and tried to remember the words directly. They were unaware that a

TABLE 2.2. The "Forbidden Colors" Experiment

Purpose: To determine when and how participants use nonverbal stimuli to control their attention

Material: A set of nine cards, each a different color

Four sets of 18 questions, seven require a color name as an answer. Examples are "Do you play with toys?" "Have you seen the sea?" "What color is the sea?"

Procedure: Experimenter asks the questions in a conversational tone. Respondents must answer as quickly as possible with a one-word response.

Rules: Respondent can only name a color once; two colors were designated as forbidden and were not to be named.

Phases in the experiment:

Phase	Components	Purpose
1	18 questions, no restrictions, no forbidden colors	Familiarize the child with the format
2	18 questions, plus green and yellow as forbidden colors; no color can be named more than once	Determine performance without the aid of external stimuli
3	(a) Same as 2 above, except blue and red are forbidden (b) Child received nine colored cards, which "may help you win" (p. 298)	Determine the child's use of external stimuli to organize his or her attention
4	Same as 3 above, except the forbidden colors were black and white	Used only if the child did show evidence of using the cards or only did so near the end of the third phase

Results: Preschool children were not successful in either phase 2 or 3, and explanations of card use in phase 4 did not help them. School-age children were not successful in phase 2 but successfully used the cards in phase 3.

Note. Summarized from Leont'ev (1932/1994).

complex task could not be addressed with elementary methods, and they were unsuccessful.

Preschool children for whom the experimenter chose the pictures were fairly successful. However, the other preschool children had high error rates. Some of the children chose pictures for the words, but later, when shown the picture, they stated a different word or did not respond. For example, one young child selected a picture of a tree for the word *night* because misbehaving children climb trees at night (Leont'ev, 1959). Later, however, the child could not recall the word. Other preschool children looked for something in the pictures that was a direct image of the word. One child selected a picture of a hatchet for the word *sun* because he found a small yellow spot in the picture and declared it to be the sun. The child had turned the task into one of direct recall.

The schoolchildren, in contrast, formed effective links that combined word and picture into an integrated structure. For example, one child selected a picture of a bird for the word *butterfly* because "a butterfly is a little bird" (Leont'ev, 1959). The auxiliary stimuli in this situation were a picture (the bird) and the verbal phrase that linked the picture to the word to be remembered.

Adults, on the other hand, created complex verbal links with the words to be remembered. For example, one person selected *candle* to represent fire and devised the sentence "Moscow burned up from a candle worth a kopek" (Leont'ev, 1959). Also, adults typically did not use the pictures in recall; they relied only on their constructed sentences or phrases.

In other words, young children could neither remember the words directly nor use the pictures as memory aids. School-age children, however, established verbal links between pictures and particular words to be remembered. Thus, they relied on an integrated visual–verbal structure. Finally, adults relied on a complex verbal structure that they created.

In the experiments on attention, preschool children were easily distracted from the task, frequently playing with the colored cards or selecting them randomly (Vygotsky, 1982–1984/1997c, p. 155). School-age children were highly accurate in using the cards to keep track of forbidden colors. However, the younger schoolchildren tended to give "mindless answers" to the questions because they were guided only by the cards (Vygotsky, 1982–1984/1997c, p. 156). In contrast, the older schoolchildren attended to the questions as well. For example, when green was a forbidden color, an older child answered the question "What color is grass?" with "In the fall, it is yellow" (Vygotsky, 1929/ 1979).

The accuracy rate was high for both the school-age children and the adults. However, the adults did not move the cards during the questioning, mentally keeping track of the colors they named. For the adults, "the process has here a sharply defined internal character and it is only supported by cards" (Leont'ev, 1932/1994, p. 308).

Conclusions

The data from the experiments on memory and attention indicated qualitative differences across the age groups. Preschool children either did not understand the psychological nature of the tasks—that is, to control one's mental processes from the outside—or were unable to form effective links between arbitrary stimuli and their responses. School-age children, in contrast, understood the role of the arbitrary stimuli and were able to master their behavior with such aids. Finally, the adults exhibited a different level of performance in that they were able to construct internal stimuli to develop new connections between the object stimuli in the task and their responses.

Further analysis of the differences in mastering one's behavior formed the basis for Vygotsky's four-stage model of the use of auxiliary stimuli to alter mental processing (Vygosky, 1960/1997i; Vygotsky & Luria, 1994). These stages are discussed in Chapter 3.

Vygotsky (1960/1997e) noted that some critics might say that the data could easily by explained be a stimulus–response (S-R) connection. That is, in recalling a set of words, the child looks at a picture of a bird and recalls the word *butterfly*. However, simply fitting the data into the S-R paradigm misses two important points. One is that the behavior of interest is the active intervention of the individual that makes the correct response possible. Second, the S-R paradigm cannot capture the "dialectical leap" that brings about a qualitative change in the relationship between the stimulus and the response (p. 39). The interventions of the school-age child and the adult in mastering their memory, for example, differ qualitatively.

Research on Concept Formation

Vygotsky, in his later years, turned his attention to the use of word meanings as a form of verbal thinking. His focus was word meanings as they are represented by concepts. Briefly, a concept is a generalization that refers to an entire group of objects and their relationships. Countless terms in any language are examples of concepts. Included are everyday words such as *brother*, *table*, and *airplane* as well as technical terms such as *osmosis*, *nuclear fission*, and *bacteria*. Through thinking in concepts, individuals uncover connections and patterns among objects and events (Vygotsky, 1930–1931/1998b, p. 48). For example, thinking with the concept *bacteria* is based on knowing that they are typically one-celled organisms that include three main forms (cocci, bacilli, spirilla). Some bacteria are required for fermentation, and others, like viruses, cause diseases.

One purpose of the experiments on concept formation was to clarify the role of the concept name, the word, in the process of forming a concept (Vygotsky, 1934/1987a, p. 127). A second purpose was to determine the extent of the child's mastery of his or her thinking (Vygotsky, 1931/1994a, p. 207). Specifically, at what point in development is the child able to use the word as a symbol for a group of objects that share some characteristics and vary in others?

Problems with Prior Research

Vygotsky (1934/1987a, 1931/1994a) found the prior research on concepts to be deficient in major ways. One approach asked the child to select all the figures from a group that shared the characteristics of a given model. Another approach asked the child either to define or to name a concept from reading or hearing the concept characteristics. However, a matching exercise or a recited definition does not indicate the child's understanding of the concept. Also, neither method addressed the process of actually learning concepts (Sakharov, 1930/1994; Vygotsky, 1934/1987a, 1931/1994a).

A third research method, developed by Narciss Ach, used a variety of three-dimensional figures (e.g., cubes, pyramids) to which he had assigned nonsense syllables as names (e.g., *ras*). The research participants spent some time turning over different figures and trying to determine which figures belonged together under one concept label. The experimenter then tested the participants with questions as "What is *gazun*?" (See Sakharov, 1930/1994, pp. 82–84, for a detailed description.)

A major problem with all three methods is that they did not address the psychological nature of concepts. That is, what does the concept mean to the child, and what are the cognitive processes involved in operating with concepts? (Vygotsky, 1934/1987a, p. 123).

The Vygotskian Experiments

Leonid S. Sakharov (1930/1994) modified the experimental–genetic method implemented in the memory and attention experiments for the study of concept formation (Vygotsky, 1934/1987a, p. 127). One set of stimuli constituted the object of the task, which were geometric figures. The other stimuli were the label(s) on upturned figure(s), which could aid the child in the task of forming a group of figures representing a concept. The concept names used in the experiments were nonsense syllables. Vygotsky's (1931/1994a) rationale for the laboratory experiments using these materials was that this approach freed the child from the guiding influence of his or her own language.

The Vygotskian experiments included more than 300 normal children, adolescents, and adults and individuals with speech and cognitive problems (Vygotsky, 1931/1994a, p. 211). The experiments used a "motley unorganized" collection of objects in which the characteristics (color, shape, height, and size) of the objects occurred an unequal number of times (Sakharov, 1930/1994, p. 95).

The experimental procedure is presented in Table 2.3. As indicated, the child's task is to select all the geometric figures that, like the upturned figure, are examples of the *bat* concept. After the child completed her selections and provided a rationale for her choices, the experimenter turned over another figure. The purpose of this step is to assist the child in identifying her selection errors. The child's selections are returned to the collection and she tries again. This process contin-

TABLE 2.3. Sequence of Events in the Vygotskian Concept Formation Experiments

Experimental materials

20–30 wooden figures differentiated by (a) color (yellow, green, red, black), (b) shape (triangle, pyramid, rectangular cube, parallelepiped, cylinder), (c) height (short, tall), and (d) size (small, large), with an artificial word written on the bottom of each. Four concepts are represented: (a) *bat* (small, short figures); (b) *dek* (small, tall figures); (c) *rots* (large, short figures); and (d) *mup* (large, tall figures). The figures are randomly arranged in one field of a game board that is divided into fields.

Procedure

1. The experimenter turns over one figure (a small, red, short parallelepiped) and asks the child to read the word on the bottom (*bat*).
2. The experimenter places the figure in a special field on the board.
3. The experimenter tells the child that (a) the pieces on the board are toys that belong to children from a foreign country; (b) some toys are called "bat" like the upturned figure; others have other names; (c) think carefully about the other toys that might be called "bat" and place them with the upturned figure in order to receive a prize.
4. The child removes a group of figures from the collection and places them beside the "bat" figure.
5. The experimenter records the time and type of each figure that is removed.
6. The experimenter then asks the child his or her rationale for the selections.
7. The experimenter then turns over another figure and reads the name on the bottom. This information indicates either (a) the nonremoved figures still include a "bat" figure or (b) the group of removed figures includes a non-"bat" figure.
8. The overturned figure is placed beside the "bat" model.
9. The figures removed by the child are taken back, and the child is asked to try again.
10. The child continues selecting groups (and receiving feedback in the form of a new upturned figure after each selection) until the child selects the correct group and states a corrected definition of "bat."

Note. Summarized from Sakharov (1930/1994).

ues until the child forms the group correctly and states an accurate definition of *bat*. Later, in reflecting on the experimental procedures, Vygotsky (1934/1987b) noted that this step introduced an artificial requirement into the concept formation process. In real life, a child's subsequent efforts do not begin from scratch but rather build on prior development. The inclusion of step 9 (see Table 2.3) in the experiment precluded any possibility of identifying transitions between stages of concept development (p. 229).

Findings

Like the experiments on attention and memory, the concept formation experiments indicated different phases or stages that preceded conceptual thinking. Very young children simply formed "an unordered heap of objects" (Vygotsky, 1934/1987a, p. 134). Vygotsky (1931/1994a, p. 217) referred to this phase as syncretic images or stockpiles of objects. In this context, the term *syncretic* refers to grouping together whole clusters or whole situations. In contrast, preschool children joined objects together on the basis of factual connections, but the connections changed from object to object. For example, the child first may join a red parallelogram to a red circle. Then he or she selects a triangle because, like the parallelogram, it has sloping sides. Vygotsky (1931/1994a, 1934/1987a) referred to these groups as complexes. At about school age, the child could group objects together on the basis of their shared characteristics (e.g., triangles; Vygotsky, 1934/1987a, 1931/1994a).

From a psychological perspective, the data indicated that concept or word meanings varied across age levels, indicated by the changing nature of the connections among the selected objects. These findings became the nucleus of Vygotsky's (1934/1987a, 1934/1987b, 1931/1994a) analyses of the phases or stages that contribute to the development of conceptual thinking. These stages are discussed in Chapter 6.

Summary

Vygotsky maintained that the transformation of primitive or elementary cognitive processes into higher forms of thinking is the principle that explains complex cognitive behavior. Also, this transformation depends on the incorporation of cultural signs and symbols into one's thinking. However, research on this principle is complicated by the fact that simple methods for mastering memory and attention have become automatic through historical development.

Therefore, one task facing the researcher is to plan research so that the studies capture the early use of signs by young children. In addition, research should identify the concrete structures of sign-using behavior. Vygotsky also identified research methods to avoid. Included are simply documenting external events, relying on research participants' self-reports on the nature of their thinking, and simply recording facts.

The research situations set up by Vygotsky and his colleagues met three important criteria. First, the situations externalized the participant's thinking without relying on self-report information. Second, the tasks could not be completed by natural cognitive processes. Third, auxiliary stimuli were placed nearby. This approach is referred to as the experimental–genetic method or the functional method of double stimulation.

The memory experiments required the recall of word or number lists. The word experiments provided pictures nearby as potential aids. In the experiments on attention, the task objective was to answer a series of rapid-fire questions without naming previously established forbidden colors. Available auxiliary stimuli consisted of colored cards. The experiments indicated qualitative differences in sign use across the age groups from early childhood to adults. The young children relied on their natural processes of memory or attention but were unsuccessful. Preschoolers attempted to use the auxiliary stimuli, but they too were not successful. School-age children, however, were highly accurate in their use of the auxiliary stimuli. Adults, in contrast, constructed internal cues. Although the data could be explained by an S-R connection, that explanation does not address the active intervention of the individual, and it also ignores the qualitative changes that occur between the stimulus and the response.

The concept formation experiments focused on word meanings as represented by concepts. The experiments used geometric figures with nonsense labels on the bottom to indicate group membership (auxiliary stimuli). The purpose was to determine when and how the research participants used the nonsense syllable to form groups of objects. In the experiments, the research participants selected various figures that they perceived as belonging to a particular group. Results indicated different phases or stages in the formation of groups from random collections of objects to the correct selection of all the examples of a concept.

IMPLICATIONS FOR EDUCATIONAL AND PSYCHOLOGICAL RESEARCH

Vygotsky's views on research and his experimental–genetic method provide suggestions for both planning and implementing research studies. Discussed in this section are a framework for action research, a framework for theoretical research, and structuring the research situation.

A Framework for Action Research

Action research is a form of systematic inquiry that is conducted by classroom teachers, principals, school counselors, and others invested in the teaching/learning environment (Mills, 2007, p. 5). Classroom teachers who conduct action research typically address their teaching and the extent to which their students are learning. The purpose is to develop insight, develop reflective practice, and improve student outcomes (p. 5).

Consider, for example, the teacher who is planning to research the situation that the children are having difficulty in math problem solving and in applying their skills to other math situations (p. 25). The teacher's theoretical orientation is that connections among math concepts and procedural knowledge are a goal of mathematics.

State Basic Assumptions or Beliefs

Vygotsky (1982–1984/1997g) advocated that researchers state their basic assumptions because they influence the character and properties of the events under study. The teacher's beliefs about math may range from a back-to-basics approach with an emphasis on correct answers to the belief that all knowledge is a construction that occurs through interaction with others. Each emphasizes different activities in the classroom.

In the area of language arts, for example, one set of assumptions supports the holistic approach to literacy known as whole language. The key assumption of this orientation is that language is easily learned through use in authentic contexts. A different set of assumptions supports a phonics-based approach in which the sound structure of the language is of primary importance. Each leads to a particular set of classroom activities and different research questions.

Determine the Essential Characteristics of the Events to Be Studied

Vygotsky (1960/1997a) maintained that appropriate research methods must address the hidden connections behind surface events. Otherwise, the research cannot identify potential problems in cognition. For example, the child in the attention experiments had to hold in her mind the forbidden colors while she quickly formulated answers to the experimenter's questions. This description identifies the hidden connections behind the phrase "controlling one's attention." In first-grade mathematics, simple word problems require an understanding of the processes of joining and separating. An example that requires joining states that Colin has five marbles and asks how many more he needs to make 13 altogether.

A Framework for Theoretical Research

In contrast to action research, educational psychologists typically research the effectiveness of particular principles. Examples are the effect
of learner self-questions about text on comprehension and the relationship of theoretical constructs such as self-efficacy to classroom events.
Suggestions for psychologists and educational researchers emphasize the
importance of conducting a thorough literature review to identify gaps
or conflicts in the findings of other related studies. Vygotsky's suggestions, however, go further.

State Basic Assumptions or Beliefs and Relevant
Theoretical Principles

Unlike Vygotsky's research design, current studies often investigate theoretical constructs, such as academic self-concept, self-regulation of learning, reading comprehension, and mathematical achievement, in group
settings through the administration of paper-and-pencil tests or surveys.
To implement Vygotsky's suggestions, researchers should review these
practices in terms of their basic beliefs about the constructs they are
studying. Specifically, for example, does the researcher view academic
self-concept as a set of beliefs about oneself or as represented by particular actions and reactions in academic situations? The researcher's basic
beliefs influence the research design and the data collection methods.

In addition to identifying basic beliefs, Vygotsky (1982–1984/
1997g) suggested that researchers should derive questions for the study
from theory and should not attempt to combine principles from different
theories. Learning theories, for example, describe activities appropriate
for learning the content in the curriculum. For example, information-
processing theory maintains that the essential elements of learning are
the mental events of attention, perception, encoding, storage in long-
term memory, and, subsequently, retrieval. Deriving research questions
from information-processing theory involves asking how well classroom
activities facilitate the identified mental events.

In contrast, cognitive-development theories do not address specific
items of content, such as the capital of Great Britain or the reasons
American colonists won the Revolutionary War. Instead, these theories
focus on the essential events that, over time, lead to major changes in the
child's thinking. In Vygotsky's theory, these outcomes are self-organized
attention, categorical perception, conceptual thinking, and logical memory. The problem with combining these two types of theories is that, for
example, classroom activities designed to attract the learner's attention
(information-processing theory) do not facilitate developing the learner's

skill in self-directing and managing his attention (Vygotsky's cultural–historical theory).

Determine the Essential Characteristics of the Events to Be Studied

Educational psychologists and other researchers often address constructs such as achievement. The research also may address possible relationships between an intervention, such as an instructional method, and other constructs, such as ethnicity and grade level.

Conducting research on these and other variables has become an ingrained practice, and the original role of these variables is often missed. Typically, that role is to serve as a surrogate variable for some unobservable and, by implication, unmeasurable process. Achievement, for example, was selected to represent learning, and the students with higher scores have presumably learned more than those with lower scores. Similarly, grade level is a surrogate for level of maturity and/or knowledge, and ethnicity is the surrogate for particular cultural patterns and socialization practices.

Vygotsky's focus on process challenges researchers to rethink such constructs. This approach begins with the question, What is the nature of the process represented by this construct? An example is grade level. Applying Vygotsky's perspective, the rationale for this variable should not be that a higher grade level simply represents an increase in the amount of a child's experience. The reason is that amount of experience does not explain psychological differences in cognitive development (Vygotsky & Luria, 1930/1993). Therefore, developmental studies should address hypothesized changes in psychological functioning. For example, Vygotsky's (1930–1931/1998a) research indicated that the transition from external to internal mastery of the processes of attention and memory is "the most essential trait that distinguishes the adolescent from the child" (p. 104). Therefore, for example, a study of grade-level differences in science achievement between 8th and 10th graders should focus on the extent to which the students demonstrate internal mastery of key cognitive processes.

Application of Vygotsky's perspective also would change the nature of the literature review in research studies. The constructs discussed in the literature would be analyzed in terms of the processes they reflect, thereby clarifying the results of prior studies.

Structuring the Research Situation

Vygotsky (1960/1997b) noted that researchers who are seeking understanding of the child's cognitive processes face a particular problem. Specifically, a basic law of behavior is stimulus-response (p. 112). Individuals respond to stimuli in the environment (e.g., What were the major events in the Revolutionary War?) or to stimuli within themselves (e.g., I need to review the chapter on basic economic principles). The problem for teachers and researchers is obtaining information about the individual's mental processes that occur between the stimulus and the response. Both the format of the experimental–genetic method and the findings inform contemporary research. Discussed in this section are problems with concurrent verbal protocols, externalizing internal processes, and assessing basic meanings.

Problems with Concurrent Verbal Protocols

Some researchers have recommended the use of concurrent verbal protocols developed by Ericsson and Simon (1984, 1993). Also referred to as "think alouds," the concurrent verbal protocol consists of the individual saying out loud everything that she says to herself silently while completing a task. The individual is *not* asked to describe or explain choices of decisions she is making.

Although implemented in several fields, concurrent verbal protocols are subject to the limitation referred to as the reactivity problem (Branch, 2000; Stratman & Hamp-Lyons, 1994). Included are factors that cause the individual difficulty in verbalizing his thoughts. One is the learning that occurs as the individual speaks aloud in which his attention to critical activities increases (Stratman & Hamp-Lyons, 1994, p. 95). Vygotsky's research on schoolchildren's egocentric speech (their spontaneous speech while problem solving) indicated that they tended to make fewer errors than in the silent condition.

Another factor is that some students are unable to attend to the task and talk at the same time, even though the verbalization excludes explanations. Vygotsky's (1934/1987d) analyses of thought and word led him to conclude that "the structure of speech is not a simple mirror image of the structure of thought. It cannot, therefore, be placed on thought like clothes off a rack" (p. 251). In other words, speech restructures the thought because the thought, in terms of actual words, is incomplete. Because thought is fleeting, speech, at the very least, slows down the process. Therefore, because it differs from the information that "pops into one's head," the overt verbalization is very likely to lose or distort the thought.

Externalizing Internal Processes

The format of the experimental–genetic method avoids the problems associated with concurrent verbalizations. Implementation of the method requires the use of concrete tasks that externalize the key principle under investigation and also do not restrict the research participant's course of action.

In this way, experiments can provide information about the meaning of the situation for the child. For example, the concept formation experiments indicated that, for the young child, grouping objects according to a concept label meant that an object only had to share one defining characteristic with one other selected object. In the child's view, all the examples need not share all the concept characteristics.

In other words, the format allows the experimenter to determine whether the child understands the psychological nature of particular cognitive tasks. This type of information is particularly important in arithmetic. One approach to researching the child's knowledge of number concepts is to provide the child with a group of 10 tokens, and then ask the child, for example, how many ways s/he can make the number 4. The child has not developed basic forms of the concept if his only strategy is to select four tokens from the group while counting 1, 2, 3, 4. Strategies also should include, for example, beginning with six tokens and taking away two, selecting a group of three tokens and adding one, and taking away six tokens from the group of 10.

Externalizing cognitive tasks also can reveal the short-cut heuristics used by the child that circumvent or substitute for the particular cognitive process under study. For example, in the memory experiments, young children searched for elements in the pictures that were replicas of the words to be remembered. As already noted, one young boy identified a yellow spot in the picture of a hatchet. He designated it as the sun, a word in the list to be remembered. In the task in the prior paragraph, the goal is to determine whether the child can use the concepts of joining and separating groups to form a particular number. If the child only counts to 4, he is substituting a more primitive process for concept knowledge.

Assessing Prior Meanings

Vygotsky's analysis of the existing concept formation research indicated that the assessment formats were inadequate in determining learner knowledge. Included were asking for a verbal definition and naming the concept on being told the concept characteristics. Then the research conducted by Vygotsky and his colleagues indicated that learning concepts is not an all-or-nothing event. Preschool children were unable to use the concept label and a concept example to select the other examples of the concept. In contrast, schoolchildren were able to correctly select the triangles from the group of geometric figures. However, this capability does not mean that the learner can, for example, compare triangles with other polygons, depict the relationships between triangles and pyramids, and so on.

This finding is important in contemporary research in which students' prior knowledge is an important factor in their understanding of new material. Assessing that prior knowledge, to be accurate, must address the learner's connections and relationships among the concepts that the researcher has identified as essential prior knowledge in the study.

In summary, teachers and researchers should first identify their basic beliefs about the events under study. This step serves to clarify the focus of the study and avoid contradictions in the framework. Second the essential acts of thinking that are required in the processes under study should be identified. Also, constructs such as grade level, ethnicity, and achievement should be described in terms of their essential characteristics. For example, ethnicity typically is a surrogate for particular cultural patterns and socialization practices.

Cognitive researchers face a problem in their studies in that they are interested in the processes that occur between the presentation of a situation (stimulus) and learner responses. Some researchers have implemented concurrent verbal protocols. In addition to reactivity, external speech is not a mirror image of thought, and some children have operated differently in silent situations and situations that included spontaneous speech.

The experimental–genetic method, in contrast, externalizes the cognitive process and implements concrete tasks that do not restrict the course of action to be taken. This procedure can determine the meaning of the task for the learner and identify those who do not understand task requirements. Equally important is to accurately assess essential prior knowledge required in the study.

REFERENCES

Berg, E. E. (1970). *L. S. Vygotsky's theory of the social and historical origins of consciousness* Doctoral dissertation, University of Wisconsin.

Branch, J. (2000, May). *The trouble with think alouds: Generating data using concurrent verbal protocols.* Paper presented at the 28th Annual Conference of the Canadian Association for Information Science, Toronto, Ontario, Canada.

Clodd, E. (1905). *The story of the alphabet.* New York: Appleton.

Ericsson, K. A., & Simon, H. A. (1984). *Protocol analysis. Verbal reports as data.* Cambridge, MA: MIT Press.

Ericsson, K. A., & Simon, H. A. (1993). *Protocol analysis. Verbal reports as data* (revised ed.). Cambridge, MA: MIT Press.

Leont'ev, A. N. (1959). *Problems of mental development.* Moscow: Publishing House of the Academy of Pedagogical Sciences RSFSR.

Leont'ev, A. N. (1994). The development of voluntary attention in the child. In R. van der Veer & J. Valsiner (Eds.), *The Vygotsky reader* (pp. 289–312). Cambridge, MA: Blackwell.

Mills, G. E. (2007). *Action research: A guide for the teacher researcher* (3rd ed.). Columbus, OH: Merrill.

Sakharov, L. (1994). Methods for investigating concepts. In R. van der Veer & J. Valsiner (Eds.), *The Vygotsky reader* (pp. 73–98). Cambridge, MA: Blackwell. (Original published 1930)

Stratman, J. F., & Hamp-Lyons, L. (1994). Reactivity in concurrent think-aloud protocols: Issue for research. In P. Smagorinsky (Ed.), *Speaking about writing: Reflections on research methodology* (Vol. 8, pp. 89–111). Thousands Oaks, CA: Sage.

Thurnwald, R. (1922). Psychologie des primitiven menschen. In G. Kafka (Ed.), *Handbuck der rergleichenden psychologie* (Vol. 1, pp. 147–320). Munich: Ernst Reinhardt.

van der Veer, R. (1991). The anthropological underpinnings of Vygotsky's thinking. *Studies in Soviet Thought, 42,* 73–91.

van der Veer, R. (1997). Some major themes in Vygotsky's theoretical work: An introduction. In R. W. Rieber & J. Wollock (Eds.), *Collected works of L. S. Vygotsky: Vol. 3. Problems of the theory and history of psychology* (pp. 1–7). New York: Plenum.

Vygotsky, L. S. (1929). The problem of the cultural development of the child. *Journal of Genetic Psychology, 36,* 415–434.

Vygotsky, L. S. (1979). The development of higher forms of attention in childhood. *Soviet Psychology, 18*(1), 67–115. (Original work published 1929)

Vygotsky, L. S. (1987a). An experimental study of concept development. In R. W. Rieber & A. S. Carton (Eds.), *Collected works of L. S. Vygotsky: Vol. 1. Problems of general psychology* (pp. 121–166). New York: Plenum. (Original work published 1934)

Vygotsky, L. S. (1987b). The development of scientific concepts in childhood. In R. W. Rieber & A. S. Carton (Eds.), *Collected works of L. S. Vygotsky: Vol. 1. Problems of general psychology* (pp. 167–241). New York: Plenum. (Original work published 1934)

Vygotsky, L. S. (1987c). The problem and the method of investigation. In R. W. Rieber & A. S. Carton (Eds.), *Collected works of L. S. Vygotsky: Vol. 1. Problems of general psychology* (pp. 43–51). New York: Plenum. (Original work published 1934)

Vygotsky, L. S. (1987d). Thought and word. In R. W. Rieber & A. S. Carton (Eds.), *Collected works of L. S. Vygotsky: Vol. 1. Problems of general psychology* (pp. 243–285). New York: Plenum. (Original work published 1934)

Vygotsky, L. S. (1994a). The development of thinking and concept formation in adolescence. In R. van der Veer & J. Valsiner (Eds.), *The Vygotsky reader* (pp. 185–265). Cambridge, MA: Oxford. (Original work published 1931)

Vygotsky, L. S. (1994b). The problem of the environment. In R. van der Veer & J. Valsiner (Eds.), *The Vygotsky reader* (pp. 338–354). Cambridge, MA: Blackwell. (Original work published 1935)

Vygotsky, L. S. (1997a). Analysis of higher mental functions. In R. W. Rieber (Ed.), *Collected works of L. S. Vygotsky: Vol. 4. The history of the development of higher mental functions* (pp. 65–82). New York: Plenum. (Original work published 1960)

Vygotsky, L. S. (1997b). Genesis of higher mental functions. In R. W. Rieber (Ed.), *Collected works of L. S. Vygotsky: Vol. 4. The history of the development of higher mental functions* (pp. 97–119). New York: Plenum. (Original work published 1960)

Vygotsky, L. S. (1997c). Mastering attention. In R. W. Rieber (Ed.), *Collected works of L. S. Vygotsky: Vol. 4. The history of the development of higher mental functions* (pp. 153–177). New York: Plenum. (Original work published 1982–1984)

Vygotsky, L. S. (1997d). Psychology and the theory of the localization of mental functions. In R. W. Rieber & J. Wollock (Eds.), *Collected works of L. S. Vygotsky: Vol. 1. Problems of the theory and history of psychology* (pp. 130–144). New York: Plenum. (Original work published 1934)

Vygotsky, L. S. (1997e). Research method. In R. W. Rieber (Ed.), *Collected works of L. S. Vygotsky: Vol. 4. The history of the development of higher mental functions* (pp. 27–63). New York: Plenum. (Original work published 1960)

Vygotsky, L. S. (1997f). The development of mnemonic and mnemotechnical functions. In R. W. Rieber (Ed.), *Collected works of L. S. Vygotsky: Vol. 4. The history of the development of higher mental functions* (pp. 179–190). New York: Plenum. (Original work published 1982–1984)

Vygotsky, L. S. (1997g). The historical meaning of the crisis in psychology: A methodological investigation. In R. W. Rieber & J. Wollock (Eds.), *Collected works of L. S. Vygotsky: Vol. 3. Problem of the theory and history of psychology* (pp. 233–343). New York: Plenum. (Original work published in 1982–1984)

Vygotsky, L. S. (1997h). The methods of reflexological and psychological investigation. In R. W. Rieber & J. Wollock (Eds.), *Collected works of L. S. Vygotsky: Vol. 3. Problems of the theory and history of psychology* (pp. 35–49). New York: Plenum. (Original work published 1926)

Vygotsky, L. S. (1997i). The problem of the development of higher mental functions. In R. W. Rieber (Ed.), *Collected works of L. S. Vygotsky: Vol. 4. The history of the development of higher mental functions* (pp. 1–26). New York: Plenum. (Original work published 1960)

Vygotsky, L. S. (1998a). Development of higher mental functions during the transitional age. In R. W. Rieber (Ed.), *Collected works of L. S. Vygotsky: Vol. 5. Child psychology* (pp. 83–149). New York: Plenum. (Original work published 1982–1984)

Vygotsky, L. S. (1998b). Development of thinking and formation of concepts in the adolescent. In R. W. Rieber (Ed.), *Collected works of L. S. Vygotsky: Vol. 5. Child psychology* (pp. 29–81). New York: Plenum. (Original work published 1982–1984)

Vygotsky, L. S. (1999). Methods of studying higher mental functions. *Collected works of L. S. Vygotsky: Vol. 6. Scientific legacy* (pp. 57–60). New York: Plenum. (Original work published 1982–1984)

Vygotsky, L. S., & Luria, A. R. (1993). *Studies in the history of behavior: Ape, primitive, and child.* Hillsdale, NJ: Erlbaum. (Original work published 1930)

Vygotsky, L. S., & Luria, A. R. (1994). Tool and symbol in child development. In R. van der Veer & J. Valsiner (Eds.), *The Vygotsky reader* (pp. 99–174). Cambridge, MA: Blackwell.

3

Cultural Signs and Symbols

A new regulatory principle of behavior must of necessity
correspond to a new type of behavior. We find it in the social
determination of behavior carried out with the aid of signs.
—VYGOTSKY (1960/1997f, p. 56)

Vygotsky, from his analysis of the writings of anthropologists and his experiments on memory and attention, identified the structural prototype of all higher cognitive behavior. Specifically, humans develop or incorporate cultural signs and symbols into their thinking to be successful in various cognitive tasks. Through the process of mastering cultural symbols for this purpose, they also raise their thinking to a higher level (Vygotsky, 1929, 1960/1997a, 1960/1997c, 1960/1997j; Vygotsky & Luria, 1994). In the human race, this process is historical (new symbol systems are being invented). In the child, this process is cultural (the child must develop the culture's ways of thinking using symbols).

The experiments on memory and attention also indicated that the process of mastering cultural signs as auxiliary stimuli for thinking is lengthy and characterized by qualitative differences at different stages. Discussed in this chapter are the role of signs and the developmental analysis of sign operations.

THE ROLE OF SIGNS

Signs are the artificial stimuli introduced into a psychological task that change the nature of the individual's cognitive processes (Vygotsky,

1960/1997f, p. 54). Vygotsky described their pivotal role in cognitive development in several ways. Discussed in this section is the first law of cognitive development and the unity of self-mastery, psychological development, and cultural development.

The First Law of Cognitive Development

On the basis of experiments on memory and attention, Vygotsky (1930–1931/1998c) formalized his first law of the structure and development of higher cognitive processes (p. 168). It is "the law *of the transmission from direct, innate, natural forms and methods of behavior to mediated, artificial, mental functions* [processes] *that develop in the process of cultural development*" (p. 168).

In other words, the developing higher cognitive processes are not simply the acquisition of some new psychophysiological processes. Instead, higher cognitive processes result from the development of new ways of thinking based primarily on some system of signs. Discussions that expand on this law are signification versus signalization, the characteristics of a mediated structure, and the concept of psychological tools.

Signification versus Signalization

Vygotsky (1931/1966, 1960/1997f) identified three primitive or elementary cognitive processes that are inborn in both early humans and today's infants. These elementary processes are involuntary attention, simple perception, and natural or direct memory. These processes are controlled by stimuli in the environment and involve concrete experiences. For example, events such as thunder, lightning, and other sights and sounds in the environment attracted or repelled the involuntary attention of early humans. Similarly, events such as a bright light or a loud noise attract or repel the attention of the infant and young child.

Also, natural or direct memory is simply a record of sense impressions and concrete experiences. A young child, for example, puts his hand on a hot stove and feels pain. On approaching the stove again, the child recalls the pain and exercises caution. Vygotsky (1960/1997f) labeled such connections between events that are totally created by natural conditions as *signalization* (p. 55). The sight of the stove, for example, signals the child's recall of the prior pain. In other words, signalization is the passive recollection of the natural connections between events (e.g., stove equals pain), but it is not the basis of human behavior (p. 55).

When early humans began to create and use auxiliary stimuli to manage and control their memory, they began to progress beyond their biological heritage. Examples discussed in Chapter 2 are the Peruvian quipu system and the notches cut into wood to remember a missionary's sermon. These and similar events were the beginning of the historical development of cognition.

These signs and others change nothing in the particular task. The signs are retrograde (Vygotsky, 1982–1984/1999, p. 46); they either redirect or reconstruct the individual's cognitive behavior (Vygotsky, 1960/1997j, p. 89; Vygotsky, 1982–1984/1997h, p. 89). For example, school-age children in the memory experiments successfully developed mental connections between words and unrelated pictures to remember a lengthy word list. The sign reconstructs the individual's cognitive behavior by establishing new mental connections in the brain.

Vygotsky (1960/1997f) labeled the creation and use of signs to redirect one's thinking as *signification*. He also referred to this use of artificial stimuli as *sign operations*. The individual's integration of simple signs that manage and control one's thinking in cognitive tasks is the beginning of the development of higher cognitive processes. Through this lengthy and ever-changing process, elementary cognitive processes (involuntary attention, simple perception, and natural or direct memory) are transformed into higher forms of thinking. Signification marks the beginning of advanced cognitive development historically in the human race and culturally in the child.

The Characteristics of a Mediated Structure

Natural memory, similar to simple perception, is a direct record of concrete events. The inclusion of an auxiliary stimulus into a situation, when it assists the individual to form new connections with the object of the task, transforms the individual's cognitive activity. The activity becomes an indirect, mediated process (see Figure 3.1). An example in the memory experiments is the school-age child who selected the picture of a chair to represent the word *house* because "a house is where one can sit" (Leont'ev, 1959).

The new intermediate link is not a way to improve or perfect the cognitive operation (Vygotsky & Luria, 1994, p. 145). Instead, the auxiliary stimulus changes the structure of the cognitive activity. The child who remembers a set of words using pictures is also relying on imagination and her capability to note similarities and differences (Vygotsky, 1982–1984/1997e, p. 95). In other words, "in mediated memorization, it is thinking which is most important" (p. 95).

This cognitive process should not be confused with the situation in which the child searches for a direct representation of the word. An example, mentioned in Chapter 2, is the child who found a small yellow dot in a picture, which he labeled the *sun*, the word to be remem-

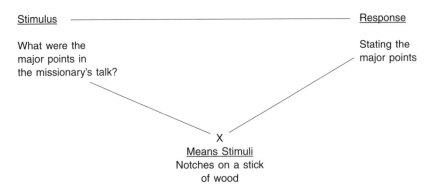

FIGURE 3.1. Example of the role of auxiliary or means stimuli. Adapted from Vygotsky (1982–1984/1997g).

bered. In this way, he turned the task into one of direct recall. In other words, the inclusion of an external object in the memory task does not necessarily mean that the child has constructed new connections in his memory.

Another important aspect of a mediated structure is that it is not cast in concrete but rather is subject to development (Vygotsky & Luria, 1994, p. 145). In the memory experiments that used lists of numbers, children who had learned to count tore bits of paper (from the strip the researcher provided) to represent the numbers. In contrast, older children who had learned the symbols for numbers tore the paper into number shapes instead of relying on a " 'tally-like' notation" (Vygotsky & Luria, 1930/1993, p. 180). Also, as indicated in the Vygotskian experiments on memory and attention, school-age children relied on external stimuli to manage their thinking. However, adults in the memory studies created complex sentences to remember the set of words. Their performance reflects the development of verbal memory mentioned previously. Also, adults in the experiments on attention did not use the colored cards. Instead, they mentally kept track of the forbidden colors through internal reminders to themselves. In other words, Vygotsky's structural principle contrasts with theories that specify particular elements of learning that are unchanging.

The Concept of Psychological Tools

Vygotsky (1960/1997f) noted that the invention and use of auxiliary stimuli (signs) to solve a problem is somewhat similar to the invention and use of tools for human labor (p. 60). Both are instruments in that they assist humans to carry out particular tasks. In Vygotsky's early writings, he referred to such cultural symbols as "psychological tools" (p. 60). Examples are the pictures and colored cards provided in the experiments on memory and attention.

However, Vygotsky cautioned that the analogy between psychological tools and tools of labor should not be carried too far. One erroneous view identified by Vygotsky was John Dewey's designation of "language as a tool of tools" (p. 61). The problem in that statement is that psychological tools and tools for labor are not equivalent. The use of a physical tool is directed outward toward some object in the environment, and the tool changes some aspect of that object. In contrast, the psychological tool does not alter the task or problem that the individual faces. Instead, it is directed inward and acts on the individual's internal activity and behavior (p. 62).

Of importance is that the signs and symbols of a culture are not automatically psychological tools. A stimulus "becomes a psychological tool by virtue of its use as a means of influencing mind and behavior" (Vygotsky, 1982–1984/1997h, p. 87). "Examples of psychological tools and their complex systems [include] language, different forms of numeration and counting, mnemotechnic techniques, algebraic symbols, works of art, writing schemes, diagrams, maps, blueprints, all sorts of conventional signs, etc." (p. 85). Each of these examples is an artificial device for mastering one's own mental processes; they are "social, not organic or individual devices . . . and they are the product of historical development" (p. 85).

The Unity of Higher Mental Functions, Self-Mastery, and Cultural Development

The tendency in psychology, noted in Chapter 2, is to analyze events of interest into their smallest elements. In contrast, Vygotsky sought to identify the essence or essential characteristics of complex events that reflect all the properties of the whole. This approach to thinking about psychological issues also allowed him to identify commonalities in processes and events.

An example is his identification of three processes that are equivalent to each other. These three equivalent processes are expressed as *"the concept of higher mental function* [process or capability], *the concept of cultural development of behavior, and the concept of mastery of behavior by internal processes"* (Vygotsky, 1960/1997i, p. 7). (See Figure 3.2.) The higher mental functions or processes identified by Vygotsky are self-organized attention, categorical perception, conceptual thinking, and logical memory. They are the outcomes of a lengthy and ever-changing

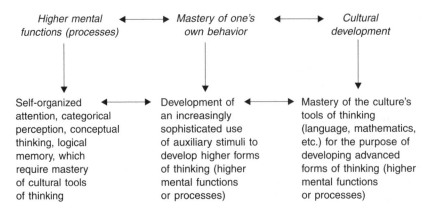

FIGURE 3.2. The equivalence of higher mental functions, mastery of one's own behavior, and cultural development.

process of cognitive development that requires the increasingly sophisticated use of cultural signs and symbols to manage one's thinking and thereby raise it to a higher level.

An example is the cultural development of attention. This process consists of changes in the devices of control and the way that attention operates (Vygotsky, 1982–1984/1997d, p. 154). School-age participants in the forbidden colors game used colored cards to focus their attention for a short period of time on the colors that could be legitimately named in response to the experimenter's questions.

Subsequently, however, individuals develop other attention-holding devices that permit them to engage in lengthy tasks. For example, an individual may continue to pay attention while reading a lengthy passage because he highlights particular sentences as he reads.

Self-Mastery

The concept of mastery of one's own behavior as Vygotsky used it differs from the use in education in the United States. In the educational system, mastery typically refers to the mastery of particular content or of identified skills, such as summarizing text and constructing a thesis statement for a paper. Students complete various kinds of assessments following identified units of instruction to determine the extent of their learning. Mastery gained prominence in the late 1960s with Benjamin Bloom's (1968) model of mastery learning. Briefly, the model varied the amount of time spent by different students on a unit, so that the majority of students could reach a predetermined standard of mastery performance. The model was congruent with classroom practice in that students were evaluated on identified curriculum priorities.

In contrast, Vygotsky addressed mastery in terms of the cognitive development of the individual. Specifically, (a) cognitive development involves attaining mastery of oneself in progressively more complex ways of thinking, and (b) mastery is attained through the incorporation of increasingly sophisticated auxiliary stimuli (signs) into cognitive tasks (Vygotsky, 1960/1997c, p. 112; 1960/1997j, p. 87).

In addition, the development of thinking indicates "a continuous perfecting" of the types of signs and the development of new devices for mastering one's cognitive processes (Vygotsky, 1930–1931/1998c, p. 168). An example is speech. When individuals develop verbal memory, they construct a verbal record rather than directly remembering concrete experiences (Vygotsky, 1982–1984/1997g, p. 189). In this process, they "abbreviate, order, and abstract and, using the word, profoundly change the form of the material to be remembered" (p. 189). Recall of the word or symbols reinstates the experience in short-term memory complete with factual and emotional detail. Examples include personal events such as the senior prom and equations and formulas such as $e = mc^2$.

Cultural Development

Typically, *cultural development* in terms of the activity of students refers to learning about one's own or another's culture. In contrast, Vygotsky used the term to differentiate natural development, the elementary cognitive processes (involuntary attention, simple perception, and direct or natural memory), from the child's efforts to develop higher forms of thinking using cultural signs and symbols. He stated that "the cultural development of any function [process] consists of a person's developing a series of artificial stimuli and signs" (Vygotsky, 1982–1984/1997d, p. 154). He also referred to "the process of cultural development of memory" (Vygotsky, 1982–1984/1997g, p. 182), "basic culture in the development of counting" (Vygotsky, 1982–1984/1997b, p. 150), "cultural development of attention" (Vygotsky, 1982–1984/1997d, p. 154), and so on.

In other words, culture refers to the tools for thinking in a particular society. The external means of cultural development and thinking include language, counting, writing, and so on (Vygotsky, 1931/1966, p. 16). The lengthy task for the child is to master "cultural forms of reasoning" (Vygotsky, 1929, p. 415) through learning to use cultural symbols for thinking, thereby mastering his own behavior.

Summary

Vygotsky's experiments on memory and attention essentially re-created the situation in which a Kaffir man altered the process of remembering. This development consisted of the use of auxiliary stimuli and the construction of verbal links between the notches and the missionary's words. Observations of the same cognitive behavior in school-age children led to Vygotsky's designation of such auxiliary stimuli as signs. They are the artificial stimuli introduced into a psychological task that change the nature of the individual's cognitive processes. This transformation is so important, from Vygotsky's perspective, that he formalized it in his first law of cognitive development.

Vygotsky also differentiated the simple or primitive mental functions (processes) from higher cognitive structures. The primitive functions, involuntary attention, simple perception, and natural memory, are primarily under the control of the environment. Vygotsky labeled the connections between environmental stimuli and these elementary or primitive processes as examples of signalization. In contrast, he labeled the higher cognitive structure as a sign operation that reflects the process of signification. Through this operation, remembering becomes an indirect or mediated process. It is a higher form of cognition because thinking is involved. The school-age child must note similarities and differences between the selected sign and the object of the task and create verbal links between them.

Vygotsky, in his early writings, also referred to cultural symbols that function as signs as psychological tools. Unlike tools for labor, psychological tools influence the individual's internal cognitive processes, not an external situation. As discussed in Chapter 2, Vygotsky maintained that theorists and researchers should move beyond the traditional meaning of analysis. Instead of subdividing a whole into elements, analysis should focus on identifying the essence or essential characteristics of the whole. This redirection also allowed him to identify shared characteristics of different processes. An example is his identification of the equivalence of higher mental function (higher cognitive processes), the cultural development of behavior, and the mastery of cognitive behaviors through internal processes. The higher mental processes develop through the appropriation of signs (cultural symbols that facilitate thinking), and mastery of cognitive behavior involves internal processing. Self-mastery, in other words, differs from the mastery of course content, and cultural development refers to the appropriation of cultural symbols in counting, remembering, controlling one's attention, and other cognitive processes.

DEVELOPMENTAL ANALYSIS OF SIGN OPERATIONS

Vygotsky (1960/1997j, p. 94; Vygotsky & Luria, 1994, p. 147) concluded from the studies of memory and attention that the cultural development of the child does not simply appear as a logical occurrence. In
addition, it is not discovered by the child as a "lightning-quick guess (the
'aha' reaction)" between a sign and the way to use it (Vygotsky & Luria,
1994, p. 147).

Instead, from early childhood to adulthood, cultural development
consists of identifiable qualitative changes. In the experiments, very
young children attempted the tasks using their natural or primitive cognitive processes but were unsuccessful. Preschool children attempted to
move away from involuntary attention and direct memory, but they too
were unsuccessful. In contrast, school-age children successfully reorga-
nized their thinking using signs, and adults constructed their own internal signs to manage their thinking. Vygotsky (1960/1997j, p. 94; 1982–
1984/1999, p. 50; Vygotsky & Luria, 1994, p. 148) referred to these
qualitative changes as the natural history of the sign to indicate that
"cultural forms of human behavior have natural roots in natural forms
[and] are tied to them by a thousand threads" (Vygotsky, 1960/1997j,
p. 95). Discussed in this section are the four stages of sign use and forms
of mediation.

The Stages of Sign Use

The qualitative differences in sign use observed in the experiments indicate that sign operations result from "a complex and prolonged process"
of actual development (Vygotsky & Luria, 1994, p. 147). Each change is
the product of a preceding transformation, which, in turn, sets the stage
for the next change. Between the natural elementary processes (involuntary attention and natural or direct memory) and the internally sign-
directed processes of the adult is an area of qualitatively unique cognitive
processes.

Vygotsky (1929; 1960/1997j; Vygotsky & Luria, 1994) concluded
from the research studies that each of the higher forms of behavior
undergoes four main stages or phases of development. However, he cautioned that these stages represent only the more important forms of cultural development; they are an abstract outline that cannot accurately
reflect the complexity of development (Vygotsky, 1960/1997j, p. 93).
The four stages, summarized in Table 3.1, are (a) primitive behavior or
natural psychology, (b) "naïve" psychology, (c) external sign use, and (d)
internal sign use (Vygotsky, 1929, pp. 425–426; 1960/1997c, pp. 113–

TABLE 3.1. The Stages of Sign Use

Stage	Description	Examples
1. Primitive behavior or natural psychology	The child tries to address new information by a natural means to the extent that he or she is interested in the situation	Efforts to (a) memorize a list of words, (b) keep track mentally of colors named, (c) gain a sense of quantity by viewing a set of objects
2. Naïve psychology	The child is unable to adequately use the external aids available for the task	Child (a) often looks at available pictures but states a different word than the word in the list, (b) becomes fixated on particular colors in the forbidden colors exercise, (c) attempts to count on his or her fingers but with many errors
3. External sign use	The child makes use of the external aids, forming his or her own method of connecting the means stimuli to the task	(a) Relationships clearly established between words and pictures, (b) color cards are systematically arranged and used, (c) accurate finger counting emerges
4. Internal sign use	After mastering the structure of some external method of sign use (symbolic activity), the child constructs an internal representation	(a) Constructs relationships between internal stimuli and words, (b) mentally tracks colors named with some support by the cards, (c) counts accurately and completes simple arithmetic problems in his or her head

119; 1982–1984/1997g, p. 187; 1930–1931/1998a, pp. 103–104). Also discussed is the development of counting. (Chapters 5 and 6 illustrate particular applications of this outline.)

Primitive or Natural Stage

The primitive or elementary mental processes (involuntary attention, simple perception, and natural or direct memory) are primarily under the control of the environment. As already noted in this chapter, the natural attention of the infant is both nonintentional and nonvolitional; it responds to strong stimuli such as a bright light or loud noise. (In contrast, artificial or cultural attention makes possible the organization of one's behavior to work on lengthy tasks in the classroom or the workplace.)

Similarly, natural memory "is characterized by direct impression of material" (Vygotsky, 1982–1984/1999, p. 46). The young child recalls concrete experiences (hot stove equals pain) or relies on a simple sequence of experiences to remember information. An example in the adult's thinking is trying to remember the main points in a missionary's sermon simply by listening to it.

Young children at the stage of natural memory attempt to solve tasks directly. For example, the young child can determine by sight that a group of seven apples is larger than a group of three apples (Vygotsky, 1960/1997c, p. 118). However, she is unable to differentiate between 16 and 19 apples. (Counting, a symbol-directed activity, is needed, but that occurs in a later stage of cognitive development.)

Vygotsky (1960/1997c) referred to this stage as primitive because the child's behavior is determined by "the natural state of his brain apparatus" (p. 114). Also, because the child is unaware of her limitations, she acts in a complex situation in the same way as she does in a simple one. She tries to address a complex structure with primitive ways of functioning, although this approach is not successful (p. 114).

Naïve Psychology Stage

This stage is an intermediate phase between solving tasks directly and accurately using signs or symbols to address cognitive tasks. Characteristics of this stage are (a) the idea of the purposefulness of using a sign to assist in the solution of a task is completely foreign to the child (Vygotsky & Luria, 1994, p. 148) and (b) the child attempts to use signs but is unaware of the psychological links that must be made between the sign and the task (Vygotsky, 1929; Vygotsky & Luria, 1994).

In some of the experiments on memory, the experimenter chose pictures that were somewhat related to the words to be remembered and placed them in sequence in front of the child (Vygotsky, 1929, p. 425). The child, regardless of her mental capabilities, easily recalled the words. However, with a new set of words for which the child was to choose pictures as memory aids, the error rate often was similar to that of direct remembering (Vygotsky, 1929, p. 425; 1982–1984/1997g, p. 184). In some cases, the introduction of pictures only confused the child because it presented a problem of greater complexity.

Even if the child turned to a picture on the presentation of a word, this action was no guarantee that the original word would be reproduced. Sometimes, instead of the original word, the child produced another word suggested by the picture (Vygotsky, 1929; Vygotsky & Luria, 1994). The child was unaware that a psychological link must be made between word and picture. In other words, the mere presence of an association was insufficient to guide the child's memory. This level of functioning is analogous to the performance of a man who is able to press on a lever but who is unable to use the skill to move a heavy rock (Leont'ev, 1959, p. 4).

Lacking at this stage is the child's realization of the purposeful nature of the operation. The child has not yet formed a "specific *sign relation* with the auxiliary stimulus" (Vygotsky & Luria, 1994, p. 146). Only when the child forms that relation does the association acquire the essential *"recursive character"* (p. 146) and call to mind the word to be remembered.

In addition, in tests in which meaningless abstract figures were presented as auxiliary memory aids, children ages 4 to 6 did not form psychological links with the words to be learned. Instead, the child looked for a sign that already had a connection with the word he was to remember or focused on turning a figure into a direct image of the word (Vygotsky, 1982–1984/1999, p. 51). For example, when the word was *bucket,* the child turned the figure △ upside down ▽ so that it resembled a bucket (Vygotsky & Luria, 1994, p. 150).

The child at this stage has not yet grasped the idea of the arbitrarily established connection of sign and meaning or the relativity of sign operations (p. 151). Also, the child is not yet at the stage where he can connect a sign to a word by constructing an auxiliary verbal structure (Vygotsky, 1982–1984/1999, p. 51). This explains the child's search for auxiliary stimuli that share properties or characteristics with the word to be remembered. However, this stage is the basis from which complete sign operations will later develop (Vygotsky & Luria, 1994, p. 151).

Research indicated similar reactions to the use of colored cards to focus one's attention. The purpose of the cards was to help the child focus on the allowable colors he could use in response to the experimenter's questions. Preschool children were at the stage of naïve psychology. They frequently played with the cards or selected them randomly (Vygotsky, 1982–1984/1997d, p. 155). One preschool child, for example, fixated on the white card and repeatedly responded "white" to all the experimenter's questions (Leont'ev, 1932/1994, p. 300).

External Sign Use

In the third stage, the child is able to use signs effectively in cognitive tasks. In the memory experiments, the child (a) selected from a group of pictures the one that she most closely associated with each word to be remembered and (b) subsequently reproduced the words accurately. Through these actions, the child demonstrates that she "is an integral part of the system" (Berg, 1970, p. 100). The child consciously controls the auxiliary stimuli (the pictures) in order to control his responses. Vygotsky's first law of cognitive development describes this stage of sign use.

The criteria for external sign use is that the child (a) chooses an auxiliary stimulus (sign) and (b) constructs a verbal link between the object of the task and the auxiliary stimulus. The construction of the verbal link also constructs new connections in the brain. In this way, the child masters an internal process through an external means.

The child's understanding of the psychological role of the pictures in the memory experiments is reflected in the meanings children developed to link the words with pictures that shared no visual or definitional features with the words. An example is the picture of a crab at the shore used to recall the word *theater* because the stones on the bottom are a theater for the crab. In other words, the child created the verbal picture–word link solely for the purpose of later recalling the word (Vygotsky, 1982–1984/1997g, p. 181). In remembering a number series, the child used peripheral neutral materials to create tallies or other numerical records. Like the word-recall tasks, the child executed external operations to solve the internal task of remembering (p. 188).

An important characteristic of this third stage is that it requires intentional actions; the child is initiating the actions to assist his or her recall. Leont'ev's example of the Chinese postman who is delivering an urgent telegram illustrates this stage of sign use in relation to attention. The postman placed a piece of coal, a feather, and some pepper at the end of a short pole, which he kept in front of him. The purpose was to "remind him that he must fly like a bird, run as if he were stepping over hot coals, or had burnt himself with pepper" (Leont'ev, 1932/1994, p. 292). This practice kept the postman on task and helped him avoid such distractions as the tempting products displayed in the shops.

Vygotsky and Luria (1994) noted that, for many mental activities, the stage of external sign use is the final stage of development (p. 154). However, they did not discuss any examples.

The concept of rearmament. The third stage of sign use, mastering an internal process through the appropriation of external stimuli, is not a once-and-for-all event. An example is the experiments on remembering a list of numbers accompanied by a wide strip of paper (potential auxiliary stimulus). As mentioned earlier, preschool children tore off bits of paper or tore notches in the edges of the paper to create a " 'tally-like' notation" (Vygotsky & Luria, 1930/1993, p. 180). In contrast, the school-age children tore out *"the shape of a number"* (p. 180). The cultural devices learned in school (numerical symbols) suppressed the child's former efforts at constructing tallies (p. 180). Moreover, when other devices were available as auxiliary stimuli, such as grains of seed, the school-age child constructed approximations of the number shapes.

Similarly, in the word-recall experiments, the child of 6 or 7 was able to establish word-picture connections when s/he found a picture with an already-established link in his or her experience. An example is a picture of a cow for the word *milk*. In contrast, the 10 to 11-year-olds were able to make use of pictures that were unrelated to the words and *"to actively connect the proposed word and the picture thus creating a new situation"* (p. 183). The link created by a 10-year-old between the word *theater* and his selected picture of a crab was that the beautiful pebbles were a theater for the crab (Vygotsky, 1982–1984/1997g, p. 181; Vygotsky & Luria, 1930/1993, p. 183).

Vygotsky and Luria (1930/1993) concluded that the child does not simply train his or her memory. Instead, he "rearms it" by shifting to new devices (p. 180). Moreover, the findings illustrate the influence of culture. Included is the school, which "creates a reservoir of experience" with sophisticated auxiliary methods for transforming the child's thinking. The substitution of numerical symbols for tallies is one example.

Internal Sign Use

The experiments on memory and attention indicated a fourth stage in which the structure of the cognitive operation changed radically (Vygotsky & Luria, 1994, p. 152). The prior stage, which may be described as an external instrumental operation, is transformed into an inner reconstructed operation (p. 152). In this stage, the individual internally generates auxiliary stimuli to complete a cognitive task. Examples are the complex verbal sentences constructed by adults in the memory studies. In one experiment, a participant remembered the words *beach, hail*, and *dress* by forming the sentence "A lady walked on the beach; it began to hail and ruined her dress" (Leont'ev, 1959, p. 94).

Vygotsky (1982–1984/1999, pp. 53–55; 1930–1931/1998a, p. 104; 1930–1931/1998c, p. 170) referred to the fourth stage as the law of revolution or the processes of revolution. During the fourth stage of sign use, in addition to a transition inward of the control of memory and attention, the adolescent begins to think in concepts. The school-age child views the meaning of a word as a collection of concrete objects connected by a factual link. In contrast, the adolescent sees the concept as a complex image that reflects ties and connections to other concepts (Vygotsky, 1930–1931/1998a, p. 89). It is this developing network of concepts and logical relations that completes the development of logical memory and self-directed attention.

In other words, the development of the inner regulation of purposeful cognitive activity is a two-pronged process (Vygotsky, 1982–1984/ 1999, p. 55; Vygotsky & Luria, 1994, p. 155). First, the natural process is transformed into an indirect operation when the child integrates external, auxiliary signs into her activity. Then the sign operation itself changes; it is subsequently transformed into a complex internal process in stage 4.

An Example of the Stages

The child's development of the process of counting is an example of the stages of sign operations. It is an early example of abstraction, which is a pivotal requirement of any form of thinking (Vygotsky & Luria, 1930/ 1993, p. 193). Counting also is "one of the most powerful tools that cultural development fosters in the mind of the human being" (p. 192).

However, the young child thinks at a concrete level. Experiments indicated that preschool children relied on forms or shapes to determine a general idea of equal quantities. They have not yet developed the abstraction aspect of counting (i.e., that number is independent of objects). In one study, a 4-year-old was asked to distribute a pile of cubes equally to four children seated at the table. She is then asked to confirm that the children have an equal number of cubes. An adult would simply count the cubes. Instead, the child solved the problem by forming a particular shape from the cubes, such as that of a bed. He then compared the beds constructed from the children's cubes to determine if they are similar (p. 194). In another case, the child who distributed the cubes formed towers and compared their heights.

In a different situation, the children had to divide several pencils that differed in color, shape, and size (Vygotsky, 1982–1984/1997b). The children, to make the groups equal in their eyes, began to make wands from the pencils, and each child received one wand. The problem was that one wand had five short pencils and another had two long pencils (p. 149).

In other words, primitive or natural counting (the first stage of sign use) is limited to "*the immediate perception of given pluralities and number groups*" (Vygotsky & Luria, 1994, p. 139). The child, for example, perceives that a group of three apples and a group of seven apples differ in quantity, but "the child does not really count" (p. 139). The child also can play dominoes by matching the numbers of dots he sees (Vygotsky, 1982–1984/1997b, p. 151).

Mastering the perception of number by counting is a different process than the perception of form. The shift from the direct perception of form to mediated number perception does not move in a straight line (Vygotsky, 1982–1984/1997b, p. 151; Vygotsky & Luria, 1994, p. 139).

Subsequent development involves the breakdown of the natural form and replacement by other processes. This transformation involves breaks and turns in the conflict between natural and cultural arithmetic (Vygotsky, 1982–1984/1997b, p. 151).

At stage 2, the stage of naïve use, the child is unaware of the meaning and implications of the counting process and makes many errors. For example, the child may accurately count the combined number of objects in two groups that consist of three objects and one object, respectively. However, when asked if the total can be a number other than four, he is likely to say "yes." The child has no clear idea of a total; he "magically assimilates a certain operation, not yet knowing its internal operations" (Vygotsky, 1982–1984/1997c, p. 118).

At stage 3, external sign use, the child begins to count accurately, typically relying on both speech and his fingers. Given a problem such as "Here are seven apples. Take way two. How many will be left?", the child typically puts out seven fingers and then pulls back two. The child is counting, using his fingers as external signs (p. 118). However, initially in this stage, the child makes mistakes in certain situations. For example, when asked to count the objects that form a cross,

$$\begin{matrix} & & \cdot & & \\ \cdot & \cdot & \cdot & \cdot & \cdot \\ & & \cdot & & \end{matrix}$$

the child typically counts the center object twice (Vygotsky & Luria, 1930/1993, p. 98; 1994, p. 140). In other words, the visual field is a stronger influence on the child's thinking than the process of abstraction. Subsequently, the child is able to count accurately regardless of the shapes formed by the objects. Eventually, the child can carry out counting operations in his head, relying on self-generated internal stimuli (stage 4: internal use).

The stages identified by Vygotsky apply to any form of cognitive activity that depends on signs and symbols for execution. In the case of counting, for example, the highest stage (counting in one's head) occurs during the elementary school years. However, more complex forms of cognition—the higher psychological functions of self-organized attention, categorical perception, conceptual thinking, and logical memory—do not reach the internal stage until late adolescence. In other words, the stages of sign use do not apply to cognitive functioning in general but to particular cognitive capabilities (Vygotsky, 1929, p. 425).

Forms of Mediation

A focus of Vygotsky's cultural–historical theory is cognitive development, the ways that individuals develop complex thinking. Pivotal in this process is the individual's increasingly sophisticated use of cultural signs and symbols to advance her thinking.

Direct Recall

In the experiments on memory, Vygotsky identified two different uses of auxiliary stimuli. One was the effort of young children to find something in the available pictures that was a likeness of the word to be remembered. Examples are turning an abstract figure upside down to resemble a bucket and designating a small yellow spot in a picture as the sun. This process does not meet the criteria for an external sign operation. To the extent that the child is successful in remembering the words, the memory process is that of direct recall. It is very similar to the process that Vygotsky labeled as signalization because it does not involve manipulation of stimuli.

Mediated Recall

The second use of available auxiliary stimuli in the experiments is the child's construction of verbal links that connected pictures to words to be remembered. An example is the child's linking the picture of a butterfly with the word *bird* by constructing the sentence "A butterfly is a little bird" (Leont'ev, 1959). Essential in this process is that the child constructed the link. It was not a link created by the teacher or other adult and simply memorized by the child.

Internal Mediation and Inner Speech

Gradually, the operation of relying on external stimuli becomes firmly established in the individual's behavior (Vygotsky, 1930–1931/1998a, p. 104). Then, depending on the extent that the operation becomes part of the general structure of one's thinking, it begins to operate primarily internally (p. 104). This operation is stage 4 in the use of signs.

However, the fourth stage of sign use is not a simple transfer inward of an external sign. Instead, the process of "using an external sign is radically reconstructed" (Vygotsky, 1982–1984/1999, p. 55). A simple example is the individual who did not rely on external stimuli to remember a set of words. Instead, he constructed a sentence that linked them together.

Vygotsky (1982–1984/1999, pp. 53–55; 1930–1931/1998a, p. 104; 1930–1931/1998c, p. 170) referred to the fourth stage as the law of revolution or the processes of revolution. It is "the law of transition of a function from outside inward" (Vygotsky, 1930–1931/1998c, p. 170). It is termed a revolution because new mental connections and new devices begin to control the individual's memory and attention.

Internal structures for controlling and mastering one's cognitive operations become, in their most developed form, inner speech. Briefly, inner speech is condensed, silent speech. To the extent that it carries out complex problem-solving strategies, it is internal verbal thinking (Vygotsky, 1934/1987b, p. 279). For example, in solving a physics problem, the student draws on her knowledge of physics concepts and principles and applies the relevant relationships to the particular problem.

Summary

The Vygotskian experiments on memory and attention involved subjects across the age range from early childhood to adulthood. The qualitative changes in their cognitive behavior led to the conclusions that the development of sign operations is not simply a logical event or an "aha" experience. Instead, each change sets the stage for the next change in a complex developmental process. Vygotsky concluded that the experiments had indicated four stages, the first two of which are different levels of nonmastery. Very young children (primitive behavior or natural psychology) relied on their natural processes, which were inadequate for the task. The young child, unaware of his limitations, acts in a complex situation in the same way as he does in a simple one. The preschool age (naïve psychology) is an intermediate stage between efforts to solve tasks directly and accurately using signs in cognition. Although the children attempted to use the available auxiliary stimuli, they did not understand the psychological role of those stimuli in the particular task. They too were unsuccessful.

Stages 3 (external sign use) and 4 (internal sign use) reflect two different forms of the self-mastery of cognition. Required for the effective use of external signs is an understanding of the psychological nature of the task and intentional actions by the child directed toward the solution of the task. In stage 3, school-age children in the memory experiments selected pictures for the words to be remembered, created a verbal link between picture and word, and later successfully used the pictures to recall the words. The children used external stimuli to master an internal process. Also, during this stage, children may progress to more sophisticated auxiliary stimuli, a process referred to as rearmament.

External sign use is transformed into an inner reconstructed operation in stage 4, referred to as the law of revolution. The individual relies on internally constructed stimuli and new devices to mastery memory and intention. Complex forms of cognition—self-organized attention, categorical perception, conceptual thinking, and logical memory—are not mastered internally until late adolescence. In other words, the stages of sign use refer to particular cognitive processes; they are not general stages of development.

The research on sign operations also identified three different forms of mediation. One is direct recall, in which some children tried to find a concrete representation of the word to be remembered in one of the pictures. However, direct recall does not meet the criteria for an external sign operation. The second form, mediated recall, consists of the individual's construction of verbal links between auxiliary stimuli and the objective of the task. The highest level, internal mediation, relies on internally constructed stimuli. In the most developed form, internal sign use becomes internal speech.

IMPLICATIONS FOR EDUCATION

The focus of Vygotsky's work was cognitive development, specifically the origins and various stages in the development of complex thinking. Therefore, his research and conclusions addressed particular acts of thinking and the transformations in those forms of thinking that emerge throughout development. Discussed in this section are (a) understanding the psychological nature of cognitive tasks, (b) mediated structures versus direct recall, and (c) the concept of self-mastery.

Understanding the Psychological Nature of Cognitive Tasks

The Vygotskian experiments indicated four qualitatively different stages in learning sign operations, the appropriation of auxiliary stimuli into cognitive tasks to master one's behavior. Stages 1 and 2, primitive or natural mental processing and naïve psychology, respectively, indicate that an essential prerequisite to sign operations is understanding the psychological nature of the task.

In the memory experiments, for example, the children were told that they were to remember a list of words or numbers. However, the children who were at the premastery levels in the memory and attention experiments either were unaware of the need for auxiliary stimuli (primitive stage) or were unable to use them successfully (naïve psychology stage). Some children, for example, searched for an exact likeness of the word to be remembered somewhere in the 30 pictures. However, those who understood the psychological nature of the task were aware that (a) the task was too complex for natural memory, (b) the selection of stimuli to aid in the task was arbitrary, and (c) the role of an auxiliary stimulus is recursive; it must influence the child's mental processes.

In other words, a failure to understand the psychological nature of cognitive tasks may occur at either of two levels. One is viewing the task itself in superficial, simplistic terms. Young children in the memory experiments, for example, viewed the complex situation simplistically. They had no doubt that the task was solvable through the application of their natural memory. Current examples of this failure are children who believe that the purpose of reading is to pronounce all the words correctly and the importance of homework is to produce a neat paper.

The second level of failing to understand psychological requirements is that of controlling specific stimuli in the task. The learner may understand the goal, such as remembering a list of words, but fail to understand that success depends on exercising control of particular stimuli. An example is the child who attempts to count using his fingers but proceeds randomly (e.g., three, one, six). He is unaware that the role of the auxiliary stimuli, his fingers, is that of an accurate visual record of an increasing quantity. In other words, assessing the learner's understanding of the psychological nature of a cognitive task is important. For the teacher, determining this information is one role of assessing the child's zone of proximal development, discussed in Chapter 4.

Mediated Structures versus Direct Recall

In the memory experiments, some children (typically the 4- to 6-year-olds) searched for a likeness of the words to be learned in the available pictures. The children were attempting to be successful through direct recall. In the classroom, mnemonic strategies provided by the teacher that rely on information already in one's memory operate in the same way. An example is the letters *f*, *a*, *c*, *e* (face) to remember the musical notes on the spaces in the treble clef. Similarly, teachers often suggest the sentence *"Every good boy does fine"* to recall the notes on the lines of the treble clef, E, G, B, D, and F. Such strategies are useful for a particular task, but they are similar to direct recall methods and do not contribute to the development of logical relationships among concepts in one's memory.

School-age children in the memory experiments typically constructed sentences to form an integrated structure of the words to be learned and available pictures. Selecting a picture of a house for the word *chair* because one can sit in a house is an example. The school-age child has constructed a legitimate verbal relationship between house and chair. Older students and adults, as already discussed, devised structures around the word to be learned that are entirely verbal.

The content of the mediated structures described by Vygotsky differs from constructions that often are suggested to students. One difference is that his approach involves verbal thinking, which is beginning to develop at school age. However, current suggestions are primarily image based. One technique is the keyword method, originally developed for foreign language learning (Atkinson, 1975). An example is constructing an image of a large egg on the crest of a wave for the Spanish word *huevo* (roughly, "wave-o"), which means egg (Jones & Hall, 1982). Others have suggested the application of image construction to other types of terminology. For example, in plant classification, the superordinate category *angiosperm* may be represented by an angel pushing a cart full of money (the image for monocotyledon). Vygotsky would likely suggest, instead, logical verbal links to represent the hierarchical relationship between the concepts. For example, plants that produce seeds in a closed pod or ovary belong to the category angiosperm; those with one seed leaf in the embryo are the subcategory, monocotyledons. Those with two seed leaves are dicotyledons. In other words, however useful images may be in initially identifying terms, they do not assist the learner in forming logical networks of concepts. These logical networks are the ultimate focus of internal sign use (see Chapter 6).

The Concept of Self-Mastery

A characteristic of cognitive development as Vygotsky described it is that individuals gain control of the stimuli in various cognitive tasks and thereby master their own behavior. For example, the school-age child who devises integrated verbal structures between pictures and words to be remembered has gained control of the available auxiliary stimuli. She also has raised her cognitive behavior to a level of thinking beyond that of direct or natural memory.

The question for education, if Vygotsky's conceptualization is not simply semantics, is the difference between saying that a child remembered the words on the list and saying that he controlled the stimuli in the task. First, as Vygotsky noted, his description addresses the cognitive activity that occurs between the stimuli and the responses in the task. The experimenter asks the child to state the words. She looks at each picture she had previously selected, thinks of the verbal link, and responds.

Second, Vygotsky's conceptualization provides a lens for educators and researchers to analyze a long-standing concern about student learning. The concern is the frequently observed lack of transfer from the instructional situation to similar contexts or situations. For example, classroom instruction sometimes includes teaching particular strategies to facilitate accomplishing a certain type of task. However, one problem with strategy instruction is that students do not continue to use the strategies (Pressley & El-Dinary, 1992). One contributing factor may be that the learners lack conscious awareness of their own thinking. Vygotsky (1934/1987a, 1930–1931/1998b, p. 65) noted that this capability appears rather late in the child. Underdevelopment of the awareness of one's own thinking means that students will not be able to master and transfer thinking strategies.

Another factor may be the nature of the strategy instruction. First, the student may view the strategy as simply another characteristic of the situation they are addressing and not view it as a generalizable process. In other words, they are unaware of the psychological nature of the task. In addition, the instruction may not have developed student mastery. An example in the experiments on memory indicated that children were able to use pictures as word cues when the experimenter chose the pictures and explained their use. However, they were unable to choose and implement pictures as cues on their own.

The task for instruction in teaching content or strategies for transfer must address two important issues in developing student mastery. They are (a) the types of external cues in the material and the self-talk demonstrated by the teacher and (b) the internal cues that the student must develop to initiate his application of the content or strategy in subsequent situations. In other words, after the teacher has demonstrated the use of particular information in addressing a cognitive task, the students must complete several practice sessions, which are necessary for the two issues just mentioned. Typically, content-transfer exercises and strategy practice have concluded when students demonstrate after instruction that they can implement the cognitive actions modeled by the teacher. Practice sessions typically end before the students have constructed the internal sign operations that will cue application of the material.

Rohrer and Thomas (1989) reflected on this issue from another perspective. They pointed out that a problem occurs when a test appears to acquire integrative processing but students have received review materials that contain the integrated propositions needed for the test (p. 113). In other words, handouts and other aids should not provide the end product of megacognitive activities. Instead, they should facilitate student construction and mastery of necessary external and internal cues (stimuli).

In other words, mastery of content or strategies using external stimuli is very different from internal control (stage 4). Implementing strategies for various tasks and manipulating content in new situations requires that the learner have internal control to the extent that she can construct cues for use of the content or strategy and the components of the content or strategy as well.

In summary, the implications of the four stages of sign use are important in two ways. First, the naïve psychology stage indicates that some children may be unaware of the psychological nature of the task. Examples are children who are unaware that the purpose of reading is to construct meaning from text and those who see homework as turning in a neat paper on time.

Second are the concepts of external mastery of an internal process and internal mastery of that process. Instruction that seeks to promote transfer must attend to both levels of mastery.

REFERENCES

Atkinson, R. C. (1975). Mnemonics in second-language learning. *American Psychologist, 30*, 821–825.

Berg, E. E. (1970). *L. S. Vygotsky's theory of the social and historical origins of consciousness.* Doctoral dissertation, University of Wisconsin.

Bloom, B. (1968). Learning for mastery. *Evaluation Comment (UCLA-CSIEP), 1*(2), 1–12.

Jones, B. F., & Hall, J. W. (1982). School applications of the mnemonic keyword method as a study strategy for eighth graders. *Journal of Educational Psychology, 74*, 230–237.

Leont'ev, A. (1959). *Problems of mental development.* Moscow: Publishing House of the Academy of Pedagogical Sciences RSFSR.

Leont'ev, A. (1994). The development of voluntary attention in the child. In R. van der Veer & J. Valsiner (Eds.), *The Vygotsky reader* (pp. 289–312). Cambridge, MA: Blackwell. (Original work published 1932)

Pressley, M., & El-Dinary, P. B. (1992). Memory strategy instruction. In D. J. Hermann, H. Weigartner, A. Searleman, & C. McEvoy (Eds.), *Memory improvement: Explications for memory theory* (pp. 79–100). New York: Springer-Verlag.

Rohrer, W. D., & Thomas, J. W. (1989). Domain-specific knowledge, metacognition, and the promise of instructional reform. In C. B. McCormick, G. Miller, & M. Pressley (Eds.), *Cognitive strategy research* (pp. 104–132). New York: Springer-Verlag.

Vygotsky, L. S. (1929). The problem of the cultural development of the child. *Journal of Genetic Psychology, 36*, 415–434.

Vygotsky, L. S. (1966). Development of the higher mental functions. In A. N. Leont'ev, A. R. Luria, & A. Smirnol (Eds.), *Psychological research in the U.S.S.R. Vol. I* (pp. 11–45). Moscow: Progress Publishers. (Original work published 1931)

Vygotsky, L. S. (1987a). The development of scientific concepts in childhood. In R. W. Rieber & A. S. Carton (Eds.), *Collected works of L. S. Vygotsky: Vol. 1. Problems of general psychology* (pp. 167–214). New York: Plenum. (Original work published 1934)

Vygotsky, L. S. (1987b). Thought and word. In R. W. Rieber & A. S. Carton (Eds.),

Collected works of L. S. Vygotsky: Vol. 1. Problems of general psychology (pp. 243–285). New York: Plenum. (Original work published 1934)

Vygotsky, L. S. (1997a). Analysis of higher mental functions. In R. W. Rieber (Ed.), *Collected works of L. S. Vygotsky: Vol. 4. The history of the development of higher mental functions* (pp. 65–82). New York: Plenum. (Original work published 1960)

Vygotsky, L. S. (1997b). Development of arithmetic operations. In R. W. Rieber (Ed.), *Collected works of L. S. Vygotsky: Vol. 4. The history of the development of higher mental functions* (pp. 149–152). New York: Plenum. (Original work published 1982–1984)

Vygotsky, L. S. (1997c). Genesis of higher mental functions. In R. W. Rieber (Ed.), *Collected works of L. S. Vygotsky: Vol. 4. The history of the development of higher mental functions* (pp. 97–119). New York: Plenum. (Original work published 1960)

Vygotsky, L. S. (1997d). Mastering attention. In R. W. Rieber (Ed.), *Collected works of L. S. Vygotsky: Vol. 4. The history of the development of higher mental functions* (pp. 153–177). New York: Plenum. (Original work published 1982–1984)

Vygotsky, L. S. (1997e). On psychological systems. In R. W. Rieber & J. Wollock (Eds.), *Collected works of L. S. Vygotsky: Vol. 3. Problems of the theory and history of psychology* (pp. 91–107). New York: Plenum. (Original work published 1982–1984)

Vygotsky, L. S. (1997f). Research method. In R. W. Rieber (Ed.), *Collected works of L. S. Vygotsky: Vol. 4. The history of the development of higher mental functions* (pp. 27–63). New York: Plenum. (Original work published 1960)

Vygotsky, L. S. (1997g). The development of mnemonic and mnemotechnical functions. In R. W. Rieber (Ed.), *Collected works of L. S. Vygotsky: Vol. 4. The history of the development of higher mental functions* (pp. 179–190). New York: Plenum. (Original work published 1982–1984)

Vygotsky, L. S. (1997h). The instrumental method in psychology. In R. W. Rieber & J. Wollock (Eds.), *Collected works of L. S. Vygotsky: Vol. 3. Problems of the theory and history of psychology* (pp. 85–89). New York: Plenum. (Original work published 1982–1984)

Vygotsky, L. S. (1997i). The problem of the development of higher mental functions. In R. W. Rieber (Ed.), *Collected works of L. S. Vygotsky: Vol. 4. The history of the development of higher mental functions* (pp. 1–26). New York: Plenum. (Original work published 1960)

Vygotsky, L. S. (1997j). The structure of higher mental functions. In R. W. Rieber (Ed.), *Collected works of L. S. Vygotsky: Vol. 4. The history of the development of higher mental functions* (pp. 83–96). New York: Plenum. (Original work published 1960)

Vygotsky, L. S. (1998a). Development of higher mental functions during the transitional age. In. R. W. Rieber (Ed.), *Collected works of L. S. Vygotsky: Vol. 5. Child psychology* (pp. 83–149). New York: Plenum. (Original work published 1930–1931)

Vygotsky, L. S. (1998b). Development of thinking and formation of concepts in the adolescent. In R. W. Rieber (Ed.), *Collected works of L. S. Vygotsky: Vol. 5.*

Child psychology (pp. 29–81). New York: Plenum. (Original work published 1930–1931)

Vygotsky, L. S. (1998c). Dynamics and structure of the adolescent's personality. In R. W. Rieber (Ed.), *Collected works of L. S. Vygotsky: Vol. 5. Child psychology* (pp. 167–184). New York: Plenum. (Original work published 1930–1931)

Vygotsky, L. S. (1999). Analysis of sign operations of the child. In R. W. Rieber (Ed.), *Collected works of L. S. Vygotsky: Vol. 6. Scientific legacy* (pp. 45–56). New York: Plenum. (Original work published 1982–1984)

Vygotsky, L. S., & Luria, A. R. (1993). *Studies in the history of behavior: Ape, primitive, and child.* Hillsdale, NJ: Erlbaum. (Original work published 1930)

Vygotsky, L. S., & Luria, A. R. (1994). Tool and symbol in child development. In R. van der Veer & J. Valsiner (Eds.), *The Vygotsky reader* (pp. 99–174). Cambridge, MA: Blackwell.

4

Development of the Higher
Psychological Functions

All of the higher psychological functions have a common
psychological characteristic that differentiates them from all
other mental processes: They are processes of mastering our
own reactions by different means.
—VYGOTSKY (1982–1984/1997e, p. 207)

Education is the artificial mastery of natural processes of
development.
—VYGOTSKY (1982–1984/1997f, p. 88)

Chapter 3 discussed the stages involved in learning to use cultural signs
and symbols to master one's thinking and raise it to a higher level. The
outcomes of this lengthy period of development were designated by
Vygotsky (1929, 1977, 1960/1997a, 1960/1997g, 1960/1997h, 1960/
1997c, 1930–1931/1998a) as the higher mental functions. The term
functions in this context means "processes." Discussed in this chapter
are the principles of development and the role of education in developing these capabilities.

PRINCIPLES OF DEVELOPMENT

Development of the higher mental functions begins with the child's first
use of signs to master his cognitive behavior, and this process continues

through adolescence. Discussed in this section are the characteristics of mental functions and the nature of their development.

Characteristics of Mental Functions

Ethnographers, sociologists, and others who were Vygotsky's contemporaries debated whether categories of thinking were universal (the Gestalt view) or whether primitive and advanced technological cultures produced different levels of cognitive development. Vygotsky's analysis of these discussions led to his identification of two general levels of cognitive functions that are distributed differently. The primitive or elementary functions—involuntary attention, simple perception, and natural memory—are innate. They also are primarily reactions to events. As stated in Chapter 3, they are reflected in the flight of early humans from thunder and lightning and the child's avoidance of a hot stove. Also, memory is directly linked to perception; it consists of simple sequences of actual experiences (Vygotsky, 1982–1984/1999a, p. 46). Because the elementary functions are biologically determined, they are universal across cultures. These basic cognitive processes formed the thinking of early humans and also characterize the thinking of the young child.

The introduction of signs by early humans into tasks that required extensive recall began to change the nature of thinking. This emergence of indirect memory mediated by signs (referred to as signification) began the lengthy development toward the formation of complex processes of thinking.

Vygotsky designated the outcomes of cognitive development as higher mental functions, and they are not universal. Included are voluntary (self-organized) attention, categorical perception, conceptual thinking, and logical memory. Voluntary attention is controlled internally and directed through symbols; categorical perception is a synthesis of concrete images and word (concept) meanings; and conceptual thinking involves working with words and ideas in terms of their connections and relationships. Also, logical memory is the recall of concepts that directly reflect one's analysis and systematic organization of material (Vygotsky, 1930–1931/1998a, p. 98).

Vygotsky's use of the word *voluntary* in relation to the higher mental functions differs from the conventional meaning. Traditionally, any action was considered voluntary if it was not an instinct or a habit; that is, a voluntary action is not automatic (Vygotsky & Luria, 1994, p. 132). However, not all actions fall into one of these two categories. Therefore, Vygotsky (1982–1984/1999c; Vygotsky & Luria, 1994) described a voluntary action as "the mastering of one's own behavior with the assistance of symbolic stimuli" (p. 135). Unlike involuntary attention, which is attracted or repelled by particular objects, voluntary attention is organized and directed "primarily by thought" (stage 4 in sign use) (Vygotsky, 1930–1931/1998a, p. 99). Development begins with the first pointing gesture whereby adults begin to direct the child's attention. Subsequently, in a much more developed form, the child masters other forms of directing attention, such as speech. During adolescence, internal mastery of attention develops (p. 104). An example is solving a problem that interests the learner, which leads to her complete absorption in the task (p. 107).

The Role of Complex Symbol Systems

The psychological tools mentioned in Chapter 3 are complex symbol systems that are essential in the development of higher mental functions. Typically, symbol systems are regarded as adjuncts to internal mental processes (Vygotsky, 1982–1984/1999c, p. 37; Vygotsky & Luria, 1994, p. 136). However, Vygotsky placed them on an equal footing with the internal mental functions. They are of "paramount importance" in the development of abstract thinking (Vygotsky, 1982–1984/1999b, p. 40). They also are unique forms of behavior that are a product of the child's cultural–social development. They are an external line in the development of symbolic activity that accompanies the internal development of attention, perception, memory, and thinking (Vygotsky, 1982–1984/ 1999c, p. 37; 1982–1984/1999b, p. 40; Vygotsky & Luria, 1994, p. 137). Writing is an example. Even at minimal levels of development, writing requires a high degree of abstraction. In addition, the child must be conscious of the structure of words, phrases, and sentences.

The inclusion of symbol use in the system of higher functions does not refer to the use of language, writing, and other symbols for everyday communication. Instead, it refers to mastering one's cognitive behavior through mastery of symbols to execute cognitive tasks. An example is drawing on appropriate formulas to determine the load on different walls in a proposed building.

In other words, the development of higher mental functions consists of two inseparably connected, but never completely merged, streams of development (Vygotsky, 1931/1966, p. 16). They are mastery of (a) the symbol systems of the culture as tools for thinking and (b) the culture's methods of reasoning (Vygotsky, 1929; 1960/1997g, p. 14).

A Comparison to Elementary Functions

In contrast to the elementary functions, the level and extent of higher or indirect forms of thinking are dependent on the kinds of symbols and their use in a particular culture. For example, currently, the Piraha in the

Lowland Amazonia region of Brazil have only a "one-two-many" counting system (Gordon, 2004). They have no specific designations for groups larger than two. Therefore, their quantitative thinking is severely limited. This example illustrates Vygotsky's belief that cultures create particular forms of cognitive behavior. Also, the extent of cultural ways of thinking sets broad limits on the potential for the development of thinking in the individual (Vygotsky, 1960/1997g, p. 18). In other words, higher forms of cognition vary historically and across different cultures. (See Appendix A for a brief discussion of this view and the cross-cultural study conducted by Luria and Vygotsky.)

The higher internal functions differ from the elementary functions in several ways (see Table 4.1). First, the elementary or primitive functions are a product of the evolution of the human race. In contrast, higher mental functions are a product of the history of the human race and of cultural development in the individual child. In addition, these two different levels of cognitive processes operate according to different laws and accomplish different purposes. The higher mental functions effect an organized adaptation to situations through the organization and control of the individual's behavior (Vygotsky, 1982–1984/1999b, p. 40).

The Concept of Psychological Systems

Vygotsky's (1982–1984/1997d) research on thinking and speech in childhood led to his identification of the concept of psychological systems (p. 92). The different functions (attention, perception, memory, conceptual thinking) "do not develop side by side like a bundle of

TABLE 4.1. A Comparison of Elementary and Higher Internal Psychological Functions

	Elementary functions	Higher functions
Source	Biological development	Cultural development
Processes	Simple perception, involuntary attention, simple memory	Categorical perception, voluntary (self-directed) attention, logical memory, conceptual thinking (verbal and mathematical)
Characteristics	Controlled by the environment; represented by the S-R model; bounded by concrete experience	Constructed by the individual through symbol use; represented by the instrumental act that includes stimuli means; emancipation from the sensory field; developed through thinking in concepts

Note. S–R = stimulus–response. Summarized from Vygotsky (1997, 1930–1931/1998a).

branches placed into a single vessel" (Vygotsky, 1930–1931/1998a, p. 84). Instead, they form a system in which different functions are dominant in their development at different ages. For example, the development of perception is dominant in early childhood, with the other functions organized around it. The 2-year-old, in particular, does "only what surrounding objects nudge him to do" (Vygotsky, 1982–1984/1998d, p. 263). As Kurt Lewin, a German psychologist, described the situation, "a ladder lures the child to climb, a door to be opened or closed, a bell to be rung" (p. 262). Attention also is linked to perception; it is riveted on the particular object until the child executes a particular action.

During school age, as indicated by the experiments described in Chapter 2, the child has the capacity to develop conscious awareness and mastery of his attention and memory through symbol use (Vygotsky, 1934/1987b, p. 187). Moreover, "the emergence of this capacity is the central feature of mental development during the school age" (p. 187). Also during school age, the child's memory becomes the dominant characteristic of his thinking. At this age, thinking means to depend on memory "to a significant degree" (Vygotsky, 1930–1931/1998a, p. 88). Children typically answer questions intended to require thinking by recalling a concrete example. One boy, when asked the appropriate course of action on missing a train, responded with a concrete experience. He replied that one must spend the night in the station, an action his family had taken on missing the evening train to Marburg (p. 92). Subsequently, during adolescence, the leading function is conceptual thinking. At that time, thinking organizes and sustains attention, and memory includes connections and relations among detailed word meanings (concepts).

In summary, the two general levels of mental functions are primitive or elementary and the higher mental functions. The elementary functions are innate, reactive, and primarily under the control of the environment. The higher mental functions include the mastery of complex symbol systems for thinking and the inner higher functions. Included in the inner higher functions are self-organized (voluntary) attention, categorical perception, conceptual thinking, and logical memory. In contrast to the elementary functions, the higher functions are not universal across cultures, and they differ in origin, structure, and purpose. They also form a psychological system in which different processes are dominant in development at different ages.

The Nature of Cognitive Development

The higher internal functions are not simply a direct continuation or improvement of the elementary functions (Vygotsky, 1930–1931/1998b,

1930–1931/1998c, 1982–1984/1999b, p. 42). Also, they are not a mechanical combination of them, nor are they a "second story" on top of the elementary functions. Instead, they are new psychological systems that develop from the transformation of elementary mental functions into higher forms of behavior, and this development is not completed until adolescence. Vygotsky (1930–1931/1998c) identified three primary laws of development and two prerequisite or foundational cognitive functions that are essential to the development of higher mental functions.

Laws of Sign Use

Vygotsky identified the first use of auxiliary stimuli by early humans to redirect and master their memory as the prototype of the development of higher mental processes. As stated in Chapter 3, he formalized this cognitive behavior as the first law of the structure and development of higher mental processes. It is the creation and use of cultural signs that begin to transform elementary mental functions into higher forms of mental activity (Vygotsky, 1930–1931/1998c, p. 168). It is represented by phase 3 in sign use: the mastery of an internal process through external auxiliary stimuli. An example is directing one's attention through oral speech. Another is the modification of perception of the environment by isolating objects through words.

The third law of development is closely related to the first. It formalizes the major change in thinking from the third to the fourth stage of sign use. From mastering an internal process though external signs, thinking is transformed into mastering those processes internally (p. 170). An example is the shift from using pictures to remember a set of words to the construction of internal cues.

The Social Nature of Cognitive Development

Vygotsky (1982–1984/1997b, 1960/1997c) described culture as the product of the social activity of humans. Therefore, addressing the issue of the cultural development of behavior leads to analysis of the social plane of development. The issue, according to Vygotsky, is how individual reactions are derived from group life (Vygotsky, 1960/1997c, p. 106).

To address this question, Vygotsky (1960/1997c) drew on a general principle stated by Pierre Janet, a French psychologist. Janet maintained that the child, in the process of development, "assimilates the social forms of behavior and transfers them to himself" (p. 102). Vygotsky (1930–1931/1998c) referred to this principle as the second law of the development of the higher psychological functions (p. 168). He presented this law of cultural development in the following way:

> Every function in the cultural development of the child appears on the stage twice, in two planes, first, the social, then the psychological, first between people as an intermental category, then within the child as an intramental category. (Vygotsky, 1960/1997c, p. 106)

Every higher mental function is the result of organizing signs and symbols in a particular way, and each form of symbol use "was formerly a social relation between two people" (Vygotsky, 1960/1997c, p. 105). An example is the early steps in developing self-directed attention. "The child begins to command herself: 'One, two, three, go!'—just as the adults commanded her before" (Vygotsky, 1982–1984/1997d, p. 96). She then follows her command. The function that originally was shared between a parent (giving the command) and the child (enacting the command) emerges as one in the child.

Vygotsky's reference to "the two planes" in which mental functions appear—social and then psychological—identifies the source of these functions. This conceptualization differs from other theories that view the psychological plane as the sole locus of learning and development.

This law of genetic development identified by Vygotsky clarified the means whereby the "ideal forms" of behavior (adult) influence the child's present forms of behavior. However, social interactions are simply the first step. The child's subsequent actions also are essential. He must imitate, invent, and practice with respect to himself the same forms of behavior that others formerly practiced with respect to him (Vygotsky, 1960/1997h, p. 88).

In other words, individual behavior is the product of a broad system of social ties and relationships that the child imitates and practices. To determine the ways that signs and symbols function in individual behavior depends on determining the ways it previously functioned in social behavior (Vygotsky, 1960/1997c, p. 103; Vygotsky & Luria, 1994, p. 138).

The Role of Conscious Awareness and Volition

Vygotsky (1934/1987b) identified two foundational cognitive functions that are essential for the development of the higher mental functions. They are conscious awareness of one's capabilities and volitional control—the ability to execute them at will. He viewed these two functions as two halves of the same coin. In the absence of cognitive awareness of his cognitive operations, the learner cannot control them. He cannot organize and direct his attention (voluntary attention), analyze and relate concepts to each other (conceptual thinking), and so on.

Vygotsky noted that the school-age child has an inadequate knowledge of his thinking (Vygotsky, 1934/1987b, 1930–1931/1998a). Awareness of one's mental activity depends on self-perception; therefore, the child develops an awareness of his cognitive operations "relatively late" (Vygotsky, 1930–1931/1998b, p. 65).

Experiments on schoolchildren's use of the words *because* and *although* supported this view. Children in the early grades were unable to use those terms when faced with incomplete sentences ending in those words. For example, the experiments conducted by Leont'ev used 16 open-ended sentences with children aged 11 to 15. The percentage of correct endings in the group ranged from 20 to 100%. One child who correctly completed 55% of the sentences wrote, " 'Kolya decided to go to the theater because although he did not have any money;' 'If an elephant is stuck with a needle it will not hurt him although it hurts all animals because they don't cry' " (p. 66). Vygotsky noted that the children's responses indicated that they were able to connect a related idea to the incomplete sentence but had difficulty in expressing the logical relation between the two ideas (p. 67). The implication for teachers is not to assume that learners can function with particular relations, such as conditional and causal, in new situations simply because they use the words correctly in everyday speech or can select related ideas.

Vygotsky's view of the development of conscious awareness of one's thinking does not refer to heuristics for particular problems or short-cut, situation-specific memory devices. These mechanisms are similar to the mnemonics discussed in Chapter 3 that depend on information already in the learner's memory. Those devices address a particular situation. However, they do not contribute to the development of the learner's thinking in addressing different kinds of problems.

Summary

Vygotsky's analysis of ethnographic writings on early cultures led to his identification of two levels of mental functions. The primitive or elementary functions, involuntary attention, simple perception, and natural memory, are primarily under the control of the environment. They are biologically determined and, therefore, are universal across historical periods and cultures. They also represent the thinking of the young child.

In contrast, the higher psychological or mental functions are the result of learning to use the symbol systems of the culture to develop complex forms of thinking. At an advanced level of thinking, the higher mental functions include self-organized (voluntary) attention, categorical perception, conceptual thinking, and logical memory. Vygotsky also placed complex symbol systems on an equal footing with the internal functions because of their critical role in that development. He viewed the symbol systems of the culture as tools for thinking and the culture's methods of reasoning as two connected streams of development. Because the development of higher forms of thinking is linked to cultural symbol systems, they are not universal. Higher forms of cognition vary historically and across different cultures.

The higher functions also form a psychological system in which different functions are dominant during different periods of development. Perception is dominant in early childhood, and memory and attention are dominant during school age. The leading function during adolescence is the beginning of conceptual thinking.

Vygotsky identified three laws of cognitive development. The first law formalizes the transformation from natural, primitive forms of cognition to the reliance on external auxiliary stimuli and the mastery of a higher form of thinking. The third law formalizes the transformation from the use of external signs to the mastery of an internal process by internally constructed stimuli.

The second law describes the cultural requirements essential for the development of higher forms of thinking. Specifically, it is the interaction between the ideal form of thinking (adults) and the present form (the child). Vygotsky's conceptualization of cognitive development as occurring on two planes differs from other views that identify only the internal psychological plane as the locus of learning and cognitive development.

Two other factors also are important in cognitive development. One is the actions of the child and the adolescent. Specifically, the learner must imitate, invent, and practice the forms of behavior that originally occurred in interaction with adults. The other is the foundational cognitive functions required for the development of advanced thinking. They are the conscious awareness of one's thinking and the capability to develop some control of one's cognitive processes. These foundational functions emerge relatively late in the child but can be developed during school age.

THE GENERAL ROLE OF EDUCATION

Vygotsky (1934/1987b, 1982–1984/1997f) maintained that education is an important factor in the child's cognitive development. Discussed in this section are determining the appropriate level of instruction, emerging mental functions and learning, and the role of the teacher.

Determining the Appropriate Level of Instruction

Important issues are the relationship between teaching/learning (obuchnie) and cognitive development, assessing cognitive processes (mental functions), assessment options, characteristics of a zone of proximal development (ZPD), and intellectual imitation.

Teaching/Learning (Obuchnie) and Cognitive Development

Vygotsky (1934/1987b) identified three prior perspectives on the relationship between teaching/learning processes and cognitive development. They are the maturational, commonality, and mutual-dependency views. The maturational view stated that a certain stage of development must be completed prior to instruction, and instruction and development do not influence each other internally. The problem with the maturational model was twofold. First, it made the dependency of instruction on development the whole issue, when it is of secondary importance (p. 195). Second, the model excluded any possibility that instruction might enhance cognitive development in any way. Writing, for example, was not viewed as an influence on thinking. The child is the same at the end of instruction as before instruction except that she is literate.

The commonality perspective, in contrast, did not ask any questions about instruction and development, and described both as the accumulation of stimulus–response connections. The third group of theories occupied a middle position between the other two. Described by Gestalt psychologist Kurt Koffka, this perspective described development as having a "dual character" (Vygotsky, 1934/1987b, p. 197). Koffka conceptualized the relationship between maturation and instruction as a mutual dependency, each influencing the other. From this idea of mutual dependency came Vygotsky's view that instruction could lead development, a cornerstone of his view of education.

The potential of instruction to contribute to cognitive development led Vygotsky (1934/1987b) to conclude that *"instruction is not limited to trailing after development or moving stride for stride along with it. It can move ahead of development, pushing it further and eliciting new formations"* (p. 198). In addition, Vygotsky went beyond the Gestalt perspective. He identified the levels in cognitive development where instruction could push development (Valsiner, 1987). Specifically, instruction can lead development when any form of higher cognition is beginning to mature (Vygotsky, 1930–1931/1998e, p. 204). Therefore, an important aspect of classroom instruction is to determine the higher cognitive processes that are emerging.

Assessing Cognitive Processes (Mental Functions)

Vygotsky (1930–1931/1998c, 1930–1931/1998e) maintained that an accurate diagnosis of a child's mental capabilities requires two types of assessment. One is an assessment of the child's independent problem solving. (In the case of concern about a child's mental capabilities, psychologists administered the well-known Binet-Simon intelligence test [now the Stanford-Binet]; Vygotsky, 1930–1931/1998e).

Assessment of the child's level of independent problem solving indicates the intellectual processes that have already matured. The other essential assessment in a clinical diagnosis of mental capabilities is to identify the functions or processes that "are in the period of maturation" (p. 200). Vygotsky referred to the second diagnostic task as that of identifying the child's ZPDs (p. 201), a concept from Ernst Meumann and other psychologists. This second task is important because it moves diagnosis from simply identifying external characteristics ("symptoms" of thinking) to include "the area of maturing intellectual functions" (p. 202). The second task, in other words, is a measure of readiness in terms of cognitive development.

At the time that Vygotsky proposed assessment to identify the learner's potential, he was heavily involved in the development of paedology (child study) in the Soviet Union. His conceptualization reflects his rhetorical effort to focus diagnosis on an estimate of the potential for subsequent development instead of focusing on test-based outcomes (Valsiner & van der Veer, 1993, p. 43).

The key to identifying maturing cognitive processes is to determine the problems that the child can solve with guidance. To illustrate this belief, Vygotsky (1930–1931/1998e) presented a hypothetical example of assessing the ZPD in the context of IQ testing. Given two children of the same age (8 years old) and the same actual level of cognitive development, each child's ZPD may be determined by his efforts to solve problems beyond his mental age through some type of assistance. Vygotsky's rationale for this approach was that children may be at the same mental age according to a standardized test, but their cognitive processes may differ in the progress of their maturation. The question then becomes one of assessing the development of these processes.

Assessment Options

Vygotsky (1930–1931/1998e) suggested four options for determining the child's ZPD. They are to (a) demonstrate the solution to a problem that is beyond the child's mental age, and see if he can begin to solve it; (b) begin to solve the problem and ask the child to complete the solution;

(c) ask the child to solve the problem with a child who is more advanced in mental age; and (d) explain the principle of the needed solution, ask leading questions, analyze the problem, and so on (p. 202).

In other words, the problem the child is asked to solve through co-operation is beyond his mental age. One purpose of the assessment is to determine "how far the potential for intellectual imitation can be stretched for the given child and how far it goes beyond his mental age" (p. 202). In Vygotsky's (1982–1984/1998e) hypothetical example, the ZPD for one child might advance his mental age forward 4 years, from 8 to 12. However, the mental age of another child may only reach the standard age-level performance of 9 years (p. 203). The theoretical significance of this diagnostic method is that it could provide information about the internal connections that advance the process of mental development (p. 202).

Although Vygotsky cast cooperative assessment in relation to the child's mental age, he noted that the practical significance of the ZPD was related to teaching. He regarded ZPDs as identifying the optimum time for teaching *at each age* (p. 204) (emphasis added). However, the process also is applicable to particular intellectual problems in the curriculum. For example, if a child has difficulty with a problem in the cooperative assessment, the teacher may conclude that the child lacks psychological awareness of the requirements of the particular task. An example is the young boy who attempts to count but assigns numbers to his fingers in somewhat random order; he is unaware of the psychological correspondence between a particular number and a certain quantity.

Assessing ZPDs refers not to procedural steps but to the child's emerging understanding of a particular cognitive process. Consider, for example, addition, which a teacher has yet to introduce in his class. If he is concerned about a child in the class, he may, working with the child alone, pose the following situation: Juan has six marbles and Marie has five more than Juan. How many marbles does Marie have? The teacher may start to solve the problem by forming a group of six tokens, add one to it, and then ask the child to continue the solution. Or, he may explain what should be done and then see if the child can complete the task.

Characteristics of a ZPD

A ZPD does not refer to particular classroom tasks, drill sheets on terms, specific homework problems, or mothers assisting young children to solve puzzles (van der Veer & Valsiner, 1991). Instead, a ZPD is "the domain of transitions that are accessible by the child" (Vygotsky, 1934/1987b, p. 211). That is, "the area of immature, but maturing processes makes up the child's zone of proximal development" (Vygotsky, 1930–

1931/1998e, p. 202). Also, mental processes in the ZPD at one stage of development are mastered by the child or adolescent and move to the actual level of development in the next stage.

Some current discussions of the ZPD refer to shared activities in different settings and initiating the child into important aspects of his or her culture (see Valsiner & van der Veer, 1993, for a discussion). However, Vygotsky (1934/1987b, 1930–1931/1998e) described the ZPD as only the mental functions that are emerging.

Vygotsky also maintained that his emphasis on the ZPD was not a new prescription for the teaching/learning process. It was only a statement to free psychologists and educators from "an old delusion that implies development must complete its cycles for instruction to move forward" (Vygotsky, 1934/1987b, p. 211). Moreover, targeting instruction to the child's emerging psychological functions is not the same as the concept of sensitive periods identified by Montessori and others (p. 212). The concept of ZPDs is not linked to biological development.

In terms of cognitive development, Vygotsky (1930–1931/1998e) designated the two assessment tasks, determining the actual level of development and determining ZPDs, as "normal age-level diagnostics" (p. 204). Along with available age norms, the child's development is described in terms of both "finished and unfinished processes" (p. 204). Also, the inclusion of internal processes in the assessment qualifies the assessment as an example of clinical diagnostics (p. 204).

Intellectual Imitation

The cooperative diagnostic tasks to determine ZPDs include imitation by the student. Vygotsky (1930–1931/1998e) rejected the view that imitating an intellectual activity is "a mechanical, automatic act" (p. 201). *Imitation*, as Vygotsky defined the term, includes understanding the implementation of the action. This definition indicates why Vygotsky was not concerned that imitative activity might erroneously identify a child's ZPD in some area. Also, the child's capacity for imitating intellectual operations is not limitless, and it changes depending on the stage of development of the learner. Therefore, each age level can be characterized by a particular zone of intellectual imitation that is associated with the child's actual level of development (p. 202).

Factors Influencing Cognitive Development

The factors associated with formal education that influence cognitive development are the role of classroom instruction, emerging functions in other settings, and the role of courses in the curriculum.

The Role of Classroom Instruction

In Vygotsky's perspective, instruction (teaching/learning) plays an essential role in cognitive development. To be successful, the appropriate threshold for instruction is the child's potential development. With this focus, "*instruction impells (sic) or wakens a whole series of functions that are in a stage of maturation lying in the zone of proximal development*" (Vygotsky, 1934/1987b, p. 212). Therefore, the child "receives instruction in what is accessible to him [or her] in collaboration with, or under the guidance of, a teacher" (p. 211).

An example is the school-age child who can select all the triangles in a group of geometric figures (described in the experiments in Chapter 2). The girl cannot yet abstract the characteristics of the concept *triangle* to apply in her thinking. However, if she can name at least one defining characteristic of the concept, abstracting the other defining characteristics is the process that is on the verge of emerging. Instruction can facilitate the abstraction process, the application of the abstracted characteristics to other situations involving triangles, and the development of connections to related concepts.

Vygotsky (1934/1987b) maintained that, like the ZPD, imitation is a component of instruction. In other words, a key factor in developing the child's emerging mental functions is the child's "persistent imitation" (Valsiner & van der Veer, 1993, p. 50). Introduced by James Mark Baldwin, persistent imitation begins with an external copy that is transformed in the process of trying again and again (Valsiner & van der Veer, 2000). For example, a musician's performance is based on reading printed notes. Much earlier, learning the meaning of the notes was based on imitating the sounds and movements made by his instructor (p. 154).

Although classroom instruction is essential in cognitive development, Vygotsky (1934/1987b) cautioned that there is not a one-to-one correspondence between the external structure of instruction and the internal structure of development that instruction brings to life (p. 206). The educational process has its own particular "sequence, logic, and complex organization" (p. 206). As a result, a particular component of instruction in arithmetic may not impact "arithmetic thinking" (p. 207). However, other components may result in the learning of a arithmetic principle or subject matter concept that leads the student to think in a new way.

Emerging Functions in Other Settings

The adult-directed interaction is one way of making use of ZPDs. In addition, given an appropriate cultural structuring of the environment, the learner can construct his own cognitive development within ZPDs (Valsiner, 1988, p. 147). For example, the school-age child operates in the ZPD when he solves problems "on the basis of a model he has been shown in class" (Vygotsky, 1934/1987b, p. 216). The "help," Vygotsky noted, is "invisibly present" (p. 216).

Another example is the 6-year-old child who grows up in a home with many books, newspapers, and magazines and with parents who are avid readers. In such an environment, she may acquire the capability of reading without explicit instruction (Vygotsky, 1956, p. 437 cited in Valsiner, 1988, p. 148). However, even this situation is socially constructed because (a) the resources are culturally prestructured and (b) the child may have frequently observed others using them (p. 148).

A third situation that can function in a ZPD is the imaginary play of the preschool child (Vygotsky, 1966, p. 16). Imaginary play can operate in this way because the child is "above his average age, above his daily behavior; in [imaginary] play, it is as though he were a head taller than himself" (p. 16). Imaginary play creates "voluntary (symbol-directed) intentions, and the formation of real-life plans and volitional motives" (p. 16). The appearance of these cognitive and motivational actions makes imaginary play "the highest level of preschool development" (p. 16). (See Chapter 8.)

The Role of Courses in the Curriculum

Vygotsky (1934/1987b) maintained that academic courses are essential for the learner's development of the higher mental functions. Specifically, "*abstract thinking develops in all [the learner's] lessons*" (p. 208). All academic subjects consist of concepts. Therefore, instruction can facilitate conceptual thinking, which requires higher forms of cognition. Logical memory, for example, develops from the learner's mastery of the connections and relationships among concepts in a particular domain of knowledge.

However, any school curriculum is not automatically appropriate for cognitive development. An example of an inappropriate curriculum identified by Vygotsky was the so-called complex method introduced in postrevolutionary Russian education (Vygotsky, 1934/1987b). Initiated in the early 1920s as an effort to move away from teaching by subjects, the Ministry of Education (Narkompros) organized the curriculum by socially oriented themes that "related directly to the child's environment and experience of the world" (Fitzpatrick, 1979, p. 20). Basic skills in reading, writing, and arithmetic were incorporated into the major themes.

Vygotsky's criticism was that the curriculum reinforced only the child's capabilities that had matured in his preschool years. A curriculum that is compatible with the child's preschool intellect is oriented toward his weakness instead of his strengths (Vygotsky, 1934/1987b, p. 211). In contrast, healthy school instruction leads the child to engage in activities that "force him to rise above himself" (p. 213).

Curriculum development in contemporary education faces two different issues. One is the rapid and continuing development of new knowledge in some areas. Typically, textbooks and other materials simply add on aspects of new developments. In the absence of some pruning of information, instruction in the classroom is highly likely to develop only fragments of information. The second issue is the introduction of content at lower levels of education. For example, probability is a concept that the curriculum formerly introduced in the eighth grade. Currently, it is found in fifth-grade textbooks. Also, some content originally taught in the early grades has been moved to preschool (Stipek, 2006). These changes raise serious questions about the child's capability to understand the psychological nature of the new tasks.

Vygotsky (1934/1987b) also emphasized that the psychological bases of school instruction develop in conjunction with instruction (p. 206). An example is written speech, which Vygotsky referred to as "the algebra of speech" (p. 204). It requires abstraction, deliberate control of words and sentences, and development of the skill in communicating to an unseen recipient (pp. 202–203). Instruction also can assist the learner in developing conscious awareness of her thinking, which is an aspect of beginning to develop concepts in academic subjects. However, the fact that higher mental functions develop in conjunction with instruction does not sanction the practice of moving content into lower levels of education. The issue in placing abstract topics in early grade levels is the child's inability to understand the psychological nature of highly abstract concepts, such as probability.

The Role of the Teacher

In today's terminology, Vygotsky viewed the teacher as the model from whom the child internalizes ways of thinking. Also, in his view, the teacher must be the agent that guides the child's thinking; this guidance takes place through many teacher–learner interactions. General steps recommended for the teacher are to (a) determine the cognitive processes required in the lesson (e.g., abstraction, classification, synthesis), (b) assess the child's potential for imitation with understanding as the teacher models these processes in relation to the concepts in the lesson, and (c) implement steps to ensure the child's conscious awareness and deliberate execution (volitional control) of those processes (discussed next). Three aspects of the teacher's role are the nature of collaboration in the instructional process, developing the learner's conscious awareness of cognitive processes, and the nature of mediation by the teacher.

Collaboration

A common misperception in some of the current literature about Vygotsky is that he advocated peer collaboration in the classroom. This misperception may have resulted from extrapolation from the word *collaboration* in translations of his work. Collaboration, when used by Vygotsky in reference to the school setting, refers to collaboration between teacher and student (Vygotsky, 1930–1931/1998e, p. 204). "The process of teaching itself is always done in the form of the child's cooperation with adults and represents a partial case of the interaction of the ideal and the present form" (p. 204). The present form to which Vygotsky refers is the stage or level of the child's thinking. The ideal form is the developed form of adult thinking that the child should achieve. In the classroom, teacher–student cooperation is an example of Vygotsky's second law of cognitive development. Higher mental functions emerge first on the social or interpsychological plane and then are imitated and reworked by the student.

Vygotsky's (1934/1987b) reference to learning in the subject areas states that "the teacher, working with the school child on a given question, explains, informs, inquires, corrects, and forces the child himself to explain" (p. 216). The importance of the teacher's explanations and questions is that they become the basis for the student's self-questioning and explaining of concepts when she is studying and reviewing materials. Specifically, "when the child solves a problem, although the teacher is not present, he or she must make independent use of the earlier collaboration" (p. 216).

The importance of these teacher–learner exchanges is beginning to be recognized by educators who are configuring school settings. Noted in Chapter 7 is the current effort to reconfigure large comprehensive middle and high schools to provide additional opportunities for teacher–student interactions.

Developing the Learner's Cognitive Awareness of His or Her Thinking

Recall from the experiments discussed in Chapter 2 that children were unable to select geometric objects that reflected a particular concept (Vygotsky, 1934/1987a). The children lacked psychological awareness of both the nature of concepts and their own thinking. At school age, the child progressed to thinking in complexes. For example, she can correctly group all the triangles together on the basis of their concrete, observable characteristics. However, that capability does not mean that the child can use the concept *triangle* in other settings or relate the concept to other polygons or other concepts. Nevertheless, accurately selecting all the examples of triangles in the group of figures is the foundation for beginning to learn connections and relationships to other concepts.

The mechanism that Vygotsky recommended in the classroom to develop the school child's awareness of his thinking is learning mature or true concepts. From Vygotsky's (1930–1931/1998b) perspective, a true concept consists of a "system of acts of thinking and some combination and processing of patterns" (p. 56). Included are connections and relationships with other concepts. Instruction that focuses on the child working out such relationships can assist her to become aware of and master her own thinking. In other words, "conscious awareness enters through the gate opened up by the scientific [academic] concept" (Vygotsky, 1934/1987b, p. 191).

Mediation

Some recommendations for teachers refer to "mediated" in the sense of an adult sharing culturally valued meanings with a child or, in the sense of scaffolding, sharing a difficult activity. In contrast, as discussed in Chapter 3, Vygotsky used the term *mediated* to mean that the individual masters a higher level of behavior through control of auxiliary stimuli, which are cultural symbols.

Vygotsky (1982–1984/1997b) also pointed out that, initially, teaching takes into consideration the concrete, graphic nature of the child's memory (p. 224). However, he emphasized that concrete memory is only a transitional step in the development of memory. Therefore, teaching should not cultivate the child's concrete memory but rather bring the child to a higher stage (p. 224). A higher stage is verbal memory and, eventually, logical memory based on thinking in concepts.

Some educators also have suggested that, as a part of instruction, the teacher should initially control or support, that is, scaffold, task elements that are beyond the learner's capability. The proposed purpose is to allow the learner to concentrate on the elements she can complete. This suggestion is not consistent with Vygotsky's recommendations. He did propose a role for task sharing in the assessment of a child's capabilities to determine the child's ZPD. However, the child's partner was a more advanced child. The implication, given Vygotsky's discussion, is that the partner had a higher IQ. Further, Valsiner and van der Veer

(1993), in their analysis of the ZPD, noted that the critical component, as stated previously, is "the child's persistent imitation that develops the emerging psychological functions" (p. 50). However, this essential aspect "is not captured in the scaffolding metaphor" (p. 50).

Summary

Vygotsky identified three prior perspectives on the relationships between teaching/learning processes and cognitive development. The problem with the maturational view is that it made the dependency of instruction on completed developmental stages the whole issue, and it is only secondary. This view also excluded any possible influence of instruction on development. The commonality perspective simply described both instruction and development as the accumulation of stimulus–response connections. The third view described a mutual dependency between development and instruction. Vygotsky believed that instruction can move ahead of development and elicit new mental formations, and he described the mechanism. Specifically, instruction can lead development when any higher mental process is beginning to mature.

The clinical diagnosis of mental capabilities, according to Vygotsky, consists of the assessment of the problems that the child can complete independently and those that she can solve in cooperation with the teacher or more advanced peer. The problems that the child can solve in collaboration represent the mental functions that are about to emerge. Vygotsky named this area of emerging functions the ZPD. It is important theoretically because it can provide information about internal connections that influence cognitive development. The ZPD is important practically because it identifies the optimum time for teaching at each age. The ZPD also is applicable to intellectual problems in the curriculum, such as learning to add.

Although imitation is a component of the diagnosis of ZPDs, the process is not mechanical. The child can only imitate a problem solution in the diagnostic task through an understanding of the intellectual operation. Also, the capacity for imitation is not limitless; it is associated with the child's actual level of development.

Classroom instruction is a key factor in facilitating cognitive development when it addresses the mental processes that are in a child's particular ZPD. Other settings in which the ZPD is manifested are the child working at home solving problems and the imaginary play of the preschool child. Courses in the curriculum also can be instrumental in facilitating cognitive development when they require the learner to rise above his or her present capabilities. An inappropriate curriculum is one that only reinforces capabilities that have already matured or that introduces concepts before the child can develop an understanding of the psychological nature of the required tasks or problems.

Particularly important in the child's cognitive development is the classroom teacher. He represents the ideal form of the cognitive behavior the child is to attain. Also, the teacher is a key individual in the interaction described in Vygotsky's second law of cognitive development. Important aspects of the teacher's role are (a) determining the cognitive processes required in the lesson; (b) assessing the child's potential for imitation with understanding; (c) working with the child, explaining, inquiring, and correcting his explanations; (d) developing the child's cognitive awareness of his thinking; and (e) moving his thinking from concrete to verbal and then to logical in adolescence.

REFERENCES

Fitzpatrick, S. (1979). *Education and social mobility in the Soviet Union 1921–1934*. New York: Cambridge University Press.

Gordon, P. F. (2004). Numerical cognition without words: Evidence from Amazonia. *Science, 306*(5695), 496–499.

Stipek, D. (2006). No Child Left Behind comes to preschool. *Elementary School Journal, 106*(6), 455–465.

Valsiner, J. (1987). *Culture and the development of children's action*. New York: Wiley.

Valsiner, J. (1988). *Developmental psychology in the Soviet Union*. Bloomington: Indiana University Press.

Valsiner, J., & van der Veer, R. (1993). The encoding of distance: The concept of the zone of proximal development and its interpretations. In R. R. Cocking & K. A. Renninger (Eds.), *The development and meaning of psychological distance* (pp. 35–62). Hillsdale, NJ: Erlbaum.

Valsiner, J., & van der Veer, R. (2000). *The social mind: Construction of the idea*. New York: Cambridge University Press.

van der Veer, R., & Valsiner, J. (1991). *Understanding Vygotsky: A quest for synthesis*. Cambridge, MA: Blackwell.

Vygotsky, L. S. (1929). The problem of the cultural development of the child. *Journal of Genetic Psychology, 36*, 415–434.

Vygotsky, L. S. (1966). [Imaginary] play and its role in the mental development of the child. *Soviet Psychology, 5*(3), 6–18. (Original work published 1931)

Vygotsky, L. S. (1977). The development of higher psychological functions. *Soviet Psychology, 16*, 60–73. (Original work published 1929)

Vygotsky, L. S. (1987a). An experimental study of concept development. In R. W. Rieber & A. S. Carton (Eds.), *Collected works of L. S. Vygotsky: Vol. 1. Problems of general psychology* (pp. 121–166). New York: Plenum. (Original work published 1934)

Vygotsky, L. S. (1987b). The development of scientific concepts in childhood. In R.

W. Rieber & A. S. Carton (Eds.), *Collected works of L. S. Vygotsky: Vol. 1. Problems of general psychology* (pp. 167–241). New York: Plenum. (Original work published 1934)

Vygotsky, L. S. (1997a). Analysis of higher mental functions. In R. W. Rieber (Ed.), *Collected works of L. S. Vygotsky: Vol. 4. The history of the development of higher mental functions* (pp. 65–82). New York: Plenum. (Original work published 1960)

Vygotsky, L. S. (1997b). Cultivation of higher forms of behavior. In R. W. Rieber (Ed.), *Collected works of L. S. Vygotsky: Vol. 4. The history of the development of higher mental functions* (pp. 221–229). New York: Plenum. (Original work published 1982–1984)

Vygotsky, L. S. (1997c). Genesis of higher mental functions. In R. W. Rieber (Ed.), *Collected works of L. S. Vygotsky: Vol. 4. The history of the development of higher mental functions* (pp. 97–119). New York: Plenum. (Original work published 1960)

Vygotsky, L. S. (1997d). On psychological systems. In R. W. Rieber & J. Wollock (Eds.), *Collected works of L. S. Vygotsky: Vol. 3. Problems of the theory and history of psychology* (pp. 91–107). New York: Plenum. (Original work published 1982–1984)

Vygotsky, L. S. (1997e). Self-control. In R. W. Rieber (Ed.), *Collected works of L. S. Vygotsky: Vol. 4. The history of the development of higher mental functions* (pp. 207–219). New York: Plenum. (Original work published 1982–1984)

Vygotsky, L. S. (1997f). The instrumental method in psychology. In R. W. Rieber & J. Wollock (Eds.), *Collected works of L. S. Vygotsky: Vol. 3. Problems of the theory and history of psychology* (pp. 85–89). New York: Plenum. (Original work published 1982–1984)

Vygotsky, L. S. (1997g). The problem of the development of higher mental functions. In R. W. Rieber (Ed.), *Collected works of L. S. Vygotsky: Vol. 4. The history of the development of higher mental functions* (pp. 1–26). New York: Plenum. (Original work published 1960)

Vygotsky, L. S. (1997h). The structure of higher mental functions. In R. W. Rieber (Ed.), *Collected works of L. S. Vygotsky: Vol. 4. The history of the development of higher mental functions* (pp. 83–96). New York: Plenum. (Original work published 1960)

Vygotsky, L. S. (1998a). Development of higher mental functions during the transitional age. In R. W. Rieber (Ed.), *Collected works of L. S. Vygotsky: Vol. 5. Child psychology* (pp. 83–149). New York: Plenum. (Original work published 1930–1931)

Vygotsky, L. S. (1998b). Development of thinking and formation of concepts. In R. W. Rieber (Ed.), *Collected works of L. S. Vygotsky: Vol. 5. Child psychology* (pp. 29–81). New York: Plenum. (Original work published 1930–1931)

Vygotsky, L. S. (1998c). Dynamics and structure of the adolescent's personality. In R. W. Rieber (Ed.), *Collected works of L. S. Vygotsky: Vol. 5. Child psychology* (pp. 167–184). New York: Plenum. (Original work published 1930–1931)

Vygotsky, L. S. (1998d). Early childhood. In R. W. Rieber (Ed.), *Collected works of*

L. S. Vygotsky: Vol. 5. Child psychology (pp. 261–281). New York: Plenum. (Original work published 1982–1984)

Vygotsky, L. S. (1998e). The problem of age. In R. W. Rieber (Ed.), *Collected works of L. S. Vygotsky: Vol. 5. Child psychology* (pp. 187–205). New York: Plenum. (Original work published 1930–1931)

Vygotsky, L. S. (1999a). Analysis of sign operations of the child. In R. W. Rieber (Ed.), *Collected works of L. S. Vygotsky: Vol. 6. Scientific legacy* (pp. 45–56). New York: Plenum. (Original work published 1982–1984)

Vygotsky, L. S. (1999b). Sign operations and organization of mental processes. In R. W. Rieber (Ed.), *Collected works of L. S. Vygotsky: Vol. 6. Scientific legacy* (pp. 39–44). New York: Plenum. (Original work published 1982–1984)

Vygotsky, L. S. (1999c). The function of signs in the development of higher mental processes. In R. W. Rieber (Ed.), *Collected works of L. S. Vygotsky: Vol. 6. Scientific legacy* (pp. 27–38). New York: Plenum. (Original work published 1982–1984)

Vygotsky, L. S., & Luria, A. R. (1994). Tool and symbol in child development. In R. van der Veer & J. Valsiner (Eds.), *The Vygotsky reader* (pp. 99–184). Cambridge, MA: Blackwell.

Part II

MAJOR CULTURAL SIGNS

5

Speech and Cognitive Development

> Speech is initially a means of socializing with those around
> the child and only later, in the form of internal speech, does
> it become a means of thinking.
> —VYGOTSKY (1960/1997e, p. 4)

Chapter 3 described the transformation of human memory from natural or elementary processes to higher forms through mastery of the culture's signs and symbols for thinking. Of the signs and symbols found in the child's culture, speech is of primary importance. It fulfills a major role in developing plans for solving problems and in organizing one's behavior. This chapter discusses the stages of speech development and the role of speech in verbal thinking.

THE STAGES OF SPEECH DEVELOPMENT

As a tool of thinking, speech develops through a sequence of stages similar to the developmental sequence of the use of signs. Discussed briefly in this section are prior views of speech and the stages of speech development.

Prior Views

Some psychologists who were Vygotsky's contemporaries maintained that intelligent action and speech developed independently on parallel tracts (Vygotsky & Luria, 1994, p. 102; Vygotsky, 1982–1984/1999c, p. 13). Also, any joint participation in some particular activity was accidental (p. 13). The problem with this view is that it leads to the unsupportable conclusion that speech is powerless to influence and alter behavior (Vygotsky, 1982–1984/1999a). Vygotsky (1982–1984/1999c; Vygotsky & Luria, 1994, p. 116) observed that speech and practical intellect do begin as separate processes. For example, the infant at about the age of 7 to 8 months can pull a string to bring an object closer. This action of practical intellect is independent of speech. However, speech and practical thinking begin to merge soon after the child begins to use simple words in adult speech.

Vygotsky also disagreed with two other views about speech acquisition. One explanation maintained that the young child simply establishes a connection between a word and its meaning (Vygotsky, 1982–1984/1998f, p. 244). For example, the child sees a lamp, hears the word *lamp*, and later recalls the particular object. The word leads to recall of the meaning in the way that a coat reminds us of its wearer (Vygotsky, 1934/1987g, p. 248; 1982–1984/1998f, p. 244). This view did not consider the idea that speech might evolve and have implications for thinking.

For Vygotsky, the problems with this view are that the emergence of speech only involves two mechanical operations. They are (a) the gradual acquisition of the movements that produce speech sounds and (b) a once-and-for-all acquisition of appropriate word–meaning connections (Vygotsky, 1982–1984/1998f, p. 245).

The second view that Vygotsky (1982–1984/1997d, 1934/1987c) rejected was the "discovery" description of speech acquisition proposed by William Stern. He described the beginning of speech as the greatest discovery of the child's life. In this "happy moment" (Vygotsky & Luria, 1994, p. 107), the child "discovers that every thing has a name" (Vygotsky, 1982–1984/1997d, p. 124). The problem is that such a discovery requires conscious effort and is a very complex operation (Vygotsky, 1934/1987c, p. 118). However, the young child's thinking is at a very primitive stage (Vygotsky, 1982–1984/1997d). She is not capable of a discovery that requires such "colossal intellectual effort" (p. 125). The child lacks the complex psychological experience required to understand the relationship between a sign or symbol and its meaning.

Furthermore, older children and even some adults fail to make the discovery that the name is an arbitrary symbol. Vygotsky (1939, 1934/1987g, p. 254) described, as an example, the story told by Humboldt about a peasant listening to two astronomy students. The peasant said he could understand how scientists using instruments were able to measure the distance from Earth to the farthest stars, but, he asked, "How did you find out the names of the stars?"

Instead of discovery, the process of linking names to objects is one in which the child obtains words (and other signs) from the adults around her. By interacting with adults, the child learns that each thing is identified by its own word (Vygotsky, 1982–1984/1997d, p. 126).

Overview of the Stages

In his various discussions of speech and thinking, Vygotsky (1934/ 1987a, 1934/1987c, 1934/1987e, 1934/1987g, 1982–1984/1997a, 1982–1984/1997d, 1982–1984/1998f) addressed different stages of speech. In one essay, Vygotsky (1934/1987c) briefly described four stages of speech development that correspond to the four stages of sign use. They are the primitive or natural stage, naïve psychology, egocentric speech (external sign operations), and internal speech (pp. 114–115). In another discussion of development at approximately the child's first birthday, Vygotsky (1982–1984/1998e) described the importance of the child's invented words (autonomous speech) as a major turning point in speech development. (See Table 5.1.)

Preintellectual

Development begins with the affective cries of the infant, which is the first vocal expression. The initial function of the cry is emotional (Vygotsky, 1982–1984/1997d, p. 122), and it expresses a physiological state, such as hunger or discomfort. The second function of the infant's vocal reactions is that of social contact (p. 122). In the early months of the child's life, babbling, laughter, and gesture begin to fulfill this function (Vygotsky, 1934/1987c, p. 110).

Autonomous Speech

This stage begins at about 12 months and ends in the second year (Vygotsky, 1982–1984/1998f, p. 256). It consists of the child's invented words, which differ from adult speech in sound structure, meaning, function, and lack of grammatical structure. An example is "boo-boo," which often refers to a bump or scrape by the child. Named by W. Eliasburg, autonomous speech refers to the child's original form of speaking.

The meanings of the child's syllables are both complex and unstable. A particular pseudoword indicates a particular object in one situation and another object in a different situation. For example, one child's

TABLE 5.1. Stages in the Child's Development of Speech

Stage	Definition
Preintellectual[a]	Prespeech, includes (a) the infant's cries, which indicates a physiological state, and (b) babbling, which fulfills the function of social contact
Autonomous or surrogate speech	Invented "words" by the child; differ from adult speech in sound structure, meaning, functions, and lack of grammatical structure
Naïve psychology[a, b]	a. Child masters the "*external structure of the sign*" (Vygotsky, 1934/1987c, p. 119). Initially, child learns that each thing has a name in the adult's language; rapid
Communicative speech	increase in vocabulary at age 2
Egocentric speech[a]	A component of the child's activity that becomes primitive verbal speech; emerges at about age 3 and continues until age 7
Naïve psychology[b]	b. Child masters the use (the external structure) of grammatical forms such as "because," "but," and "when" but has not mastered the corresponding causal, conditional, and temporal relationships (internal structure) (p. 114)
Inner speech[a]	Internal operations begin to form from developed egocentric speech at about age 7, mastered at about age 12

Note. Compiled from Vygotsky (1934/1987c, 1982–1984/1997d; 1982–1984/1998e).
[a]Stages that correspond to the four stages in the development of sign operations.
[b]Recurs with each new language structure (Vygotsky, 1934/1987c, p. 114).

word, *ka* had 11 meanings over a period of months. Among them were a yellow stone, egg soap, and stones of any color or shape (Vygotsky, 1982–1984/1998f, p. 253). Then it was applied to a pencil or a bobbin, for which "ka" is the first syllable of the words for those objects ("karandish" [pencil] and "katushka" [bobbin]; p. 253).

This example illustrates the limited effectiveness of autonomous speech. It is only useful between the young child and adults around him who understand the particular meanings. Moreover, it is effective only in concrete situations, when the object it represents is in plain sight (p. 250). Nevertheless, it is important for two reasons: (a) It fulfills an indicative function and (b) the child is making an effort to communicate with adults using the consonants and vowels in the adult language.

Current discussions of child development do not refer to autonomous speech as a separate stage of speech development. Instead, they note that the infant's babbling, by the end of the first year, does include the consonants, vowels, and intonation patterns of adult speech. Hart and Risley (1999), in their monthly observations of 42 children and their families over 2½ years, found that the children were "highly vocal" before they said their first words (p. 74). Parents variously referred to this development as babbling, gibberish, or jabber. The observers noted that "the children acted as though their gibberish were a 'bona fide' language" (p. 35). Also, during parent–child interactions, the child's nonword utterances typically were treated by the parents as though they understood them (p. 82).

Naïve Psychology

This stage of speech development is the period in which speech and practical intellect merge. It begins between 18 and 24 months, with the child's first use of simple words in adult language. The child learns that objects are referred to by name. However, she is unaware of the symbolic function of object names. She treats the name as simply another characteristic of a thing along with the object's other features (Vygotsky, 1934/1987c, p. 119).

Unlike the other stages in the development of speech, naïve psychology is not restricted to a particular time period. It reappears whenever the child first learns a new sign or a new speech structure. The child masters the external structure (naïve psychology), but only later, through using the speech form, does she master its functional meaning (p. 119). An example is the child's use of subordinate clauses (p. 114).

Egocentric Speech

Another transforming change occurs at about age 3. The child's speech differentiates into two types: communicative and egocentric (Vygotsky, 1934/1987e, p. 74). Communicative or external speech is for others; egocentric speech is talking aloud for oneself. Egocentric speech is a lengthy phase in development, beginning at about age 3 and continuing until about age 7. (See the discussion later in this chapter.)

At about age 7, the child's talking aloud during a practical activity ceases. It begins to be transformed into inner speech. However, inner speech is not fully developed before the age of 12 or older.

Summary

Vygotsky disagreed with the view that intelligent action and speech develop independently on parallel tracks. In his view, they initially are separate processes but merge when the child begins to use simple words in adult speech. Vygotsky also rejected the views that the child establishes a word–meaning connection once and for all or that the child suddenly discovers the link between words and their meanings. He noted that, instead, the child learns to link objects and names from the adults in his or her world.

Vygotsky's analyses identified five stages of speech development, each of which is a major transformation. They are preintellectual, autonomous speech, the stage of naïve psychology, and egocentric speech, which eventually becomes inner speech. The preintellectual stage consists of the infant's cries and subsequent babbling. The next stage, autonomous speech, occurs at about 12 months. The child invents artificial words, but the meanings are unstable. However, the child can communicate with an adult about objects in the visual scene. The child's practical intellect and speech begin to merge at about 18 to 24 months as the child uses simple adult words. This transformation is the naïve psychology stage. Unlike the other stages, naïve psychology re-emerges whenever the child begins to use a new speech structure. The lengthy stage referred to as egocentric speech follows. The child talks aloud to himself during particular activities that he undertakes. At about age 7, egocentric speech begins to be transformed into inner speech.

SPEECH AND VERBAL THINKING

Vygotsky (1930–1931/1998c, 1934/1987d) identified speech as initially a means of communication. However, at the same time, the child's brief thoughts also emerge in the form of simple words in adult speech (Vygotsky, 1930–1931/1998c, p. 169). The three stages of speech development that are related to the child's thinking are naïve psychology, egocentric speech, and inner speech.

The Naïve Psychology Stage

As stated earlier, naïve psychology refers to the child's initial learning of forms of speech. The term *naïve psychology* is similar to the term *naïve physics*, which refers to inadequate inferences about events in the physical environment. Young children, for example, often assert that swaying trees are creating the wind they feel. Naïve psychology, in terms of speech, refers to the inadequate understanding and lack of logic in the child's forms of speech. For example, the young child rejects the idea that ink could be called cow; ink is for writing and has no horns.

Naïve psychology is most prominent between 18 and 24 months when the child begins to use simple words in adult speech. However, this stage reappears when the child begins to use more complex forms of speech, such as subordinate clauses.

Initial Phase

The child begins to talk and the adults around her talk with her about the things she sees (Vygotsky, 1982–1984/1998d, p. 280). As the child begins to name things, connections between words and objects develop. In this way, the word begins to intrude into the child's perception. It isolates separate elements, going beyond the natural structure of his sensory field (Vygotsky, 1982–1984/1999b, p. 29). For example, when the child says "kitty-cat" to the family pet, speech is directing his perception, separating the cat from the child's visual field.

Second, during this period, the young child's thought "is born as a dim and undefined whole," and the first expression is a simple word (Vygotsky, 1939, p. 34). For example, when the young child says "Mama!" it may mean "Mama, pick me up," "Mama, I'm hungry," and so on (Vygotsky, 1960/1997f, p. 88). As the child's thoughts become differentiated, he gives up using individual parts of speech to express his entire meaning. At about age 3, he can formulate simple requests in the form of short, simple sentences (Vygotsky, 1934/1987f, 1939).

With these developments, intellect and speech begin to coincide, and this new relationship is an important event in the development of thinking and speech (Vygotsky, 1934/1987c). Vygotsky summarized this development in the statement, "Speech becomes intellectual, connected with thinking, and thinking [becomes] verbal and connected with speech" (Vygotsky, 1982–1984/1997d, pp. 123–124). However, the child's thinking stage is quite primitive. A major limitation is that the child has only mastered the external structure of the word (Vygotsky, 1934/1987c, p. 118). That is, the child connects the word to concrete objects it represents (Vygotsky, 1982–1984/1998d, p. 279). S/he does not develop conscious awareness of the internal structure, the symbolic function of words, until much later (Vygotsky, 1934/1987c, p. 118). For example, a young boy may refer to both his pet and the pet of his friend as "doggie." He is unaware of the internal structure of the meaning of *dog* (a mammal, member of the canine family, and so on).

In the child's view, the name is simply another characteristic of the particular thing. He is unaware that the name is an arbitrary choice. For example, young children are asked if a "cow" could be called "ink" (Vygotsky, 1939). They responded that the exchange would be impossible because a cow gives milk and ink is used for writing (p. 36). From the child's perspective, the name is part of the meaning of the object; the young child explains the names of objects by their qualities. For example, an animal has the name "cow" because it has horns (Vygotsky, 1939, p. 36; Vygotsky, 1934/1987g, p. 254; Vygotsky, 1982–1984/ 1998d, p. 279). Similarly, a herring is so named because it is salted (Vygotsky, 1982–1984/1998f, p. 246).

In other words, early in the child's development, the two planes of speech—the external, auditory and the internal, semantic planes—are merged (Vygotsky, 1934/1987g, p. 254). The child's inability to differentiate the external auditory aspect of the word from the inner, semantic aspect is linked with his limited potential to express and understand thought (p. 254).

Nevertheless, a key development of this initial period is that the child can now form a stable picture of the external environment that is organized in terms of objects (Vygotsky, 1982–1984/1998d, p. 277). An indicator of this development is that the child "begins to *actively expand his vocabulary* by asking the name of each new thing he encounters" (Vygotsky, 1934/1987c, p. 111).

Subsequent Phases

Unlike egocentric speech, which occurs between the ages of 3 and 7, naïve psychology reappears whenever the child begins to use new forms of speech. Shozefina I. Shif, a student of Vygotsky, found that children were able to use the word *because* accurately in their spontaneous speech. However, when presented with partial sentences to complete, they made errors. For example, given the partial sentence, "The cyclist fell and broke his leg because . . ., " the child responded, "he was taken to the hospital" (Vygotsky, 1934/1987b, p. 216). Such errors indicate that the child's accurate use in his everyday speech did not mean that she was consciously aware of the functional use of subordinate clauses.

In other words, children use conjunctions correctly in their spontaneous speech to express causal, temporal, adversative, and conditional relations (Vygotsky, 1934/1987g, p. 251). However, the child is unaware of the semantic aspects of subordinate conjunctions. Therefore, she is unable to use them on demand to complete presented sentences.

Summary

Vygotsky identified three stages in the development of speech that also are related to the child's thinking: naïve psychology, egocentric speech, and inner speech. The initial phase of the child's naive use of adult speech is an important stage in cognitive development. It is the phase when thinking, however primitive, and speech merge. As the child begins to name things, particular elements in the child's sensory field are identified. The child begins to associate particular words with certain objects and she begins to form a stable picture of the external environment in terms of objects. However, the child has no conception of the symbolic function of words. He is unaware that words are symbols for groups of objects that share certain characteristics. The word is simply another characteristic of the object.

Unlike the other stages of the development of speech, naïve use of the language reappears when the child begins to use new and more complex structures. The child is able to implement the structure in his daily speech. However, she is unable to use the structure on demand, a result that indicates the child has not mastered the internal meaning of the structure.

Overview of Egocentric Speech

The term *egocentric speech*, selected by Jean Piaget, refers to the child talking aloud to himself. It occurs in the presence of other children involved in the same activity, such as playing in a sandbox. It also occurs when the child is engaged in a practical tool-using activity, such as attempting to get a piece of candy from the top of a cupboard (Levina, 1968/1981; Vygotsky, 1930–1931/1998a, p. 114). In both types of activities, the child's talk is a monologue; it is not intended to be communicative speech.

Comparison with Piaget's View

Vygotsky and Piaget held different views of the basic nature of development from infancy through childhood. Piaget maintained that the child, from birth, is only involved in his own states and experiences, and accepts everything around him as part of himself (a state known as *solipsism*). Only very slowly does the child become aware of external reality. He also is unable to understand the viewpoints of others. Gradually, the child's thinking becomes socialized, as adult thinking and adult speech begin to push aside his egocentric speech.

In contrast, Vygotsky viewed the child from birth as a social being and an integral part of the lives of those around him (Vygotsky, 1934/ 1987g, 1982–1984/1998f). The child's thinking begins in the form of social interactions with others. Therefore, the child does not begin as an isolated independent being who is gradually socialized from the outside into adult ways of thinking. Instead, thinking is transformed from the social interactions where it originated into individual thinking (see Table 5.2).

Piaget maintained that the child's egocentric speech was an out-

TABLE 5.2. A Comparison of the Views of Piaget and Vygotsky
on Egocentric Speech

	Piaget	Vygotsky
1. Basic belief about child development	The child from birth is only involved in his or her own states and experiences and only slowly becomes aware of external reality	The child, from birth, is a social being, whose thinking begins in the form of social interactions
2. Belief about children's thinking	Gradually moves from being primarily independent of reality to become socialized and like adult thinking	Through several transformations, moves from social interactions to individual thinking
3. Characteristics of egocentric speech	a. An outgrowth of the child's egocentric thought, which is the inability to see the perspectives of others	a. The expression of the child's effort to understand a situation in words, to find an answer to a problem or determine the next step in a task
	b. Stands halfway between the child's undirected thinking and later socialized intelligence	b. Initially is a commentary on the child's own activity and later becomes a plan for addressing a practical task
	c. Disappears at about age 7 when the young child's unique ways of thinking gradually are replaced by adult forms of cognition	c. Does not disappear but is transformed into inner speech, beginning at about age 7

growth of his egocentric thought, and this monologue is often observed during children's play activities. To explore the role of the child's talking aloud, Vygotsky and his associates conducted experiments on the relationship between the child's speech and her practical activity. Like the experiments on attention and memory, the child faced a situation to resolve, and a tool essential to the task was nearby. Examples are reaching a piece of candy on top of a cupboard and getting a ball from behind a net. Each activity required the use of a stick. Other studies required children to draw pictures to help them remember different sentences.

During the experiments, a major increase in egocentric speech occurred when the researcher left the room during the experiment (Vygotsky & Luria, 1994, p. 118). Also, the amount of egocentric speech was higher in activities that required tool use than in the activity of drawing (p. 114). Vygotsky (1982–1984/1999c) maintained that the experimental findings indicated an important psychological role for egocentric speech. Specifically, egocentric speech, during its development, "begins to fulfill the function of primitive verbal thinking—thinking aloud" (p. 15).

The Preschool Period

The lengthy period of egocentric speech begins at age 3 and continues until age 7. These years are the period that Vygotsky (1982–1984/ 1998g, p. 196) later identified as the preschool period. It is a period of several developmental changes (see Chapter 8). At the beginning of this period, as indicated by the experiments on children's classification of objects described in Chapter 2, the child forms "unordered heaps." By age 7, he can organize objects into groups based on shared concrete characteristics.

Also, as described in Chapter 3, the preschool child is unable to use auxiliary stimuli to manage and control her memory or attention. However, at school age, she begins to master these cognitive operations using external signs.

The preschool period is also the stage when imaginary play develops. As the child takes on different roles, such as doctor or soldier, her thought is beginning to be free from social situations. Imaginary play, together with the development of egocentric speech during this period, contributes to the beginning of abstract thought.

In summary, the term *egocentric speech* refers to the child talking aloud to himself while engaged in some practical activity, often in the presence of other children. Piaget introduced the term because he maintained that such speech is related to the child's egocentric thought. Piaget's view stemmed from his belief that the child, from birth, accepts everything around him as part of himself. In contrast, Vygotsky maintained that the child, from birth, is a social being and part of the surrounding social environment. From his perspective, egocentric speech initiates the child's primitive verbal planning. Finally, egocentric speech and the preschool period identified by Vygotsky coincide. During this phase of development, the child moves from forming random groupings of objects to forming complexes and begins to engage in imaginary play.

Phases of Egocentric Speech

During the preschool period, egocentric speech and its relationship to the child's actions and thinking is also transformed. Vygotsky identified three phases in this dynamic relationship. The first phase is referred to as syncretism of action (Vygotsky, 1930–1931/1998a, p. 114; Vygotsky, 1982–1984/1999c, p. 21; Vygotsky & Luria, 1994, p. 116). The second is that of a reflecting, accompanying form of speech, and the final form is the verbal planning stage (Vygotsky, 1930–1931/1998a, p. 114; Vygotsky, 1982–1984/1999c, pp. 24–25; Vygotsky & Luria, 1994, pp. 120–121; see Table 5.3).

Syncretism of Action

The young child's speech in this phase does not produce a sign system that can assist him in his actions. Instead, his speech is "a chaotic hodge podge" (Vygotsky & Luria, 1994, p. 116). The child typically attempts to attain a goal, such as getting a piece of candy from the top of a cupboard, by direct means. The child's activity is interspersed with some statements about the task (e.g., "It's too high up"), emotional speech, appeals to the object of the problem, and appeals to the experimenter for help (social speech). One 3-year-old, for example, maintained that his wish would be met by itself. He said, "It will climb down now and drop down to us, it will come to us on the floor" (research conducted by S. A. Shapiro and E. D. Gerke, colleagues of M. Basov, reported in Vygotsky, 1930–1931/1998a, p. 116). The basic trait of this phase is a merging of the social and physical situations "into one nonsystematized whole" (Vygotsky, 1930–1931/1998a, p. 118).

In a different type of situation, drawing a picture, the young child first completed the picture and then became aware of and stated the subject of the drawing. In other words, the child did not have a particular goal for the activity in advance (Vygotsky, 1930–1931/1998a, p. 115).

The Reflecting, Accompaniment Phase

In this second phase, speech accompanies action. It also begins to shift to the beginning of the activity and to guide parts of the child's effort. For example, the child comments that she cannot reach the candy on top of the cupboard. She stands on a chair, reaching up to the cupboard, saying "on the chair." A few sentences later she says "I could get it with the stick." She then picks up the stick and gets the candy (Levina, 1968/1981, p. 291). Similarly, in the activity of drawing, the child begins to talk about the parts of his drawing as he is producing it (Vygotsky, 1982–1984/1997a, p. 201).

The movement of speech to the beginning of the child's activity is the beginning of the domination of speech over action (Vygotsky & Luria, 1994, p. 120). This relationship is the first step toward the third stage of sign use discussed in Chapter 3. In stage 3 of sign use, the child solves an internal task (e.g., adding numbers and remembering a list of words) using an external sign, such as counting on one's fingers and us-

TABLE 5.3. Phases of Egocentric Speech

Stage	Description
1. Syncretism of action	During a practical activity, the child's speech is a mixture of emotional speech, appeals to the experimenter, and appeals to the object of the activity.
2. Reflecting, accompanying phase	At about age 4 or 5, speech and thinking begin to occur simultaneously. Speech fluctuates between accompanying the child's actions and appearing at the beginning of the activity.
3. Verbal planning	The child begins to plan the needed actions and then to implement the plan. Speech frees the child from the immediate visual situation and allows him to consider his relevant past experience and to formulate a goal for his efforts.

Note. Summarized from Vygotsky (1930–1931/1998a, 1982–1984/1999c) and Vygotsky and Luria (1994).

ing external mnemonic signs (Vygotsky, 1934/1987c, p. 115). Similarly, egocentric speech, which is external in form, is beginning to guide the child's mental effort in a practical activity.

However, the child's egocentric speech may not always be effective (Vygotsky, 1930–1931/1998a). Instead, the child's speech may divert him or her from using the resources in the situation. He may, for example, ask the experimenter for help or end up conversing with the experimenter about something else (p. 116).

The Verbal Planning Phase

The transformation of speech in the third phase is that the child identifies essential elements of the task and needed actions in advance. The child first plans his actions in a practical situation and then implements them (Vygotsky, 1982–1984/1997a, p. 201; Vygotsky, 1983-84/1999c, p. 24; Vygotsky, 1930–1931/1998a, p. 115; Vygotsky & Luria, 1994, p. 121). Between the object of the activity and the child's actions stand *"stimuli of the second order*, [speech] now directed not immediately at the object but at the organization and personal *planning of the child's behavior"* (Vygotsky & Luria, 1994, p. 121).

The verbal planning phase of egocentric speech is another form of the symbol use described in Chapter 3. Second-order stimuli (speech) reflect the child's new course of mental processes; with the help of speech, thinking becomes more complex. The child formulates a goal, brings past practical activity to bear on the situation, and devises a plan. Her actions are no longer limited by the visual field. Levina (1968/1981) noted that some children informed the experimenter of their intended actions and then implemented them (p. 292). Also, in tasks in which the child must make drawings in order to recall sentences, children began to plan silently. When asked by the experimenter, they revealed the recall indicators they had chosen and were illustrating in their pictures (p. 293).

Chapter 3 discussed the role of simple signs and symbols in shifting the recall of specific items from direct to indirect memory. Similarly, as children begin to use verbal stimuli to plan a course of action, these auxiliary stimuli (speech) redirect a complex practical activity onto a completely new foundation. First, the child is freed from the immediate visual situation. Second, the child can draw on her similar past experiences. Third, the child can look to the future by establishing a goal for her efforts (Vygotsky & Luria, 1994).

Conclusions

The three phases of egocentric speech identified by Vygosky indicated that the child does not construct the merging of speech and thinking through logical operations (Vygotsky, 1982–1984/1999c, p. 24; Vygotsky, 1930–1931/1998a, p. 115; Vygotsky & Luria, 1994). Neither does the child invent new forms of behavior (Vygotsky & Luria, 1994, p. 115). Instead, in the second stage, speech begins to fix certain points of the action as it accompanies that action. An example is "Look! I got the chair," following the child's first step in attempting to get the candy on top of the cupboard. Vygotsky and Luria (1994, p. 121) concluded that this and similar statements serve as a verbal model of parts of the operation. Specifically, the points noted by the child in stage 2 begin to be formed as a preliminary strategy for the problem. This strategy is improved in subsequent experiments and is converted into advance verbal planning (Vygotsky, 1982–1984/1999c, p. 24). In other words, instead of an "unexpected discovery by the child," the process consists of a lengthy complex development (p. 24). The emotional and communicative roles of primary speech are followed by reflecting on situations and creating a model from such situations (pp. 24-25).

Finally, and perhaps most important, is that egocentric speech is linked to the "profound reconstruction of the whole behavior of the child" (p. 25). These verbal stimuli are directed toward the planning and organization of the child's behavior, and the mental field in which the child is operating "changes radically." The result is changes in the psychological functions of attention and memory (p. 25). The indicative function of words assists the child in controlling his attention. In other words, control of his attention moves from elements in the visual field to his direction. This shift reflects Vygotsky's (1982–1984/1997c) statement that "the history of the child's attention is the history of the development of the organization of his behavior" (p. 153).

Speech also permits the child to focus on different parts of the visual field and to include in his field of attention "elements of past and future sensory fields" (Vygotsky, 1982–1984/1999b, p. 35). For example, the child who must reach the candy on top of a high cupboard views the candy, the height from her location, and the nearby chair. She also may recall that she previously had reached a toy that had fallen behind her bed with a yardstick. This inclusion of successive past, present, and future (the goal) related to the task also separates the field of attention from the field of perception. Attention is no longer governed by the concrete visual field of the activity.

The inclusion of the child's speech formulas from prior tasks and actions precipitates a reconstruction of the field of memory (Vygotsky, 1982–1984/1999b, p. 35). These speech formulas from past situations do not simply extend the past into the present. Instead, the child synthesizes and merges elements of prior experience with the present situation in a new way (p. 35). The child who recalled using a yardstick to retrieve a fallen toy merges that memory with the task of retrieving the out-of-reach candy. A past formula is merged into a present situation.

Another characteristic of egocentric speech that is related to the child's thinking is the progressive abbreviation that takes place during the preschool period. At age 3, the child's egocentric speech does not differ from his social speech (Vygotsky, 1934/1987g, p. 261). However, by age 7, as egocentric speech becomes the guiding force of the child's planning in practical situations, its structure changes and vocalization becomes superfluous (p. 261). In other words, egocentric speech moves from resembling social speech to only verbs or predicates (e.g., "Get chair" or "chair") to the disappearance of sound.

Vygotsky (1934/1987g) cautioned that the lack of vocalization did not mean that egocentric speech itself disappears. This conclusion is like assuming counting disappears when the child stops using his fingers (p. 261). Like counting, egocentric speech moves inward. It is one aspect of the general development from the child's social interactions with adults to his individual forms of thinking.

Inner Speech

For Vygotsky, the psychological nature of inner speech is important because it represents the most advanced level of the relationship between speech and thinking. From this perspective, egocentric speech "is an early form of internal speech" (Vygotsky, 1934/1987g, p. 258).

Other Views

Vygotsky's emphasis on the psychological nature of inner speech differs from other approaches. One definition equated inner speech with verbal memory. In this view, memorizing a poem and only reciting it in memory would be an example of inner speech. However, this task is not an example of thinking. A second meaning refers to inner speech as simply unpronounced, silent speech (Vygotsky, 1939, p. 37; Vygotsky, 1934/1987g, p. 256). However, the motor act of inner speaking does not account for the thinking function in inner speech. Some contemporary researchers in cognitive science, also defining inner speech as subvocal speech, are investigating the areas of the brain activated during this activity. However, requiring research participants to mentally generate sentences (e.g., Verstichel, Bourak, Font & Crochet, 1997) and other similar tasks does not address the thinking role of inner speech.

A third perspective, identified by Vygotsky (1939, p. 37; Vygotsky,, 1934/1987g, p. 256), is quite broad and includes all activity that precedes the actual motor act of speaking aloud. The problem with this definition is that it applies to all forms of speech activity and, therefore, cannot differentiate inner speech as a unique psychological function.

Characteristics

Vygotsky (1934/1987g) referred to inner speech as "an internal plane of verbal thinking" (p. 279). In terms of the form of execution, it is "mute, silent, speech" (p. 262). It is abbreviated, like egocentric speech, and is formed from both the child's external social speech and his egocentric speech. At school age, inner speech is weak and unstable. Also, it is not fully functional (Vygotsky, 1930–1931/1998b, p. 70). At about age 12, verbal thinking begins to become stable and begins to be logical in abstract situations. However, Pierre Janet, a French psychologist, maintained that the transition from external to internal speech in humans had required thousands of years of evolution. He also doubted that many people had mastered internal speech. "The idea that internal speech is well developed in all people [is] a great illusion" (Vygotsky, 1930–1931/1998c, p. 170).

Support for the nature of inner speech came from experiments with preschool and elementary schoolchildren. The schoolchildren, faced with a concrete situation, paused for a time before enacting a plan. Queries about their thoughts indicated they were very similar to those expressed aloud by the preschool children (Vygotsky, 1934/1987e, p. 70).

Summary

Vygotsky maintained that speech is a major psychological tool in the child's development of thinking. The three stages of speech development that are related to the child's thinking are naïve psychology, egocentric speech, and inner speech. Naïve psychology begins with the child's use of simple adult words and his expression of thoughts in one-word sentences. The child's vocabulary expands rapidly; however, he masters only the external structure of words, not their symbolic meaning. Naïve psychology also emerges at other times when the child encounters complex sentence structures, such as subordinate clauses.

From about the age of 3 to 7 is the lengthy period of the development of egocentric speech. The three phases of egocentric speech are syncretism of action, the reflecting/accompaniment phase, and a verbal planning phase. In these transformations, speech changes from being a chaotic hodgepodge to accompanying the child's activity to a strategy-development activity. The third stage is particularly important because the child's actions are no longer limited by the visual field, he can formulate goals and apply prior experience to the activity. In this stage, second-order stimuli (speech) stand between the object of the activity and the child's actions, and these stimuli organize the child's behavior.

During the preschool period, from age 3 to about 7, egocentric speech becomes increasingly abbreviated. Vocalization eventually ceases, and egocentric speech moves inward as inner speech. In that form, it is condensed like the third stage of egocentric speech and a silent form of verbal thinking. However, it does not become fully functional until after age 12.

EDUCATIONAL IMPLICATIONS

Vygotsky (1960/1997b) identified the source of cognitive development as "a social relationship between two people" (p. 105). The child then imitates and reworks the behavior and subsequently implements it. This principle is essential in the development of speech for thinking. Discussed in this section are facilitating speech in early childhood and speech in the classroom.

Early Childhood

The environment in which the young child develops her speech is important for three reasons. First, only the child's early prattling is spontaneous, but articulate speech in adult language does not develop in this way (Vygotsky, 1982–1984/1998d, p. 272). In other words, the child's speech is not an individual activity. It emerges in the young child's need for communication and develops through personal contact (p. 273).

The basis for the young child's need for communication is described in Chapter 8. It begins during infancy and continues in early childhood in the relationship that Vygotsky (1982–1984/1998e) referred to as the "Great-we" (p. 233). It is the perception of an indivisible mental communication with the primary caregiver, and it provides a motive for the young child to communicate fully with important adults in her environment.

Second, speech is a major tool in thinking. In the absence of early language development, the child, on entering school, is at risk for subsequent learning. This issue was one impetus in the late 1960s for the establishment of Head Start.

Third, as the child begins to gain some proficiency in speech, s/he is then able to learn more. The speech of the adults around the child typically does not change, regardless of whether the child is 6 months old, 18 months old, or 3½ years old. However, this unchanging factor holds a different meaning for the child depending on whether he is only beginning to understand speech or is at a later stage (Vygotsky, 1935/1994, p. 339). In other words, the environment is a dynamic influence on the child's speech and thinking (p. 346).

Contributions to Thinking

A major role of speech is that it contributes to the semantic and systemic construction of the child's thinking. The learning of new words through speech contributes to the semantic aspect of consciousness (Vygotsky, 1982–1984/1998d). This development begins with the young child asking the names of everything he sees (Vygotsky, 1934/1987c, p. 111). Although, initially, the child perceives the word as a property of the object, verbal perception begins to replace nonverbal perception (Vygotsky, 1982–1984/1998d, p. 280).

In the child, speech contributes to the systemic construction of the child's thinking by altering the relationship between the psychological functions of perception and attention. In the young child, affect, attention, and action are bound up with perception. Objects in the environment perceived by the child either attract or repel his attention. For example, as stated in Chapter 4, a door lures the child to open or close it, a box to be uncovered or covered, and so on (Vygotsky, 1982–1984/1998d, p. 262). However, through words, the child begins to focus on different objects in the environment, thereby separating perception, attention, and action.

As the child grows older and her speech structure becomes more complex, she can begin to think at higher levels. Early supporters of Vygotsky's position, Ausubel, Novak, and Hanesian (1968), described verbalization as an integral component in acquiring abstract ideas. It influences the products of cognition (e.g., concepts and propositions) as well as the nature of thinking itself.

The Role of Adults

The importance of parents and other caregivers talking to young children cannot be overemphasized. As already stated, the child cannot develop articulate speech on her own. Cooperation with adults "nudges the child onto a new path of communication, to mastering speech" (Vygotsky, 1982–1984/1998d, p. 272). Vygotsky (1935/1994, p. 348) referred to adults' developed form of speech as the "ideal." It represents the final or completed form of speech that the child is to attain at the end of development. In addition to serving as a continuing presence, the ideal form determines and guides the first steps that the child takes along the path of development (p. 348). In other words, rich dialogues with parents or other caregivers are essential in the development of speech.

The absence of opportunities for such dialogues leads to impoverished forms of speaking and, therefore, impoverished ways of thinking. Vygotsky (1935/1994, p. 350) expressed concern about children in a day nursery with only one adult for several children. They have far fewer opportunities for interactions with finished or ideal forms of speech. The children talk with each other, but they speak neither well nor very much (p. 350). Their conversation cannot function as a source of language development because they are not at a higher level and cannot lead development.

The importance of a rich language environment that involves adults is indicated by the wide differences in speech use and vocabularies among children. For example, low-income children in one study of language development did not talk 59% of the time in their preschool and kindergarten programs (Dickinson & Tabors, 2001).

Researchers have conducted various studies of children's language development, many of which rely on cognitive measures of the children's vocabulary. However, Vygotsky (1982–1984/1998d) maintained that the study of children's speech should not be taken out of the social context. His rationale was that the child's socializing with adults is the mechanism of the development of the child's speech. Therefore, separating the child's speech from that of adults would be "a major mistake" (p. 273). One study that implemented his suggestion is the multiyear study of 1- and 2-year-olds and their families by Hart and Risley (1995). The researchers spent 1 hour per month in each home documenting the quantity and quality of the speech.

The data indicated major differences in the number of words heard by the children of professional, working class, and welfare parents. They found that children in families on welfare heard half as many words (an average of 616 words per hour) as the average working-class child (an average of 1,251 words per hour) and less than one-third as the average child in a professional family (an average of 2,153 words per hour) (Hart & Risley, 1995, p. 197). This number also remained consistent throughout the study. Also, by age 3, the children in professional families had much more experience in "hearing different objects, actions, attributes, relations, and conceptual categories named and described" (p. 246). Ausubel et al. (1968) also noted that disadvantaged children use few parts of speech that are essential for thinking. Their speech lacked "conjunctions, adjectives, adverbs, and qualifying phrases of clauses" (p. 218). These speech forms are important prerequisites for manipulating and understanding *relations* between abstractions (p. 218).

Recommendations

The young child (between 18 and 24 months) begins to become aware that different things are called by different names. This awareness emerges in social interactions with caregivers. For example, daily life includes communications from parents such as "Drink your milk" and "Where's your teddy bear?" An important requirement for caregivers is that the connection between word and object must be used functionally as a way of socializing with the child. This requirement helps to ensure that the word has meaning for the child and is internalized by him or her (Vygotsky, 1960/1997b, p. 105).

The child may be speaking in syllabic creations or in single words. However, in the ideal developmental situations, the child's mother or caregiver speaks to her in language with a complex grammar and syntax. Her language also has a large vocabulary, although it may be scaled down for the child (Vygotsky, 1935/1994, p. 348).

Children from homes in which conversation is minimal need opportunities to learn to express themselves. One study trained Head Start teachers in intensive monthly coaching sessions to use open-ended questioning to complement book reading and related activities (Wasik, Bond, & Hindman, 2006). One goal was to engage the children in conversations with the teachers and their assistants. Findings indicated that children expressed their ideas and elaborated on their feelings and reactions to stories and other activities.

However, one study of low-income 4-year-olds in early childhood programs found that more than 25% lacked any story time. Moreover, although teachers were involved with the children approximately two-thirds of the time, individual interaction occurred only 10% of their time (Layzer, Goodson, & Moss, 1993).

In preschool and first grade, oral language experiences, such as shared storybook reading, are an effective means for children to learn new words. One intervention, known as dialogic reading, involves introducing a new storybook with beautiful pictures each week. First, the teacher reads the story to groups of 2 to 4 children 3 to 5 times during the week. Second, the teacher engages the children in conversations about the story during the readings. The adult asks questions, provides additional information, and encourages more sophisticated responses by the children through more challenging questions. The goal is for the child to become the storyteller (Whitehurst, Zevenbergen, et al., 1999, p. 262).

The Issue of Television

A recent development in television is the production and marketing of programs and DVDs targeted to the child younger than age 2. One program, The Teletubbies, features brightly colored creatures who babble baby talk. Thus, the very young viewer sees characters that vocalize at or below his or her level of speech development.

The increase in programming for the under 2 set has led the American Academy of Pediatrics (AAP) to repeat their earlier policy statement against any television for that age group (Committee on Public Education, 1999). Their rationale is that research on early brain development indicates that infants and toddlers have a critical need for interactions with parents and caregivers. These interactions are essential for brain growth as well as the development of cognitive and social skills.

The AAP policy statement supports Vygotsky's position about the importance of cooperation and dialogue with adults. These interactions, in addition to introducing the child to the world and the role of language, are important for two other reasons. One is that these interactions begin the separation of attention from perception, an essential development in early childhood. Television viewing, in contrast, does not facilitate this separation. Second, in dialogue, the child has many opportunities to develop word meanings, initiate questions, make comments, and change the direction of the conversation.

Close (2004), in an extensive literature review of the relationship between television and language development for Britain's National Literacy Trust, supports the AAP position. She noted that the research indicated little benefit for television for very young children. Also, children who are heavy viewers of programs for adult or general audiences have a poor vocabulary and poor expressive language development (p. 6). Some studies have reported benefits for receptive vocabulary development as measured by such tests as the Peabody Picture Vocabulary Test. Receptive vocabulary is measured by requiring children to point to the correct picture for an unusual word (such as viola) introduced through video. Vocabulary gains on such tests are minimal, and the static vocabulary measure provides no information about children's language use in communication with adults. Further, Krcmar and Grela (2004) found that children younger than 22 months could not learn from television in comparison to real-life interactions with adults (p. 19). Also, the auditory stimulation of television, even if in the background, may inhibit children's vocalizations.

Speech in the Classroom

Two major issues involving speech in the classroom were identified by Vygotsky. First and foremost is that "the development of the child's thinking depends on his mastery of the social means of thinking, that is, on his mastery of speech" (Vygotsky, 1934/1987c, p. 120). This relationship has important implications for children with little experience using English and those whose primary language is a dialect of English (nonstandard English) or a language other than English. The child lacks the basic tools of thinking in the print language of the culture. This situation presents a major challenge to education. Data from the 1990 census indicated that more than 21 million individuals from the age of 5 and older speak English less than "very well" (U. S. Bureau of the Census, 1992). This number constituted 18% of the population in that age group, and the number is likely to increase.

Second, the stage of naïve psychology refers to the child's mastery of the external structure of the sign, a speech structure, for example, but not the functional meaning. Vygotsky's examples are the young child's initial learning of words in adult speech and the schoolchild's initial use of subordinate clauses in sentences. These examples indicate that, in the classroom, instruction must be sensitive to the disconnect between initial word use and mastery of functional relations (e.g., causal, conditional, and temporal). In Vygotsky's day, grammar, which addresses such relations, was routinely taught in elementary schools. This is often not the case in contemporary education. As already stated, accurate use of such words as "because" and "although" in everyday speech is no guarantee that the child can accurately conclude incomplete sentences that end in "because" or "although" (Vygotsky, 1934/1987c). The child is not yet conscious of his or her own thinking with those relations and is also unaware of the symbolic meaning.

This finding supports the encouragement and training of parents and other adults to use more complex syntactical structures and more complex vocabulary in their verbal interactions with children in both informal and formal instructional settings. Classrooms often emphasize learning new vocabulary words. However, Stipek (2006) noted that one curriculum standard referred to the number of new words a child should learn. This narrow focus leads to teaching words out of context, which is of little utility in developing children's speech (p. 458).

The benefits of formal instruction in grammar and syntax remain a controversial issue and the focus of discussions about the impact of such instruction on children's writing (Hudson, 2001; Hartwell, 1985). One activity, sentence combining, has produced positive results from Grade 2 to adulthood (Hudson, 2001). According to Saddler (2005), sentence combining provides conscious practice in reworking "basic or kernel sentences into more syntactically mature or varied forms" (p. 468). For example, "My cat is playful" and "My cat is named Sassy" can be combined to form the more complex sentence "My cat, Sassy, is playful."

Sentence combining can be prompted by underlining the word in the modifying sentence to be integrated into the kernel sentence, or it can be open with many possible sentence combinations. The activities may be oral or written, individual or with another person. Saddler (2005) suggested the following progression of grammatical types in sentence-combining activities: (a) compound sentences with coordinating conjunctions such as "like" and "but"; (b) possessive nouns; (c) sentences with adverbial clauses using subordinating conjunctions like "because" and "after"; (d) sentences with relative clauses; and (e) appositives, as in the prior example with Sassy the cat. However, from Vygotsky's perspective, real opportunities for students to implement their constructions in both oral dialogues and meaningful writing projects also are needed, and symbolic as well as structural properties should be addressed.

A third issue is that the research conducted by Vygotsky and colleagues indicated that inner speech is not fully formed until about age 12 and is less effective than egocentric speech in addressing practical tasks and problems. This finding is useful in the classroom when children are solving problems silently during seat work. Vygotsky (1930–1931/ 1998b) referred to the student who has obtained an "absurd answer" in working a problem. The teacher asks him to solve it aloud, which introduces self-awareness of his operations, and, in tracing their course, to take control of his thinking (p. 71).

Summary

A major role of speech is that it contributes to the semantic and systemic construction of the child's thinking. Cooperation and conversation with adults are essential in the development of the child's speech and thinking. The major differences in the number and type of words in different home environments support Vygotsky's view of the importance of a rich speech environment. Also supportive of Vygotsky's position is the policy of the AAP, which advocates no television watching by children younger than 2.

Speech is essential in the classroom because it is the primary tool of thinking. Although classrooms often focus on the learning of vocabulary, verbal constructions are equally important. Suggestions include the use of complex verbal constructions in speech with students and sentence-combining exercises. Also important in the classroom are opportunities to think aloud when children have difficulties in silent problem solving. The rationale for solving the problem aloud is that the inner speech of the school-age child is not yet fully formed.

REFERENCES

Ausubel, D. P., Novak, J. D., & Hanesian, H. (1968). *Educational psychology: A cognitive view.* New York: Holt, Rinehart & Winston.

Close, R. (2004, March). *Television and language development in the early years: A review of the literature.* Retrieved January 16, 2007, from http://www.literacytrust.org.uk/Research/TV.html

Committee on Public Education. (1999). Media education. *Pediatrics, 104,* 341–343.

Dickinson, D. K., & Tabors, P. O. (Eds.). (2001). *Beginning literacy with language: Young children learning at home and school.* Baltimore, MD: Brookes.

Hart, B., & Risley, T. R. (1995). *Meaningful differences in the everyday experience of young American children.* Baltimore, MD: Brookes.

Hart, B., & Risley, T. R. (1999). *The social world of children learning to talk.* Baltimore, MD: Brookes.

Hartwell, P. (1985). Grammar, grammars, and the teaching of grammar. *College English, 47*(2), 105–127.

Hudson, R. (2001). Grammar teaching and writing skills: The research evidence. *Syntax in the Schools, 17,* 1–6.

Krcmar, M., & Grela, B. (2004). Teletubbies teaches first words? *Literacy Today, 39,* 19.

Layzer, J., Goodson, B., & Moss, M. (1993). *Life in preschool: Volume one of an observational study of early childhood programs for disadvantaged four-year-olds.* Cambridge, MA: Abt Associates.

Levina, R. E. (1981). L. S. Vygotsky's ideas about the planning function of speech.

In J. Wertsch (Ed.), *The concept of activity in Soviet psychology* (pp. 279–299). Armonk, NY: M. E. Sharpe. (Original work published 1968)

Saddler, B. (2005). Sentence combining: A sentence-level writing intervention. *The Reading Teacher, 58*, 468–471.

Stipek, D. (2006). No Child Left Behind comes to preschool. *Elementary School Journal, 106*(5), 455–465.

U.S. Bureau of the Census. (1992). *Statistical abstract of the United States* (112th ed.). Washington, DC: U.S. Government Printing Office.

Verstichel, P., Bourak, C., Font, V., & Crochet, G. (1997). Inner speech and left brain damage: Study of the phonological analysis of word aphasic and non-aphasic patients. *Revue de Neuropsychologie, 7*(3), 281–311.

Vygotsky, L. S. (1939). Thought and speech. *Psychiatry, 2*, 29–54.

Vygotsky, L. S. (1987a). Stern's theory of speech development. In R. W. Rieber & A. S. Carton (Eds.), *Collected works of L. S. Vygotsky: Vol. 1. Problems of general psychology* (pp. 93–99). New York: Plenum. (Original work published 1934)

Vygotsky, L. S. (1987b). The development of scientific concepts in childhood. In R. W. Rieber & A. S. Carton (Eds.), *Collected works of L. S. Vygotsky: Vol. 1. Problems of general psychology* (pp. 167–241). New York: Plenum. (Original work published 1934)

Vygotsky, L. S. (1987c). The genetic roots of thinking and speech. In R. W. Rieber & A. S. Carton (Eds.), *Collected works of L. S. Vygotsky: Vol. 1. Problems of general psychology* (pp. 101–120). New York: Plenum. (Original work published 1934)

Vygotsky, L. S. (1987d). The problem and the method of investigation. In R. W. Reiber & A. S. Carton (Eds.), *Collected works of L. S. Vygotsky: Vol. 1. Problems of general psychology* (pp. 43–51). New York: Plenum. (Original work published 1934)

Vygotsky, L. S. (1987e). The problem of speech and thinking in Piaget's theory. In R. W. Rieber & A. S. Carton (Eds.), *Collected works of L. S. Vygotsky: Vol. 1. Problems of general psychology* (pp. 53–91). New York: Plenum. (Original work published 1934)

Vygotsky, L. S. (1987f). Thinking and its development in childhood. In R. W. Reiber & A. S. Carton (Eds.), *Collected works of L. S. Vygotsky: Vol. 1. Problems of general psychology* (pp. 311–324). New York: Plenum. (Original work published 1934)

Vygotsky, L. S. (1987g). Thought and word. In R. W. Rieber & A. S. Carton (Eds.), *Collected works of L. S. Vygotsky: Vol. 1. Problems of general psychology* (pp. 243–285). New York: Plenum. (Original work published 1934)

Vygotsky, L. S. (1994). The problem of the environment. In R. van der Veer & J. Valsiner (Eds.), *The Vygotsky reader* (pp. 338–354). Cambridge, MA: Blackwell. (Original work published 1935)

Vygotsky, L. S. (1997a). Development of speech and thinking. In R. W. Rieber (Ed.), *Collected works of L. S. Vygotsky: Vol. 4. The history of the development of higher mental functions* (pp. 191–205). New York: Plenum. (Original work published 1982–1984)

Vygotsky, L. S. (1997b). Genesis of higher mental functions. In R. W. Rieber (Ed.),

Collected works of L. S. Vygotsky: Vol. 4. The history of the development of higher mental functions (pp. 97–119). New York: Plenum. (Original work published 1960)

Vygotsky, L. S. (1997c). Mastering attention. In R. W. Rieber (Ed.), *Collected works of L. S. Vygotsky: Vol. 4. The history of the development of higher mental functions* (pp. 153–177). New York: Plenum. (Original work published 1982–1984)

Vygotsky, L. S. (1997d). The development of speech. In R. W. Rieber (Ed.), *Collected works of L. S. Vygotsky: Vol. 4. The history of the development of higher mental functions* (pp. 121–130). New York: Plenum. (Original work published 1982–1984)

Vygotsky, L. S. (1997e). The problem of the development of higher mental functions. In R. W. Rieber (Ed.), *Collected works of L. S. Vygotsky: Vol. 4. The history of the development of higher mental functions* (pp. 1–26). New York: Plenum. (Original work published 1960)

Vygotsky, L. S. (1997f). The structure of higher mental functions. In R. W. Rieber (Ed.), *Collected works of L. S. Vygotsky: Vol. 4. The history of the development of higher mental functions* (pp. 83–96). New York: Plenum. (Original work published 1960)

Vygotsky, L. S. (1998a). Development of higher mental functions during the transitional age. In R. W. Rieber (Ed.), *Collected works of L. S. Vygotsky: Vol. 5. Child psychology* (pp. 83–149). New York: Plenum. (Original work published 1930–1931)

Vygotsky, L. S. (1998b). Development of thinking and formation of concepts in adolescence. In R. W. Rieber (Ed.), *Collected works of L. S. Vygotsky: Vol. 5. Child psychology* (pp. 29–81). New York: Plenum. (Original work published 1930–1931)

Vygotsky, L. S. (1998c). Dynamics and structure of the adolescent's personality. In R. W. Rieber (Ed.), *Collected works of L. S. Vygotsky: Vol. 5. Child psychology* (pp. 167–184). New York: Plenum. (Original work published 1930–1931)

Vygotsky, L. S. (1998d). Early childhood. In R. W. Rieber (Ed.), *Collected works of L. S. Vygotsky: Vol. 5. Child psychology* (pp. 261–281). New York: Plenum. (Original work published 1982–1984)

Vygotsky, L. S. (1998e). Infancy. In R. W. Rieber (Ed.), *Collected works of L. S. Vygotsky: Vol. 5. Child psychology* (pp. 207–241). New York: Plenum. (Original work published 1982–1984)

Vygotsky, L. S. (1998f). The crisis of the first year. In R. W. Rieber (Ed.), *Collected works of L. S. Vygotsky: Vol. 5. Child psychology* (pp. 243–259). New York: Plenum. (Original work published 1982–1984)

Vygotsky, L. S. (1998g). The problem of age. In R. W. Rieber (Ed.), *Collected works of L. S. Vygotsky: Vol. 5. Child psychology* (pp. 187–205). New York: Plenum. (Original work published 1982–1984)

Vygotsky, L. S. (1999a). Methods of studying higher mental functions. In R. W. Rieber (Ed.), *Collected works of L. S. Vygotsky: Vol. 6. Scientific legacy* (pp. 57–68). New York: Plenum. (Original work published 1982–1984)

Vygotsky, L. S. (1999b). The function of signs in the development of higher mental functions. In R. W. Rieber (Ed.), *Collected works of L. S. Vygotsky: Vol. 6. Scientific legacy* (pp. 27–38). New York: Plenum. (Original work published 1982–1984)

Vygotsky, L. S. (1999c). The problem of practical intellect in the psychology of animals and the psychology of the child. In R. W. Rieber (Ed.), *Collected works of L. S. Vygotsky: Vol. 6. Scientific legacy* (pp. 3–25). New York: Plenum. (Original work published 1982–1984)

Vygotsky, L. S., & Luria A. R. (1994). Tool and symbol in child development. In R. van der Veer & J. Valsiner (Eds.), *The Vygotsky reader* (pp. 99–174). Cambridge, MA: Blackwell.

Wasik, B. S., Bond, M. A., & Hindman, A. (2006). The effects of a language and literacy intervention on Head Start children and teachers. *Journal of Educational Psychology, 98*, 63–74.

Whitehurst, G. J., Zevenbergen, A. A., Crone, D. A., Schultz, M. D., Velting, O. N., & Fischel, J. E. (1999). Outcomes of an emergent literacy intervention from Head Start through second grade. *Journal of Educational Psychology, 91*, 261–272.

6

Development of Thinking in Concepts

Cognition, in the true sense of that word, science, art, various spheres of cultural life may be adequately assimilated only in concepts.
—VYGOTSKY (1930–1931/1998, p. 42)

The road leading from the initial familiarity with a new concept to the moment when the word and the concept become the child's property, is a complex internal psychological process.
—VYGOTSKY (1935/1994a, p. 358)

The signs and symbols of a culture are the mechanisms whereby its members can develop higher cognitive processes—in today's terminology, thinking skills. Initially, as mentioned in Chapter 3, Vygotsky identified artifacts (e.g., graphs, charts, drawings), symbol systems, and language as potential signs for assisting individuals to develop their thinking. Chapter 5 described the role of speech in initiating verbal thinking, specifically the role of verbal planning in addressing practical problems.

During the last years of his life, Vygotsky began to emphasize the importance of concepts or word meanings as a form of verbal thinking (Valsiner & van der Veer, 2000, p. 375). Cognitive development, from the child's early (and sometimes mismatched) groupings of objects to a rich understanding of the concept as a symbol and then to the construction of connections and patterns among concepts, is a lengthy process. However, it is "an issue of tremendous theoretical importance" (Vygotsky, 1934/1987b, p. 167). This lengthy process, from Vygotsky's perspective, "contains the key to the whole history of the child's mental development" (p. 167). When this process is completed in late adolescence, the individual has mastered "the most advanced form of the sign created by human thinking" (Vygotsky, 1934/1987a, p. 159). Discussed in this chapter are the phases in concept development and the role of subject matter or academic concepts in thinking.

PHASES IN CONCEPT DEVELOPMENT

Vygotsky (1930–1931/1998) rejected the traditional psychological view of concepts, which was taken from formal logic. In that perspective, a concept is an abstract mental category that is unrelated to "all the wealth of concrete reality" (p. 53). For example, the definition of a bed as a piece of furniture used for resting or sleeping does not reflect the rich meanings of the concept. That is, the word *bed* represents bunks, four posters, baby cribs and king size, as well as creek beds and planting beds. As indicated by this example, concept names (words) in the traditional view served as substitutes for the rich meanings of concepts in the same way that "credit cards substitute for gold coins" (Vygotsky, 1930–1931/1998, p. 54).

Traditional research and concept formation treated the task as that of simply learning the name and characteristics of a defined collection of objects. For example, students were expected to learn that triangles are flat, three-sided, closed figures. This perspective also served as the basis for the concept-learning research in the United States in the 1950s and 1960s.

Vygotsky's (1930–1931/1998, 1935/1994a, 1934/1987b) thinking, in contrast, differed from the traditional view in two major ways. First, as indicated by the experiments described in Chapter 2, word meanings grow and develop. Second, identifying concept examples accurately is not an indication of true conceptual thinking. In the case of *triangle*, for example, conceptual thinking involves working with triangles in terms of the connections and relationships to other polygons. The student who has developed the concept *triangle* can (a) determine that the sides of pyramids are triangles, (b) subdivide hexagons and other polygons into a particular number of triangles, (c) relate triangles to other polygons, and so on. These acts of thinking are more sophisticated than simply matching concept examples visually.

Early Phases of Concept Formation

From a psychological perspective, the experimental data described in Chapter 2 indicated three major findings. First, concept or word meanings varied across age levels, and second, the nature of the connections among the selected objects also varied. Very young children relied on subjective impressions, whereas older children classified objects by their concrete connections.

Third, the research indicated that concept formation is a unique process and cannot be reduced to an elementary cognitive operation. The processes of association, attention, and the cooperation of judgment and representation contribute to the formation of concepts, and none is an explanation by itself (Vygotsky, 1934/1987a, p. 131; Vygotsky, 1931/1994b, p. 212). Also, words are essential for concepts, and thinking in concepts cannot take place outside of verbal thinking.

The experiments and Vygotsky's further analyses indicated two different roots that lead to actual conceptual thinking, which he labeled as thinking in true concepts. One root consists of grouping particular objects together on the basis of visual characteristics. The other root consists of the child beginning to abstract defining characteristics of the concept, which he labeled a potential concept (Vygotsky, 1931/1994b, p. 247; Vygotsky, 1934/1987a, p. 157). A key difference is that, in abstraction, the child is able to transcend the physical, visual situation. An abstracted attribute or characteristic can then be applied to other examples or situations.

Syncretic Images and Complexes

The experiments briefly discussed in Chapter 2 indicated that very young children connected objects on the basis of irrelevant perceived features (Vygotsky, 1931/1994b, p. 217). (See Table 6.1.) An example is the set of objects joined by the syllable "ka" described in Chapter 5.

The collection of objects picked out by the child indicates that he treats his association of subjective impressions as though they were actual connections among things. The child's selections are not guided by observable, objective associations among objects. Instead, the child is guided by his own perceptions (Vygotsky, 1931/1994b, p. 217).

The next phase in the child's thinking is the formation of complexes. This stage stands "heads and shoulders" above the preceding phase of syncretic images (Vygotsky, 1931/1994b. p. 219). As indicated in the experiments, the child forms groups on the basis of concrete, observable connections rather than subjective impressions.

However, the process in the formation of complexes differs from

TABLE 6.1. Types of Preconceptual Thinking

Type of thinking	Description	Internal process
I. Recognition of object characteristics		
Syncretic images	Appear in the behavior of very young children; the child "isolates an unordered heap of objects" (Vygotsky, 1934/1987a, p. 134).	The child's perceptions suggest the subjective connections whereby he or she links objects. The child takes association of thoughts and impressions for the associations between things (Vygotsky, 1931/1994b, p. 216).
Thinking in complexes	Grouping objects on the basis of concrete similarities; connections are "empirical, accidental, and concrete" (p. 137). Any observable connection may lead to inclusion in a group.	Recognition of concrete, observable connections, but the connections often vary across the group of objects. *Example*: Child joins a red triangle to a red circle and then selects a parallelogram because, like the triangle, it has two sloping sides.
Pseudoconcept	"The most widespread, dominant, and often almost exclusive form" of complexive thinking (Vygotsky, 1931/1994b, p. 227). The pseudoconcept serves as a bridge to true conceptual thinking.	Reliance on stable, unvarying characteristics to match objects to a model. *Example*: Given a yellow triangle, child selects all the triangles from a group of figures.
II. Abstraction of defining concept features		
Potential concepts	Abstraction of a single defining concept characteristic	Child typically defines a potential concept in terms of the action of that concept in a situation or the way the child uses it. The child defines reason as "when one is very hot and doesn't drink water" (Vygotsky, 1931/1994b, p. 249). (A common belief was that drinking cold water when one was hot was unhealthy; p. 265).

Note. Summarized from Vygotsky (1934/1987a, 1931/1994b).

that of forming concepts. First, the choice is accidental and may vary from one selected object to another. For example, the child may join a red square and a green triangle to a green semicircle because those figures each share a characteristic with the semicircle (straight side, green color). Also, in the experiments conducted by Vygotsky's colleagues (Sakharov, Kotelova, and Pashkovashkaya), the children typically included objects in two or more groupings. Vygotsky (1934/1987a, p. 150; Vygotsky, 1931/1994b, p. 236) referred to this aspect of thinking as "participation."

As indicated by the prior example, the underlying characteristic of complexes is a concrete connection between individual elements, which is a product of direct experience (Vygotsky, 1931/1994b, p. 220). In contrast, concepts are formed on the basis of abstracted, logical connections (p. 219).

Relationship to the Development of Speech

A key characteristic of the young child's speech, described in Chapter 5, is that he has mastered only the external structure of words but not the symbolic function. As mentioned in Chapter 5, the child who refers to family pets as doggies is unaware of the detailed meaning of the word "dog." This situation, referred to as object relatedness (Vygotsky, 1931/1994b, p. 256), is similar to the child's thinking in complexes. She has a partial meaning of the word and, therefore, is able to communicate with adults. However, she is far from developing true concepts. The words of the child and the adult refer to the same object, but they do not have the same meanings (p. 240).

The Pseudoconcept

The most advanced level of complexive thinking is the pseudoconcept, which is found in both experimental and real-world situations (Vygotsky, 1931/1994b, p. 226). Also, in the real-life thinking of preschool children, the pseudoconcept is the dominant form of complexive thinking (p. 227). The pseudoconcept is so named because the end result of selecting objects exactly corresponds to examples that represent the concept.

However, pseudoconcepts cannot be considered concepts in terms of the cognitive processes used by the child and the nature of the associations that link the examples together. The child forms a pseudoconcept by correctly selecting concrete examples that match a particular pattern. For example, in the experimental situation, given a yellow triangle, the child chose all the triangles in a group of geometric figures. This group, formed by accurately matching concrete characteristics of the figures to the model, is a pesudoconcept (Vygotsky, 1934/1987a; Vygotsky, 1931/ 1994b). The child has grouped the objects on the basis of their concrete, observable connections. However, simply recognizing concrete examples of a concept does not mean that the learner has developed a category of thinking that he can apply in other situations.

Vygotsky (1931/1994b) referred to the pseudoconcept as "a shadow of a concept, its contours" (p. 229). As the most widespread form of children's complexes, the pseudoconcept, and the superficial similarity to a concept, can lead to misjudgments about children's thinking. The fact that the child can communicate with adults and can establish some mutual understanding may lead to "the impression that *the end point in the development of the meaning of a word coincides with the starting point*" (p. 229). That is, the adult may assume that there is no need for development, because he views the child as functioning with a ready-made definition of the concept (p. 229). The pseudoconcept, however, is simply "a bridge that lies between the child's concrete and abstract thinking" (Vygotsky, 1934/1987a, p. 146).

When the child can think with pseudoconcepts and also has mastered the process of abstracting a key attribute of an object (potential concept), he is "able to reach a stage where he can form real concepts" (Vygotsky, 1931/1994b, p. 250). The process of abstracting a key characteristic is similar to the way that new words appear in the child's vocabulary. A single attribute or characteristic attracts the child's attention, and the word can then become a foundation for constructing a generalization for other objects identified by the same word (p. 250). For example, the young child may learn the word *doggie* for his pet, which he then applies to his neighbor's pet, having noticed the characteristic of, for example, its wagging tail. In the case of triangles, at the stage of identifying examples (pseudoconcept), the child may, for example, abstract the characteristic of three pointed ends (angles).

In summary, Vygotsky rejected the traditional view of a concept as a word label and a set of defining attributes or characteristics. Data from the Vygotskian experiments indicated that word meanings and connections among concept examples varied across age levels. One root of conceptual thinking consists of syncretic images (subjective connections among objects) and complexes (concrete, observable connections that are unstable). At the most advanced level of complexive thinking—the pseudoconcept—the child can accurately group concept examples together. However, the selections are based on matching examples to a model, not conceptual thinking. Together with the potential concept (abstracting a defining concept characteristic), the pseudoconcept contributes to the foundation for learning concepts.

Characteristics of True Conceptual Thinking

As with syncretic images, complexes, and pseudoconcepts, Vygotsky defined a concept in terms of the acts of thinking that it represents. His rationale for this approach is that the concept label, the word, is a sign, and it can be used in various mental operations (Vygotsky, 1931/1994b, p. 251). These different cognitive operations reflect fundamental differences between each of the forms of preconceptual thinking (syncretic images and complexes) and conceptual thinking.

In other words, a concept is "a new form of intellectual activity" (p. 259). It arises through the learner's activity in processing various examples, a process that includes determining connections and relationships of a particular object with others (Vygotsky, 1930–1931/1998, p. 56). Therefore, a concept only develops through "a long process of thinking and cognition" and is the "result of multiple operations of judgment" that include "apperception, interpretation, and recognition" (p. 56). For example, conceptual thinking in relation to the term *triangle* means that the individual can identify such diverse examples as icicle-shaped figures, as well as other sizes and colors, and determine relationships with other polygons. Examples of interconnections include information such as the facts that squares can be divided into two triangles, hexagons into 10, and the area of an octagon or hexagon is the area of one triangle multiplied by 8 or 10, respectively, and so on.

In other words, Vygotsky (1931/1994b) set a high level of intellectual activity in his criteria for the attainment of a true concept. First, the learner has abstracted and resynthesized the essential attributes of the concept. Second, the "newly acquired abstract synthesis becomes the basic form of thinking" (p. 250). Third, and a corollary of the prior criterion, is that the individual then applies the abstracted synthesis to understand and interpret related events (p. 250). A concept, in other words, "is a predisposition for quite a number of judgments" (Vygotsky, 1982–1984/1997b, p. 100). An example is the number 9. It appears in concrete form in a set of playing cards. However, the concept 9 encompasses judgments that are not reflected in the number on the playing cards. Examples include that it is divisible by three but not by even numbers, and it is the square of the number 3, the square root of 81, and so on. In terms of teaching, the pseudoconcept 9 is the ZPD for learning the concept 9 (p. 100).

Vygotsky also noted that accepting his definition of conceptual thinking meant that the cognition associated with the system of judgments in a concept is logical thinking (Vygotsky, 1930–1931/1998, p. 57). In other words, logical thinking is "a concept in action" (p. 57). Logical thinking is not an add-on to concepts; it does not develop after concepts. Instead, logical thinking is in the concepts themselves, which includes their external connections and relationships (p. 57).

The forms of cognition associated with forming true concepts means that this goal is not accomplished prior to adolescence. As true concepts do begin to develop, the student approaches the point of thinking in concepts (Vygotsky, 1934/1987a, p. 160; Vygotsky, 1930–1931/1998, p. 38). This development coincides with a major emphasis on academic subjects in the student's education, and these subjects (e.g., mathematics, science, and art) can be adequately understood only in concepts (Vygotsky, 1930–1931/1998, p. 42). Forming concepts also is the key factor in the development of higher mental functions, discussed in Chapter 4.

However, Vygotsky (1934/1987a, pp. 160–161; Vygotsky, 1931/1994b; 1930–1931/1998, pp. 51–52) cautioned that the capability of forming true concepts during adolescence is a "young and unstable acquisition of the intellect" (p. 51). Concepts do not become the dominant form of thinking until the end of that period. In other words, the more elementary processes coexist with concepts for a time.

In terms of intellectual activity, Vygotsky also was a realist. He noted that human behavior does not always operate at the upper levels of development (Vygotsky, 1931/1994b, p. 251). Often typical for adults is that their thinking functions at the level of complexes and sometimes occurs with more elementary forms of thinking (p. 252).

Commonalities between the Stages of Sign Use and Concept Development

The processes involved in the stages of sign use share several characteristics with the stages of concept development (see Table 6.2). As indicated, the young child's thinking consists of the primitive or natural mental processes: involuntary attention, simple perception, and natural memory. These processes are responsible for the child's selection of concept examples on the basis of subjective perceptions. Similarly, at the stages of naïve psychology (signs) and complexes, the child attempts to solve cognitive tasks. However, she either does not understand the psychological nature of the task or is unable to carry it through.

At the stage of external sign use, concrete, observable, auxiliary stimuli guide the child's thinking. Similarly, the child can group concept examples accurately by relying on the observable concept characteristics. However, the child's thinking is tied to the concrete visual situation. Finally, relying on internal, constructed stimuli to guide one's thinking occurs at best at adolescence. The student also constructs internal connections and relationships among concepts.

TABLE 6.2. Commonalities between Stages of Sign Use
and Concept Development

Stages of sign use	Processes	Stages of concept development
Primitive or natural	Cognition consists of inborn processes and concrete experience.	Syncretic images
Naïve psychology	Child attempts to manage her thinking but is unaware of the psychological nature of cognitive tasks.	Complexes
External sign use	Child masters his thinking with the aid of external stimuli; forms groupings of concept examples guided by observable characteristics.	Pseudoconcepts
Internal sign use	Adolescent masters his thinking through internally created stimuli; forms concepts and interrelationships in the same way.	True concepts

Summary

Vygotsky rejected the traditional view of a concept as an abstract mental category. From that perspective, students were to simply learn the concept name and a set of characteristics or attributes. Vygotsky's view of concepts differed from the traditional perspective in two major ways. They are that (a) concept (word) meanings grow and develop and (b) accurate identification of concept examples is not an indicator for true conceptual thinking.

On the basis of experimental data, Vygotsky identified two different roots of conceptual thinking. One root consists of syncretic images, formed on the basis of subjective impressions, and complexes. At the level of complexive thinking, the child groups objects on the basis of concrete, observable characteristics. However, the characteristics for selection are unstable; they change from one example to the next. At the highest level of complexes—pseudoconcepts—the characteristics are stable across the examples. The pseudoconcept differs from true conceptual thinking in that the child selects the concept examples through matching, not through abstracting and synthesizing the concept attributes. Nevertheless, the capability of forming pseudoconcepts, together with being able to abstract a single attribute, is the foundation for learning to form concepts.

True concepts result from a lengthy developmental process that is not concluded prior to adolescence. The true concept is a reflection of an object in its diversity and its connections and relationships to other objects and concepts. It arises through a lengthy process that involves several acts of thinking. Of importance is that the acts of judgment involved in forming and using true concepts is logical thinking. Thus, the development of true concepts in adolescence leads to a new form of intellectual activity, that of thinking in concepts.

A comparison of the stages in sign use and concept development indicate similarities between them. The young child's thinking in both areas is a reliance on primitive or natural processes. At the stages of naïve psychology (signs) and complexes, the child lacks an understanding of the psychological nature of the particular task. Moreover, the stage of external sign use is similar to the formation of pseudoconcepts. The learner's thinking is tied to the concrete situation. Finally, internal sign construction and the internal construction of true concepts occur during adolescence.

EVERYDAY AND ACADEMIC (SCIENTIFIC) CONCEPTS

The second period of Vygotsky's work on concept formation began in the 1930s. This work addressed a particular issue: the differences between everyday and scientific or academic concepts. In addition to the importance of academic concepts in cognitive development, they are an important practical issue for education (Vygotsky, 1934/1987b, p. 167).

Vygotsky (1934/1987b, p. 168) defined everyday concepts as developing through the child's practical activity and social interaction with others. Some theorists had referred to these concepts as spontaneous because they arise naturally in daily life and the child uses them without consciously thinking about them. Vygotsky preferred the designation "everyday concepts" because they were not spontaneously invented by the child (van der Veer & Valsiner, 1991, p. 270). In contrast, academic concepts develop in school as part of learning a particular subject area.

Vygotsky questioned the two then-current views on the development of academic concepts in instruction. One view rejected the idea of any internal cognitive development of academic concepts; students simply internalized information presented during instruction. The other view maintained that the steps in learning everyday concepts (such as dog, table, or chair) were merely repeated for academic concepts. However, Vygotsky (1934/1987b, 1935/1994a) noted that research findings on everyday concepts had simply been extended without any further research to academic concepts.

Research conducted by Shozefina I. Shif used open-ended sentences that ended in "because" or "although." Some of the sentences used everyday concepts and others used academic concepts from social sciences instruction (see Appendix B). Similar to the findings in Leont'ev's research, some children who used "because" accurately in their spontaneous conversation were unable to complete the sentences with either everyday or academic concepts (Vygotsky, 1934/1987b, p. 215). Furthermore, situations with "although" were more difficult for the children. Also, if the child had not mastered the relationship in his everyday thinking, he was unable to develop conscious awareness of this relationship with academic concepts. The child cannot gain conscious awareness of relationships that he does not have (p. 216). Discussed in this section are the characteristics of everyday and academic concepts and limitations of Piaget's views.

Characteristics of Everyday and Academic Concepts

Vygotsky's analyses led him to identify several differences between everyday and academic concepts. Summarized in Table 6.3, these differences indicate opposite developmental paths for the two types of concepts (p. 217).

Everyday Concepts

The child's everyday concepts are complexes that are learned in the preschool years (p. 238). They emerge in contact with real objects and things, such as flower and dog, and they are saturated with personal experience. The child's attention is directed toward the object that is represented by the concept in the course of daily life. However, the child's capability to define the concept and master its use in establishing logical relationships with other concepts occurs late in the developmental process. For example, when faced with an abstract problem involving "the brother of a brother," the child is confused (p. 218). This task in the Binet-Simon test required the child to solve the contradiction between a family that included three brothers and the statement "I have three brothers: Paul, Ernst, and me" (Rieber, 1998, endnote 55, p. 335).

Academic Concepts

In contrast to everyday concepts, the child's development of the academic concept "begins with work on the concept itself" (Vygotsky, 1934/1987b, p. 217). The child "defines it, applies it in various logical

TABLE 6.3. A Comparison of Everyday and Scientific (Academic) Concepts

	Everyday (spontaneous) concepts	Scientific (academic) concepts
Origin	Emerges in the child's immediate experience with things	Begins with a verbal definition in classroom instruction
Development	Develops from the more elementary characteristics to the higher, from below to above; develops in the child's rich daily experience with those around him or her	Develops from the more complex characteristics to the elementary, from above to below; develops through instruction in systematic cooperation between teacher and child
Nature	Linked to concrete experience, an act of thought involves memories of concrete experience rather than the concept's logical structure	Linked to other concepts in a system of logical categories and oppositions (Vygotsky, 1935/1994a, p. 366)
Relationship to verbal thinking	Often used without conscious awareness of the meaning; child often cannot state a verbal definition; attention is directed toward the object that the concept represents	Introduced through verbal means; child can verbalize the concept but may not be able to use it fluently. Use is both conscious and voluntary; attention is directed toward one's own thinking
Strength	The saturation with experience	The conscious awareness of one's thinking and volition
Weakness	The lack of abstraction, the child's inability to act on the concept with volition	The insufficient saturation with concrete experience, verbalism
Relationship to cognitive development	Serves as an initial linking of verbal symbols to concrete experience (development of word meaning)	Serves as the gateway to conscious awareness of cognitive processes through systematization (connections with other concepts)

operations, and identifies its relationships to other concepts" (p. 218). It develops through instruction, in systematic cooperation between teacher and child, and the child's attention is directed toward her own thinking. The weakness of the academic concept is insufficient saturation with concrete experience.

The development of academic concepts is similar to learning a foreign language, which requires conscious awareness and attention. In the process of learning a second language, awareness and thought are often applied to the child's native language. Academic concepts also are learned with conscious awareness, and Vygotsky (1934/1987b) maintained that learning them as part of a system blazes the trail for the further development of everyday concepts. The structural formations are in place that can lead to the development of subordinate and superordinate relationships among everyday concepts (p. 219). (However, van der Veer and Valsiner, 1991, noted that the ways the learning of academic concepts would "reform" the child's everyday concepts are unclear [p. 275]).

The Importance of a System

Vygotsky (1934/1987b) maintained that the essential difference in the psychological nature of (everyday and academic) concepts is that the child's everyday concepts do not form a system (p. 234). The lack of a system means that the only possible relationships are connections among the objects themselves. For example, "the relationship of the word 'flower' to the object is completely different for the child who does not yet know the words rose, violet, lily than it is for the child who does" (p. 234). The lack of a system of concepts, according to Vygotsky (1934/1987b, p. 234), is the explanation for syncretic thinking in the young child.

In contrast, from the outset, academic concepts are identified as part of a system. They have links to higher order concepts in a hierarchical relationship as well as links to concepts at the same level. For example, square, rectangle, and pentagon are instances of the higher order concept *polygon*. The learning of academic concepts is characterized by the child's conscious awareness of such relationships.

Conclusions

Vygotsky's analyses of everyday and academic concepts led to three specific conclusions. One, discussed in the prior paragraphs, was his identification of the lack of a system in the child's everyday concepts. Second, the development of academic concepts does not repeat the developmental sequence of everyday concepts (Vygotsky, 1934/1987b, p. 220). If it did, then the acquisition of academic concepts would result in only an enrichment of the child's vocabulary and an extension of the child's store of concepts. Instead, the acquisition of academic concepts and their systemic nature influence the child's thinking and lead to a new stage of mental development. Therefore, because instruction is essential to the development of academic concepts, it plays a vital role in the child's mental development (p. 220). Third, the research by Shif established a bridge between the experimental study of concepts and the study of the child's actual concepts (p. 239).

Limitations in Piaget's View

Vygotsky agreed with several of Piaget's views on cognitive development. However, he maintained that Piaget had made some errors in his discussions of the role of concepts in children's thinking. Vygotsky (1934/1987b) stated that one of the goals of his research was to overcome the limitations "in what was one of the best contemporary theories [Piaget's thinking] of the development of the child's thought" (p. 176)

The Significance of Children's Contradictory Statements

First, Piaget recognized the unsystematic nature of the young child's thinking, but he did not recognize its importance (Vygotsky, 1934/ 1987b). For example, the child states that a bead sinks because it is small. At another point, observing a larger bead sink, the child maintains that it sinks because it is big. Piaget believed that the reason for the child's behavior is egocentrism, an inability to view the world objectively. In contrast, Vygotsky (1934/1987b) maintained that the child perceives his statements about the beads to be mutually exclusive judgments. The child lacks a single superordinate concept of the situation (objects sink because they are heavy), which would permit his awareness of the contradictory statements, and then the child could correct them. The contradictory statements can exist side by side for the child because his thinking is determined by the logic of perception. Specifically, the only relationships among concepts for the child are those that she perceives among objects (p. 232). "The child takes the connections between [his or her] impressions for the connections between things" (p. 235). In other words, the child lacks a system of concepts, which is the "root cause" of the flaws in the child's thinking described by Piaget (Vygotsky, 1934/1987b, p. 234).

The Role of the Child's Spontaneous Concepts

Second, Piaget maintained that only the child's everyday concepts provide direct knowledge of the child's thinking (Vygotsky, 1934/1987b, p. 174). The child's nonspontaneous concepts are learned from adults and reflect adult thinking (p. 174). Therefore, they cannot reflect the child's thinking. However, Vygotsky (1934/1987b) noted that this inference by Piaget contradicted his statements that a child, in learning a new concept, reworks it (p. 174).

Third, to accept the view that the child's nonspontaneous concepts do not represent the child's thinking leads to another problem. The researcher must then accept the related situation of a barrier between the child's spontaneous and nonspontaneous concepts. Vygotsky (1934/ 1987b) noted that this situation had led Piaget to view concept development as occurring on two separate channels (p. 174).

The Course of Cognitive Development

Fourth, Vygotsky noted that Piaget represented mental development as a gradual dying out of the child's inaccurate thinking (the egocentric thinking mentioned in Chapter 4). The more powerful thinking of the adult gradually replaces the particular characteristics of the child's thinking. Vygotsky described the process of forcing out one form of thinking by another as similar to replacing one liquid in a container by forcing in another liquid from the outside (p. 175). However, as discussed in Chapter 5, Vygotsky (1982–1984/1997a) described the child's egocentric speech as an early form of verbal thinking that becomes inner speech.

Vygotsky further argued that extending Piaget's belief to instruction implied an antagonistic relationship between instruction and development. That is, nonspontaneous concepts, the material of instruction, must force out the child's spontaneous representations (Vygotsky, 1934/ 1987b, p. 175), an action that is neither logical nor practical.

Summary

The second period of Vygotsky's work on concept formation addressed the differences between everyday concepts and the academic or subject matter concepts learned at school. Everyday concepts are those that are learned in the child's daily life, and she uses them without consciously thinking about them. Vygotsky disagreed with the two existing views of concept formation. One view maintained that academic concepts did not undergo any development, and the other perspective equated the steps in learning academic concepts.

In contrast, Vygotsky identified major differences between everyday and academic concepts. Among them are that learning an academic concept typically begins with the definition, learning requires conscious awareness of one's thinking, and the academic concept is part of a system that includes hierarchical, subordinate, and coordinate relationships with other concepts in the content domain. Learning academic concepts and their relationships is important because this conceptual effort leads to a higher level of mental development.

Although Vygotsky agreed with several of Piaget's views on cognitive development, he maintained that Piaget had made errors in his discussions about children's concepts. Vygotsky noted that (a) the child's contradictory statements about situations do not result from egocentrism (instead, the child views his judgments as mutually exclusive); (b) the child's everyday concepts do not provide direct knowledge of her thinking; and (c) mental development is not a gradual dying out of the child's inaccurate thinking. Moreover, according to Vygotsky, the child's contradictory statements about the world result from the lack of a system in his everyday concepts.

EDUCATIONAL IMPLICATIONS

Vygotsky's analyses of the development of concepts and the psychological differences between everyday and academic concepts have implications for research and theory as well as educational practice.

Implications for Research and Theory

In addition to information about general issues for research and theory, Vygotsky (1934/1987b) described a framework that could capture the level and nature of the child's thinking.

General Issues

Vygotsky (1934/1987b) cautioned that psychological research had relied on superficial methods in addressing children's actual concepts (p. 181). He called for the sophisticated study of children's actual concepts, and Shif's research on the child's uses of "because" and "although" was a first step. These experiments indicated differences between the spontaneous and self-directed (voluntary) production of causal and adversative relations. Also important is his description of the different intellectual processes involved in the learning of everyday and academic concepts and the role of academic concepts in thinking.

Therefore, information about the child's learning of everyday concepts should not be applied to the learning of academic concepts. However, contemporary models and theories do not meet Vygotsky's criteria. Bruner, Goodnow, and Austin (1956) defined concept attainment as finding the attributes that identify concept examples (p. 22). Robert Gagné's (1977, 1985) theory described concrete concepts as having observable characteristics; evidence of learning requires the identification of concept examples. The second concept type in his theory—defined concepts—are abstract and cannot be identified by observable characteristics. Examples include prime number, transportation, and justice. To acquire defined concepts, the student must learn the classifying rule that determines concept membership (Gagné, 1985). Finally, Herbert Klausmeier's (1992; Klausmeier, Gatala, & Frayer, 1974) model identified four levels of concept attainment. However, the levels reflect emerging expertise in identifying examples and learning the concept definition. For example, at level 2 (identity), the child recognizes a previously encountered item when presented in a different context. At level 4 (formal concept), the learner can identify all examples as well as nonexamples, name the concept and the defining attributes, and differentiate the concept from closely related concepts (Klausmeier et al., 1974).

Applying Vygotsky's perspective, three problems may be identified with these models. First, they focus on a product of concept formation: identifying examples or stating definitions or classifying rules. However, such responses cannot indicate whether the learner is at the level of complexive thinking or the level of true concepts. The learner may be matching observable characteristics instead of abstracting and synthesizing defining concept attributes. Second, a focus on individual concepts does not address the connections and relations among concepts. In the absence of developing connections to other concepts, the student's learning is incomplete.

Third, contemporary models focus on concepts as categories to be learned, not the psychological operations the child activates when she uses the concept in her thinking. Therefore, contemporary models lack a mechanism for ensuring that learners can actually think in concepts. The difficulty is that the learner may be thrust too soon into solving problems with new concepts before he is able to use the concepts to understand and interpret various situations. A second potential problem is that the learner does not reach the stage of developing the judgments that are made in using a concept. The learner, therefore, does not make the concept his own and can only use the concept in a narrow way.

A Framework for Determining Children's Levels of Concept Development

Any concept is a generalization; that is, it represents a group of objects, events, or activities as well as relations with other concepts. Thinking begins with syncretic images, then progresses to complexes and then, hopefully, to true concepts. Vygotsky (1934/1987b) sought a way to determine the level of the child's or adolescent's level of thinking in relation to concepts (p. 228).

Vygotsky based one aspect of his solution to this task on the fact that any concept can be expressed in terms of other concepts. He labeled this principle as "the law of concept equivalence" (p. 226 [emphasis added]). Particularly important is that the law of concept equivalence is unique for each stage in concept development. At the syncretic stage, the child is likely to have no equivalents of the syllables she attaches to various collections of objects. In contrast, at the complexive stage, the child may understand that roses and daisies are both flowers, a hierarchical arrangement.

The second aspect of analyzing the child's thinking in relation to concepts is based on the view that thinking may range from extremely graphic to extremely abstract. For example, a young child may describe her grandmother's lap as a soft pillow (graphic). An auto mechanic, in contrast, refers to a car's problems in technical terms that include both descriptive and abstract elements (graphic/abstract). A scientist, in discussing her work, may speak entirely in scientific terms. One example is Einstein's presentation of his theory of relativity (abstract).

The nature of children's thinking can be determined for each stage of concept development by identifying (a) the extent of concept equivalence and (b) the range of thinking from extremely graphic to extremely abstract. Vygotsky (1934/1987b) referred to this information as the measure of generality of a concept (p. 227). The advantages of such research are that (a) the nature of syncretic, complexive, potential or true concepts is more fully revealed; (b) differences in this measure indicate differences in the transition from one stage of concept development to the next; and (c) a different set of operations is possible for different measures of generality (pp. 228–229). For example, in the young child's autonomous speech, there are no levels of generality; everything is on the same plane. Vygotsky also recalled one child who understood the concepts *table, chair,* and *bed,* but he was unable to subordinate them to *furniture.* Instead, the child placed *furniture* alongside the other concepts.

Implementing Vygotsky's conceptualization requires the identification of the words that children and adolescents use and either the objects to which their words refer or their definitions and examples of those words. This information can be obtained from parents, teachers, observations in school settings, and written or oral questioning. Then, in conversations with individual children or adolescents, protocols can be developed that indicate the extent of equivalence of the learner's words (concepts) and the nature of his thinking from graphic to abstract.

Applications to Educational Practice

Two key principles of concept formation are important for classroom instruction. They are (a) the early ways of thinking of the child (syncretic, complexive) and (b) suggested activities in the classroom. In addition, Vygotsky's work has implications for the current classroom practice known as concept mapping.

Word Use and Abstract Thinking

Of major importance is that "use of the general word does not in any sense presuppose the mastery of abstract thinking" (Vygotsky, 1934/1987a, p. 163). Throughout Vygotsky's discussions, he cautioned against the error of equating the child's word use with conceptual thinking. The child simply uses the same words as the adult and refers to some of the objects or events that are concept examples. In contrast, interpreting reality through true concepts is on the plane of abstract–logical thinking.

The capability of accurately identifying some concept examples by preschool children may mislead parents and other adults to conclude that the child has a fairly complete understanding of everyday concepts. However, the child, prior to the age of 7, is thinking in the form of syncretic images or complexes (Vygotsky, 1930–1931/1998). At about the age of 7, the child makes a transition to using pseudoconcepts (the most advanced level of complexive thinking). Also, he may be able to identify a common trait of the examples of some concepts. However, this capability does not constitute a concept, although it is an important step in the development of concepts (p. 61). In other words, the schoolchild externally seems to deal with devices of logical thinking (concepts), but she "has not mastered logic in the true sense of the word" (p. 66).

Addressing Concept Formation in the Classroom

The research conducted by Vygotsky's associates indicated that the thinking of the schoolchild has not yet matured. The child is insensitive to contradictions in his statements, has difficulties in establishing logical relationships between ideas, and matches ideas syncretically according to subjective, not objective, criteria (Vygotsky, 1930–1931/1998, p. 52).

The mechanism for addressing these cognitive limitations is appropriate instruction in academic concepts. The rationale for this approach is threefold. First, the psychological equivalent of the [true] concept is "a system of acts of thinking and some combination and processing of patterns" (p. 55). In other words, thinking of some object with the help of a concept means that the object is included in an organized system of connections and relationships (p. 53). Second, learning concepts is the mechanism whereby the higher mental processes—self-organized attention, categorical perception, conceptual thinking, and logical memory— are developed. One reason for the key role of academic concepts is that "true" concepts "are not simply acquired or memorized by the child and assimilated by his memory" (Vygotsky, 1934/1987b, p. 176). Instead, academic concepts require "an extraordinary effort" of the child's thought (p. 176). Working with academic concepts in a hierarchical system of connections and relations with other concepts develops the learner's perception of categories and logical memory as well as the deliberate focusing of attention on the elements of situations.

Third, mathematics, the natural sciences, and the social sciences can only be communicated and presented adequately in the form of logical verbal thinking: the system of connections and relationships among concepts. In other words, this new content plays a role in the development of cognition because it presents problems that only can be resolved through the formation of concepts (Vygotsky, 1930–1931/1998, p. 39).

Mastery of academic concepts means that the student can define them easily, implement them in various logical operations, and identify the relationships among them (Vygotsky, 1934/1987b, p. 218). One implication for instruction is that attempting a direct communication of concepts from the teacher's head to that of the child is a practice that is "educationally fruitless" (Vygotsky, 1935/1994a, p. 356). All that is accomplished is simply a "meaningless acquisition of words" and "mere verbalization" that, in reality, hides a vacuum (p. 356).

Instead, the teacher explains the new concept, places it in a context with related concepts, poses problems that include the concept, and requires the student to explain and work with the concept. In other words, instruction should move from verbal definitions to working with concepts in various situations. In this process, the student develops a conscious awareness of the logical relationships among concepts and also of her own thinking. Equally important, the student begins to master her own thinking. Instruction that addresses the logical relationships in academic subjects is the mechanism for addressing the student's lack of awareness of his thinking and the need to master the logical relationships in the particular domain.

Some science educators suggest using analogies to facilitate students' understanding of relationships among concepts. For example, Venville and Donovan (2006) relate the chromosomes comprising a genome to the chapters of a book. Although an analogy may be used to introduce a relationship, an analogy is not an exact representation. Extraneous information from the analogy may inhibit students' learning.

A second approach in mathematics and the natural sciences is the use of interactive, computer-based representations that provide concrete, graphic representations of implicit features of concepts. "Skaterworld," for example, illustrates velocity–time relationships through the movements of a skater alongside velocity–time graphs. Another example,

"Numberspeed," illustrates motion, velocity, and acceleration through the movement of two turtles racing on a track that students manipulate (Parnafes, 2005). The program poses challenges to students such as "Can you make the top turtle get to 20 first, and then the bottom turtle get to 40 first?" (Parnafes & DiSessa, 2004). The program provides numerical and visual feedback to the students. Of importance in the implementation of these approaches is that the student's thinking must move beyond the graphic auxiliary stimuli that illustrate concept relationships to his or her construction of internal stimuli that symbolize the interrelationships. In other words, instruction must build on the relationships introduced in the computer program. Also, the capability of *thinking* in concepts develops over a period of time. Many situations that explore relations among concepts are necessary to develop thinking to that level.

Relevance for Concept Mapping

The technique of concept mapping was introduced in 1979 as a way to increase students' meaningful learning in science (Novak, 1979). The elements of a concept map are nodes that identify concepts and links connecting the nodes that are labeled to illustrate the relationship between concepts. For example, in one concept map, the node "calcium homeostasis" is joined to the two nodes "osteoclasts" and "osteoblasts" with a link labeled "maintained by" (Cliburn, 1990).

The elements of concept maps, concept nodes, and labeled links indicating relationships such as "has," "is," "involves," "inhibits," and so on are also the components of propositional networks. In psychology, propositional networks are one conceptualization of the organization of knowledge in long-term memory (see Anderson, 1990; DiVesta, 1987).

In the classroom, concept maps may be (a) teacher made, serving as guides to course content and as diagnostic and testing guides, or (b) student constructed, reflecting the student's perceived organization of meaningful information. Educators and researchers have noted that concept maps reflect the organizer's conceptual perspective of a subject area; therefore, they are somewhat subjective (Santhanam, Leach, & Dawson, 1998; Schmid & Telaro, 1990). Some positive benefits for concept mapping have been reported. However, teaching the technique is time-consuming (Schmid & Telaro, 1990; Santhanam et al., 1998) and can be very difficult for students who have had only a sketchy exposure to a topic (Cliburn, 1990). To be able to construct concept maps, students also must be familiar with ways to organize knowledge (p. 213).

Vygotsky (1934/1987b) noted that learning relationships of generality among concepts (superordinate, subordinate, parallel) requires extraordinary effort by the student. Therefore, asking students to map causal relationships before they have learned the relationships of generality among concepts results in errors and misconceptions. This problem is indicated by the difficulties in teaching concept mapping and the subjectivity found in concept maps.

An alternative is for the class to construct a large visual diagram of the concepts in the course material as the semester progresses. As the students learn new concepts, they are added to the diagram. This exercise allows students to flesh out their understandings of the relationships among concepts, an essential aspect of concept learning as Vygotsky defined it. However, a necessary prerequisite to this activity is that the teacher prioritize the extensive information presented in the textbook, which, typically, is loaded with terms. The purpose of this teacher planning activity is to identify the terms that are to be developed to the level of true concepts because that level of thinking includes the connections and relationships to other concepts.

Summary

Vygotsky's perspective on the development of conceptual thinking can inform issues in both research and theory and the classroom. His view calls into question models of concept formation that rely on the identification of concept examples as evidence of learning. Three problems with that perspective are that such tasks cannot indicate whether the learner is at the level of complexive thinking or true conceptual thinking; a focus on individual concepts does not address connections and relationships among concepts; and the models focus on concepts as categories, not the psychological operations undertaken by the child.

Vygotsky's law of concept equivalence can assist researchers and theorists in identifying typical knowledge levels for different age groups. The researcher determines the extent to which the child can express a concept in terms of other concepts and the type of concept examples (extremely graphic to extremely abstract) he names.

Implications for the classroom include the relationships of the word (concept label) to abstract thinking, addressing concept formation in the classroom, and the role of concept mapping. Vygotsky cautioned that accurate word use by the learner to refer to particular concept examples is no indication that she has mastered the logical thinking represented by true conceptual thinking.

Academic or subject matter concepts are the basis for the development of conceptual thinking. These concepts cannot be acquired through simple memorization. Mastery of academic concepts means that the student can easily define them, implement them in logical operations, and identify interrelationships. Classroom practice, therefore, must include teacher explanations of new concepts, placing them in a context with related concepts, presentation of problems that include the concepts, and student explanations of the concepts. Interactive computer-based representations of abstract concepts that also provide feedback to students can introduce such concepts to the learner. Then classroom activities should be implemented to move the child's thinking beyond the graphic representations in the computer-based exercise.

Concept maps in the classroom may be teacher or student constructed. Issues identified in relation to concept maps are that they are somewhat subjective because they reflect the organizer's perspective; teaching the technique is time-consuming; and the technique is difficult for students who have sketchy information about a topic. Vygotsky emphasized that learning connections and relationships among concepts requires extraordinary effort by the student. An alternative practice is for the students to construct one large visual diagram of the concepts in their subjects as the semester progresses. This activity requires preplanning by the teacher on identifying the terms in the content that are to be learned at the level of true concepts.

REFERENCES

Anderson, J. R. (1990). *Cognitive psychology and its implications* (3rd ed.). New York: Freeman.

Bruner, J., Goodnow, J., & Austin, A. (1956). *A study of thinking*. New York: Wiley.

Cliburn, J. W. (1990). Concept maps to promote meaningful learning. *Journal of College Science Teaching, 19*(4), 212–217.

DiVesta, F. J. (1987). The cognitive movement and education. In J. Glover & R. Ronnings (Eds.), *Historical foundations of educational psychology* (pp. 203–233). New York: Plenum.

Gagné, R. M. (1977). *The conditions of learning* (3rd ed.). New York: Holt, Rinehart & Winston.

Gagné, R. M. (1985). *The conditions of learning* (4th ed.). New York: Holt, Rinehart & Winston.

Klausmeier, H. (1992). Concept learning and teaching. *Educational Psychologist, 27*(3), 267–286.

Klausmeier, K. J., Gatala, E. S., & Frayer, D. A. (1974). *Conceptual learning and development: A cognitive view*. New York: Academic Press.

Novak, J. (1979). Applying psychology and philosophy to the improvement of laboratory teaching. *The American Biology Teacher, 41*(8), 466–470.

Parnafes, O. (2005, April). *Constructing understanding of physical phenomena through the interpretation of dynamic and interactive representations*. Paper presented at the meeting of the American Educational Research Association, Montreal, Quebec, Canada.

Parnafes, O., & DiSessa, A. (2004). Relations between types of reasoning and computational representations. *International Journal of Computers and Mathematical Learning, 9*, 251–280.

Rieber, R. W. (Ed.). (1998). Notes to the Russian edition. In *Collected works of L. S. Vygotsky: Vol. 5. Child psychology* (pp. 319–353). New York: Plenum.

Santhanam, E., Leach, C., & Dawson, C. (1998). Concept mapping: How should it be introduced and is there evidence for long-term benefit? *Higher Education, 35*, 317–328.

Schmid, R. F., & Telaro, G. (1990). Concept mapping as an instructional strategy for high school biology. *Journal of Educational Research, 84*(2), 78–85.

Valsiner, J., & van der Veer, R. (2000). *The social mind: Construction of the idea.* New York: Cambridge University Press.

van der Veer, R., & Valsiner, J. (1991). *Understanding Vygotsky: A quest for synthesis.* Cambridge, MA: Blackwell.

Venville, G., & Donovan, J. (2006). Analogies for life: A subjective view of analogies and metaphors used to teach about genes and DNA. *Teaching Science, 52*(1), 18–22.

Vygotsky, L. S. (1987a). An experimental study of concept development. In R. W. Rieber & A. S. Carton (Eds.), *Collected works of L. S. Vygotsky: Vol. 1. Problems of general psychology* (pp. 121–166). New York: Plenum. (Original work published 1934)

Vygotsky, L. S. (1987b). The development of scientific concepts in childhood. In R. W. Rieber & A. S. Carton (Eds.), *Collected works of L. S. Vygotsky: Vol. 1. Problems of general psychology* (pp. 167–241). New York: Plenum. (Original work published 1934)

Vygotsky, L. S. (1994a). The development of academic concepts in school-aged children. In R. van der Veer & J. Valsiner (Eds.), *The Vygotsky reader* (pp. 355–370). Cambridge, MA: Blackwell. (Original work published 1935)

Vygotsky, L. S. (1994b). The development of thinking and concept formation in adolescence. In R. van der Veer & J. Valsiner (Eds.), *The Vygotsky reader* (pp. 185–265). Cambridge, MA: Blackwell. (Original work published 1931)

Vygotsky, L. S. (1997a). Development of speech and thinking. In R. W. Rieber (Ed.), *Collected works of L. S. Vygotsky: Vol. 4. The history of the development of higher mental functions* (pp. 191–205). New York: Plenum. (Original work published 1982–1984)

Vygotsky, L. S. (1997b). On psychological systems. In R. W. Rieber & J. Wollock (Eds.), *Collected works of L. S. Vygotsky: Vol. 3. Problems of the theory and history of psychology* (pp. 91–107). New York: Plenum. (Original work published 1982–1984)

Vygotsky, L. S. (1998). Development of thinking and formation of concepts in the adolescent. In R. W. Rieber (Ed.), *Collected works of L. S. Vygotsky: Vol. 5. Child psychology* (pp. 29–81). New York: Plenum. (Original work published 1930–1931)

Part III

THE CYCLE
OF DEVELOPMENT

7

Structure and Dynamics of Age-Related Development

Development is a continuous process of self-propulsion characterized primarily by a continuous appearance of the new which did not exist at previous stages.
—VYGOTSKY (1982–1984/1998j, p. 190)

The environment of the child must be studied: most of all we must study what it means for the child.
—VYGOTSKY (1982–1984/1998g, p. 293)

Vygotsky (1982–1984/1997a) noted that the research studies of his collaborative group had always followed an analytical path (p. 241). The goal had been to identify and determine the path of cultural development of particular mental functions that were linked to (a) the mastery of external symbolic functions, such as speech and arithmetic, and (b) "internal changes in memory, attention, abstract thinking, [and the] formation of concepts" (p. 241).

Vygotsky then turned his attention to paedology, typically referred to as child study. Other Soviet psychologists viewed paedology as interdisciplinary. However, Vygotsky purposefully differentiated it from other disciplines by defining it as the science of child development (van der Veer & Valsiner, 1991, p. 308). Further, he identified three research problems of importance in paedology. They are (a) the role of the environment in development, (b) the development of consciousness in terms

153

of the child's world view and personality, and (c) the problem of age-related changes in development. Of interest is that, in 1930, the Paedological Section of the First All-Union Congress on the Study of Human Behavior had identified two important topics for researchers in the discipline. The closing resolution of the Paedological Section called for the study of the environment of the child from the perspective of the child's class background and children's world views as they experienced the "increasing 'class struggle' " in Soviet society (van der Veer & Valsiner, 1991, p. 301).

Vygotsky (1982–1984/1997a, 1982–1984/1998g, 1935/1994, 1930–1931/1998a) developed his own definition of the child's world view, but not from the class-based foundation specified in the resolution. Vygotsky's conception of the relation between the child and the environment and his descriptions of world view and personality are discussed in the first part of this chapter. The chapter then introduces key developmental concepts and Vygotsky's outline of the cycle of developmental periods. These periods of development are elaborated in Chapter 8.

THE CHILD–ENVIRONMENT RELATIONSHIP

Discussed first in this section is Vygotsky's conceptualization of the nature of the environment, followed by a discussion of the unity of environmental and personal characteristics. The section concludes with the changing role of the child's world view and personality in the development of human consciousness.

Nature of the Environment

Vygotsky (1982–1984/1998g) identified three problems in both the theoretical and practical study of the role of the environment in relation to the child (p. 293). First, for the most part, educators and researchers viewed the environment in terms of its absolute physical features. A social report, for example, might include the size of the living space in the home, whether the child has her own bed, the level of the parents' education, whether they read newspapers, and other similar features. The rationale for this approach is that documentation of these indicators would provide information about their role in the child's development (p. 293). Similarly, both theories of learning and theories of development viewed the environment as a set of conditions external to the child that typically play a particular role. Some writers did acknowledge that, as the child moves from one age to another, the *"environment in the direct sense of this word keeps changing"* (Vygotsky, 1935/1994, p. 339).

However, they were referring to the external, physical characteristics of the child's environment that change from infancy through the school years. From the restricted space of the infant to the school classroom, the child's environment does broaden as he grows older.

However, Vygotsky maintained that these changes in the physical environment are only part of the story. First, the child's environment is not restricted to physical features. Instead, the environment is social and is characterized by a variety of social interactions. Therefore, for Vygotsky, an important factor that differentiates the elementary school situation from the home is the nature of the social interactions between adult and child.

The second problem was the view that the environment is external to the child. A third, related problem was that the environment functions only as the setting in which developmental changes in the child occur. In contrast, Vygotsky (1982–1984/1998g, p. 293) maintained that the child is part of the environment. In other words, characteristics of the child interact with characteristics of the environment to determine its influence on the child. From the perspective of development, the environment "is completely different for a child at age one, three, seven, or twelve" (Vygotsky, 1982–1984/1998g, p. 293). An example, discussed in Chapter 5, is the development of speech. The speech of the adults in the child's environment does not change, but it takes on different meanings for the child as his own speech patterns develop (Vygotsky, 1935/1994). Similarly, as the child's thinking moves from syncretic images to complexes and then to mature or true concepts, the learner is better equipped to make use of modeled behaviors in the environment. The development of the child's internal processes changes the nature of his experience of the environment, and the changing experiences, in turn, affect the child's thinking (Vygotsky, 1982–1984/1998g, p. 294). In other words, the child's relationship to the environment is reciprocal and relative rather than absolute and objective (Vygotsky, 1982–1984/1999, p. 55). This reciprocal, relative influence is characteristic of a dialectical relationship.

Vygotsky (1935/1994) also maintained that the environment is the source of development; not merely the setting. This view explains the central role of adults, or "ideal forms," who interact with the child's more rudimentary behavior (Vygotsky, 1935/1994, p. 348). This interaction with adults is critical because the child learns to master her own processes of behavior "from the example of how an adult masters it" (Vygotsky, 1982–1984/1997a, p. 248).

Vygotsky viewed this presence of ideal forms at the beginning of a child's development as unique to cultural development. There was no comparable condition in biological evolution. Primitive man did not biologically change because "a man of the future" was present to influence him (Vygotsky, 1935/1994, p. 349). However, *"in child development that which is possible to achieve at the end and as the result of the developmental process, is already available in the environment from the beginning"* (pp. 347–348). For example, as mentioned in Chapter 5, the complex, articulated speech of adults in the child's environment acts as both a model and a guiding force for the child's speech development.

The absence of ideal forms of behavior is detrimental to a child's development, thus supporting the concept that the social environment is the source of development. A child who only develops his concept of numbers among other children will not develop higher levels of mathematical thinking (Vygotsky, 1935/1994, p. 351). For the child's thinking to become more abstract and logical, adults must use these forms of thinking in their interactions with the child.

The Unity of Environmental and Personal Characteristics

In different discussions, Vygotsky (1929, 1934/1987a, 1935/1994) pointed out the error in subdividing a complex mental activity into specific elements (as discussed in Chapter 2). The reciprocal and relative relationship between the child and the environment is a complex whole that also should not be decomposed into specific elements for study. Vygotsky used the Russian term *perezhivanie* to reflect this unity. Van der Veer and Valsiner (1994, p. 354, note 1) stated that the term was used to convey "the idea that one and the same objective situation may be interpreted, perceived, experienced, or lived through by different children in different ways" (p. 354).

Lacking a comparable term in English, the editors used the term *emotional experience*, which, they indicated, only addresses the affective and not the interpretive, rational aspect of the relationship. For Vygotsky (1935/1994), *perezhivanie* is *"a unit where, on the one hand, in an indivisible state, the environment is represented, . . . and on the other hand, what is represented is how I, myself, am experiencing this* [the environment]" (p. 342). In other words, experience is a unity of the environment, or situational characteristics, and the individual's personality, or personal characteristics (p. 342). This unity is key to understanding individual differences in development.

As an example, Vygotsky presented the case of three siblings treated in his clinic who experienced their mother's abusiveness and alcohol dependency in very different ways (Vygotsky, 1935/1994, p. 340). The youngest reacted to the mother's physical abuse with complete depression and helplessness. In contrast, the middle child was ambivalent and conflicted. This child, in his attitudes and in his behavior, exhibited both a strong attachment and a strong hatred for the mother. Finally, the oldest child, although somewhat limited in his mental capabilities, was the only one of the three who understood the situation. He understood that his mother was ill and felt pity for her. He also acted to protect the two younger children and thus became the "senior member of the family" (p. 341). His behavior was not typical for his age but was more like that of an adult, even though his mental capacities were limited. Of importance is that these three children developed totally different relations to the same environmental influence. In other words, their emotional experiences differed.

In this example, the children differed in their emotional reactions to a dysfunctional situation. However, the child's experience with the environment involves more than an affective reaction. As mentioned, events, such as beginning to develop speech, alter both the child's functioning and his interpretation of the environment.

World View and Personality

Vygotsky (1982–1984/1997a) identified the content of the process of cultural development as consisting of two mental syntheses that he named world view and personality. He introduced these two general concepts as a preliminary orientation to the cultural development of the child (p. 242). Stated another way, world view and personality are two aspects of the developing consciousness of the child.

World View

Vygotsky (1982–1984/1997a) did not consider world view to be a "logical thought-out view of the world . . . developed in a deliberate system" (p. 242). Instead, world view refers to the individual's behavior as a whole in terms of his cultural relation to the world, and it functions as a synthesis. When fully formed, which does not occur prior to adolescence, world view consists of the individual's consciousness of an external reality and his method of relating to that reality (Vygotsky, 1930–1931/1998a, p. 147).

At the moment of birth, the child does not have a world view (Vygotsky, 1982–1984/1997a, p. 242). This development begins when he begins to react to people and objects in the environment. Initially, the world view of the infant and the young child is subjective. One 8-month-old, for example, raised and dropped his body repeatedly in an effort to move a distant object. Also, a young child may squint her eyes in an attempt to turn on a light (Vygotsky, 1982–1984/1997a) or may attempt to influence objects through speech.

The child's world view becomes more stable at school age. Egocentric speech has reached the verbal planning stage. In addition to planning his actions through speech, he can provide an accounting of the steps he has taken (p. 250). Then, during adolescence, the learner is beginning to relate to the world in terms of concepts (Vygotsky, 1930–1931/1998b).

At the end of adolescence, he draws on a comprehensive system of knowledge in dealing with the world. The adolescent also can develop a life plan, a form of adaptation to the external world (Vygotsky, 1982–1984/1997a, p. 251). This view is consistent with the social situation in the USSR at that time, in which adolescents typically joined the work force formally at the age of 15.

Personality

In contrast to world view, which is external, personality is internal. (See Figure 7.1.) However, Vygotsky defined personality in a different sense than the typical use of the term. His definition does not include particular traits that reflect a certain personality type (Vygotsky, 1982–1984/1997a, p. 242). Instead, personality is a social concept; it is not innate but is a product of cultural development.

Personality consists of two components. One component is the unity of behavior mastered by the child (p. 242). Any step in the development of a mental function assumes development of the personality, however small (p. 242). Vygotsky's (1934/1987b) rationale for this view is that the ways the child's mind "partitions, analyzes, connects, and reworks" her experience, both internal and external, depends on the knowledge system that apprehends that experience (p. 324). For exam-

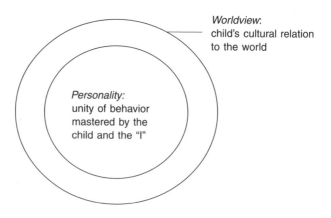

FIGURE 7.1. Components of the child's developing consciousness.

ple, the young child does not relate logically to her experiences. Recall the young child described by Basov who faced the task of getting a piece of candy from the top of the cupboard. As noted in Chapter 5, the child assured the experimenter that the candy would soon come down from the top of the cupboard to where they were.

The preschool child's mastery and direction of his behavior involves more complex events than the elementary or primitive mental processes. Through egocentric speech, the child begins to plan her actions in practical situations. Then, by school age, the child's memory and attention are no longer bound up with perception. He also has the capacity to master his attention, memory, and so on. The term *personality* captures the mastery, individual control, and directing of one's higher capabilities, such as verbal memory (Vygotsky, 1982–1984/1997d, p. 91).

The other component of personality is the individual's development of his sense of "I." Described in Chapter 8, the connectedness the very young child experiences with her mother or primary caregiver is followed by the beginning of the separation of the personal "I" (Vygotsky, 1982–1984/1998d, p. 266). Personality becomes more diversified when the child begins elementary school and social experiences become more varied (Vygotsky, 1982–1984/1997a, p. 250). During adolescence, cognitive activity acquires a personal nature (Vygotsky, 1930–1931/1998c, p. 176) as the individual develops the capacity for self-reflection.

The development of the child's sense of "I" is also a social product. Vygotsky (1982–1984/1997a) agreed with James Baldwin, American psychologist and sociologist, that the child's concept of "I" develops from his concept of other individuals (p. 245). The child first becomes conscious of the actions of others and only later becomes conscious of himself as an actor and a thinker.

Summary

Following work on the cultural development of mental functions, Vygotsky turned his attention to paedology. In his view, three important questions were the role of the environment in development, the development of consciousness in terms of the child's world view and personality, and the problem of age-related changes in development. In relation to the first question, Vygotsky rejected views of the environment that defined it in terms of absolute, physical features external to the child, and simply the setting for the child's development. In his view, the environment that influences child development is primarily social. Also, the child's relationship to the environment is reciprocal and relative. Development of the child's internal processes changes the nature of his experience of the environment, and the changing experiences, in turn, influence the child's thinking. Moreover, adults who serve as the ideal forms of behavior interact with the child and are the source of changes in her cognitive behavior. The term *perezhivanie* reflects the child's particular emotional/interpretive experience of the environment.

Two concepts that form the content of development are the individual's world view and her personality. Both are syntheses that are social products; they are two aspects of the developing consciousness of the child. World view refers to the person's awareness of an external reality and his method of relating to that reality. Initially, the child's world view is subjective but becomes more stable at school age. By the end of adolescence, according to Vygotsky, the individual can formulate a life plan, a form of adaptation to the external world.

Personality, in contrast, consists of two components: the unity of behavior mastered by the child and her development of the "I." The aggregate of the cognitive processes mastered by the child is important because this knowledge system determines the ways that the child analyzes and reworks her experiences. The development of the "I" begins with the child's connectedness to her mother or primary caregiver and becomes more diversified during the elementary school years. Personality reaches the final stage during adolescence with the development of the capacity for self-reflection.

FRAMEWORK FOR AGE-RELATED DEVELOPMENTAL PERIODS

In the last 2 years of his life, 1932 to 1934, Vygotsky was preparing a book on developmental psychology from birth through adolescence (see Rieber, 1998, endnote 1, p. 329). His goal was to present a schematic of the sequence of development that identified meaningful, internal, age-related changes (Vygotsky, 1982–1984/1997a, p. 241). However, the work remained incomplete at his death. Published in the *Collected Works* are two chapters and four lectures that were to be a part of this book. The chapters present his system for the identification of age-related internal developmental changes and his analysis of infancy. The four lectures address the first year, early childhood, age 3, and age 7. However, discussions of age-related development, especially at adolescence, are available from other essays in the *Collected Works*.

Vygotsky identified age periods that are associated with specific internal changes and with changes in the child–environment relationship. First discussed are the problems Vygotsky identified in other views that divided development into periods. The framework that he developed for determining age-level periods follows. Discussed in this section are identifying criteria for determining age-related periods, the role of the social situation, and the sequence of age-level periods.

Identifying Criteria for Determining Age-Related Periods

As in his other work, Vygotsky identified issues and concerns, in part, from the shortcomings he identified in other perspectives. Discussed in this section are problems in prior views and criteria for age-level periods.

Problems in Prior Views

Vygotsky (1982–1984/1998j) categorized the approaches to dividing child development into periods in three groups. The first group did not address the actual course of psychological development. Instead, this approach used levels of training and education, such as preschool age, primary school age, and so on (p. 187). Although fairly close to actual developmental periods, levels of education are external features of childhood. They are not internal developmental changes.

The second approach selected a particular trait as the standard for defining levels of development. However, the problem is that the trait may be important for making a judgment about the child's development at one age and less important or insignificant at another age. For example, changes in children's teeth are an easily observable trait. Categories are toothlessness, milk teeth, permanent teeth, and wisdom teeth. The appearance of teeth at the boundary between infancy and early childhood is indicative of the child's early development. However, the eruption of wisdom teeth at a later age has no developmental significance (p. 188). This issue led Vygotsky to differentiate central and peripheral aspects of development. For example, speech development in early childhood is a central line of development. However, during school age, it is peripheral (Vygotsky, 1982–1984/1998j, p. 197).

Vygotsky also faulted the "single-trait" approach for failing to consider a basic feature of development. Specifically, the nature of development is not static; development reorganizes itself as it progresses. Finally, the single-trait approach focuses on observable characteristics of children instead of studying "the internal essence" of development (p. 188). As noted by Karl Marx and Friederich Engels, if the external characteristics of a thing reflected its essence, then science would not be needed. Therefore, in studying development, psychology must reject attempts to identify symptoms of different age levels and "move on" (p. 189).

A third group did focus on determining the substantive characteristics of development. However, although they stated the problem correctly, they did not solve it. An example is Arnold Gesell's perspective. He separated childhood into waves of development that, in his view, reflected changes in the child's "internal rhythm." However, he also believed that the most important accomplishments occur in the first years of life, followed by a gradual slowdown (Vygotsky, 1982–1984/1998j, p. 189). This goal is not unlike that of some late 20th-century perspectives whose proponents view early childhood as the most crucial period in development. Vygotsky chided Gesell for his "half-hearted attempts at periodicity" (p. 190), and pointed out the importance of the development of higher mental functions, which does not occur until adolescence. Therefore, the pinnacle of development does not occur in the early years.

In summary, two of the approaches to defining development failed to address internal processes. In addition, one of those approaches attempted to identify a single indicator that would serve as a marker for different periods of development. Particular problems are that the selected indicator is not equally important throughout development, and this approach also ignores the complexity of development. The third perspective addressed internal processes but did not go beyond early childhood.

Criteria for Age-Level Periods

Vygotsky (1982–1984/1998j) rejected the view that child development is simply the growth and regrouping of existing factors. Instead, he maintained that the process of development is self-propelled; it consists of "a continuous appearance and formation of the new which did not exist in previous stages" (p. 190). In addition, the developmental process reflects a unity of (a) the physical and the mental and (b) the social and the personal as the child advances through the various periods of development (p. 190).

This emergence of new formations reflects the dialectical conception in which unique formations emerge from a synthesis of prior and new events or qualities. An advantage of the perspective that development consists of the appearance of new formations is that it can accommodate the unities identified previously.

Vygotsky (1982–1984/1998j) identified three important criteria for identifying periods of psychological development. First, each period should be determined by internal changes, not simply external observable characteristics. Specifically, developmental periods should be described in terms of changes in the child's consciousness (Vygotsky, 1982–1984/1998i, p. 258). Vygotsky's rationale was that the development of personality, the child's relationship to the environment, and his basic activities during any particular period are linked to the development of this internal framework (p. 258).

Second, "only breaks and turning points" in the flow of development can serve as a reliable benchmark for identifying age-level periods

(Vygotsky, 1982–1984/1998j, p. 190). An example is the emergence of autonomous speech at about one year of age. The young child's prattling is replaced by her conscious effort to identify and label objects in the environment. This early labeling by the child, although it lacks consistency, is a turning point in the development of the child's consciousness.

Third, descriptions of developmental periods must address both the structure and dynamics of development. Structure refers to the integral dynamic formation of consciousness that emerges in a particular developmental period (p. 196). The dynamics of development consist of all the laws that govern the appearance, changes, and connections of the new structure in each period of development (p. 198). Two foundational concepts in this process are the social situation of development and the concept of neoformations.

The Social Situation of Development

Vygotsky (1982–1984/1998j) had identified problems in prior views of development and the criteria that a theory of development must meet. The result is that any theory of development he might propose faced several challenges. It must address internal changes in the child's affective and mental framework, identify breaks and turns in development, and address the complexity of development. In addition, an adequate theory must illustrate the structure and dynamics of change and avoid relying on a single observable characteristic as a marker of change. Finally, for Vygotsky, the concepts must be compatible with the principles of his cultural–historical theory.

To address these requirements, Vygotsky identified the social situation of development as the "engine" of development. Chapter 3 in this text discussed the essential role of interactions between adult and child as the source of the child's cognitive development. For example, from the beginning of the child's life, adults direct the child's attention. Then, with the gradual mastery of language, the child begins to direct her attention in the same way (Vygotsky, 1982–1984/1997c, p. 167). In other words, the adult, the ideal form of behavior, interacts with the child's present form of behavior. The interactions between adult and child are imitated, practiced, and reworked by the child in the process of becoming new internal mental processes within the child.

Definition

In defining the social situation of development, Vygotsky expanded on the basic adult-child interaction. His definition states that it is the social relations between the child of a particular age and social reality

(Vygotsky, 1982–1984/1998j, p. 199). Specifically, the social situation of development refers to the nature of the personal contact between child and adult at a particular period in time (Vygotsky, 1930–1931/1998d, p. 273). The nature of this social relation is not constant, and changes in the relationship between child and adult introduce new periods of development. For example, the infant's behavior indicates a strong need to communicate but lacks speech. Later, when the young child develops autonomous speech, he can communicate with adults in a new, albeit limited, way about concrete objects in his visual field. The social situation of development has changed, because autonomous speech, although limited, opens the door for the child's development of words in adult speech.

The earliest example of the social situation of development in the child's life marks the end of the newborn period and is the initial *social* connection between the baby and his primary caregiver. This event occurs at about 2 months of age. It is the baby's awareness of the presence of humans in her world (Vygotsky, 1982–1984/1998f, p. 215). This awareness is reflected in the social smile of the infant in response to a human voice or a human face. This initial social contact opens the door to the potential for cognitive and affective development for two reasons. The social smile indicates the infant's need for communication as well as a particular receptivity in the infant to the actions and words of his primary caregiver.

Vygotsky (1982–1984/1998j) described the social situation of development as an original, exclusive relation between the child and social reality that is unique to a particular period of development. It is the "initial moment" for all the dynamic developmental changes during a particular period (p. 198).

The Nature of "Critical" Periods

Vygotsky accepted the view of Pavel Blonsky, a Russian educator, that age-level periods of development are either stable (slow, gradual change) or crisis (critical) periods. The term had been used in psychology in a negative way, for example, the obstinacy of a 3-year-old. However, Vygotsky thought that the emphasis should be on the positive developments of critical periods. For example, the 3-year-old's stubborn behavior is a necessary aspect of reconstructing his or her social position with respect to adults and the authority of the parents (Vygotsky, 1982–1984/1998h, p. 288).

The defining characteristic of critical periods is that the changes are abrupt, major shifts that are turning points in development. The essential content of development in the critical periods is "unique and specific to a high degree" (1982–1984/1998j, p. 194). Specifically, the essential content in the critical period is a *"reconstruction of the child's social situation of development"* (italics added) (p. 199). In the newborn, for example, the social smile in response to a human changes the newborn–adult relationship, and it initiates the development of a close connection between the baby and her primary caregivers. It sets the stage for the small changes that occur in the subsequent stable period of development.

Some psychologists suggested that external conditions might be responsible for critical periods because these periods are dissimilar in different children (Vygotsky, 1982–1984/1998j, p. 192). Vygotsky addressed this issue by stating that external conditions do determine the concrete manifestations of each critical period. However, development is guided by the logic of the internal process itself. For example, one child may undergo the critical period at age 3 with many confrontations and disruptions targeted to the adults in her world, whereas others achieve some independence with relative calm. In other words, development is guided by the logic of the internal process itself. The end result, in both cases, is the increased autonomy of the child and a more developed personality.

The Sequence of Age-Level Periods

Prior to Vygotsky's analysis, psychologists had identified four critical periods, occurring at ages 1, 3, 7, and 13. Vygotsky added the newborn as a critical period because the act of birth propels the newborn into a completely different environment that "changes the whole tenor of his life" (Vygotsky, 1982–1984/1998j, p. 193). Vygotsky also noted that stable periods compose most of childhood, and psychologists had studied these periods more extensively than the critical periods. Moreover, in those efforts, the critical periods were not a part of the general sequence of periods of child development. One of Vygotsky's goals was to systematize the critical periods and include them in a portrayal of child development (p. 191). Another important goal was to identify and describe the internal changes in the child's consciousness (his affective and mental framework) that occur in each period.

The Concept of Neoformations

Vygotsky's criterion for determining the concrete periods of development in the child is the new developments that he named *neoformations*. Each neoformation is "a new type of structure of the personality and its activity" (Vygotsky, 1982–1984/1998j, p. 190). It consists of the mental and

social changes that appear during a particular age-level period and primarily determine "the consciousness of the child, [and] his relation to
the environment, his internal and external life " (p. 190).

In critical periods of development, the central neoformation is a
change in the child's social situation of development that emerges in the
middle or at the end of a period and sets the course of development in
the subsequent stable period in a particular direction. Examples are the
social smile of the newborn, which initiates communication between the
young baby and her caregivers, and the resistant behavior to the decisions of adults about her activities that occurs in the critical period
about age 3, initiating a new autonomy.

Stable periods, in contrast, are marked by primarily "microscopic
changes that accumulate to a certain limit" and then appear in the form
of some sort of neoformation (p. 190). An example of change during a
stable period is the child who is learning words in adult speech, the stage
referred to as early childhood. The young child's vocabulary expands
during this period, and the result is the development of semantic and systemic content in the child's mental framework.

Vygotsky's descriptions of the changes in critical and stable periods
are examples of two forms of dialectical change described by the philosopher Hegel. One is the conflict between opposites that results in a new
synthesis, which describes the transformation in Vygotsky's critical periods. The most easily observable is the critical period at age 3, when the
child's emerging sense of self conflicts with the rules established by his
caregivers. The other form of change is the transformation of quantity
into quality. An example is a teakettle on the stove. The temperature of
the water in the teakettle gradually becomes hotter and hotter and subsequently changes into steam. Changes in stable periods, such as the child
increasing her vocabulary during early childhood, are an example. As already stated, the outcome is an enhanced organization of the child's
mental framework.

The Alternating Sequence

Vygotsky's analyses led to a sequence of age-level periods in which critical periods alternate with stable periods (1982–1984/1998j). They are illustrated in Figure 7.2. Although stable periods typically have distinct
boundaries, the boundaries that separate the beginning and end of critical from adjacent periods are not as definite. The culmination point typically occurs in the middle of the critical period but may occur near the
end of the period.

Several features differentiated Vygotsky's scheme of age-level peri-

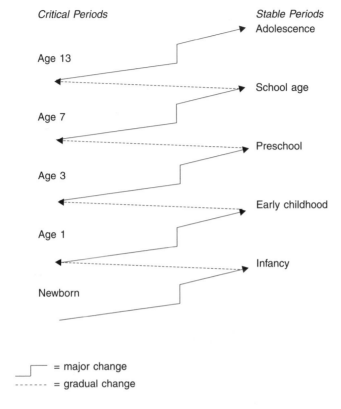

FIGURE 7.2. The sequence of age-level periods (Vygotsky, 1982–1984/1998j). (*Note.* Bozhovitch, 2000, stated that Vygotsky designated the ages of 13 and 14 as a critical period and ages 15 to 17 as adolescence.)

ods from other views of child development. Two major differences are (a) the use of age-related neoformations as the criteria for dividing development into age periods and (b) the introduction of critical periods into the sequence. He also excluded prenatal development and the years from 18 to maturity. In his view, the age period from 18 to 25 is likely the first link in the chain of mature age periods and not the final period of child development (Vygotsky, 1982–1984/1998j, p. 196). Vygotsky also viewed the period of the newborn as a critical age, and he described adolescence as a stable, rather than a critical, age (p. 195). Bozhovich (2004), a colleague of Vygotsky, noted that Vygotsky had divided adolescence into two parts: negative (13–14 years of age) and positive (15–17 years) (p. 40). This description corresponds to

Vygotsky's designation of the thirteenth year as a critical period and the subsequent years as stable.

Summary

Vygotsky identified three criteria for determining age-level periods. First, each period should be determined by internal changes and described in terms of changes in the child's consciousness. Second, the reliable benchmark for identifying age-level periods is the breaks and turning points in the flow of development. Third, descriptions of developmental periods must address both the structure and dynamics of development.

The engine of development identified by Vygotsky is the social situation of development. Expressed as the second law of development (Chapter 3), the social situation of development refers to the nature of the personal contact between the child and the adult at a particular period in time. The nature of the social situation of development is not constant, and changes in that situation introduce new periods of development. Further, Vygotsky defined critical periods of development as those periods in which the child's social situation of development is reconstructed. For example, the emergence of the social smile in the young infant reflects a critical developmental period because it indicates a recognition of adults in the young infant's environment. It is a turning point in development because it initiates the affective and cognitive relationship with primary caregivers.

In contrast to critical periods, which are major turning points in development, stable periods are characterized by small changes. These changes accumulate to a certain point, which precipitates a change in the child's thinking. An example is the child who is learning words in adult speech, the stable period of early childhood. The child's vocabulary expands during this period, which results in the development of semantic and systemic content in the child's consciousness. The stable periods also compose most of childhood.

Prior to Vygotsky's analysis, psychologists had identified critical periods at ages 1, 3, 7, and 13. Vygotsky added the critical period of the newborn and described development as an alternating sequence of critical and stable periods. He referred to the new developments in each period as neoformations. They are the new structures of the personality and its activity that determine the consciousness of the child and his relationship to the social environment. In the critical periods, the neoformations are reconstructions of the child's social situation of development. In stable periods, small changes add up to a recognizable change in the child's thinking or activity.

EDUCATIONAL IMPLICATIONS

Educational implications include Vygotsky's concept of the social situation of development and implications for assessment.

The Social Situation of Development

Vygotsky (1982–1984/1998g) identified three problems with the concept of the child's environment held by educators and researchers. The problems are (a) focusing primarily on physical characteristics instead of documenting the nature of the social interactions, (b) viewing the environment as external to the child, and (c) considering the environment as the setting for development, not the source. These concerns currently are particularly important for two levels of education: preschool programs and middle school.

Preschool

Vygotsky noted that social reports about young children primarily focused on the physical characteristics of the child's home environment. In contemporary society, fewer children remain at home during their preschool years. Many young children attend prekindergarten (beginning at age 4) and kindergarten programs. Two questions about these environments that should be asked are (1) What is the child's interpretation/emotional view of the pre-first-grade experience? and (2) Are the relations between child and teacher or caregiver appropriate for fostering the child's cognitive development?

Researchers have begun to develop observational instruments intended to assess the quality of programs for young children. One instrument, the Observational Record of the Caregiving Environment, does note the frequency of some practices at different times, such as caregivers talking to children. It also includes global ratings of teacher characteristics, such as teacher sensitivity (National Institute of Child Health and Human Development, 2002). Some other instruments focus primarily on features of the physical environment, such as available curriculum materials, their reported use, and the organization of materials and activities (Pianta, 2003).

Determining the nature of the preschool experience for the child is even more important given federal legislation. Specifically, preschools feel pressured to teach academic skills as a result of the No Child Left Behind legislation (Stipek, 2006). This pressure emanates from the belief of policymakers that an early start on teaching academic skills can help children meet the standards set for elementary school (p. 455). A major concern of educators is that efforts to teach academic skills in preschool have the potential to undermine children's confidence and their enthusiasm for learning. In addition, the standards for K–12 are "overly narrow" and often are merely laundry lists that can lead to fragmented teaching (p. 457).

Documenting the nature of the preschool experience for the children under these conditions as well as the nature of the relations between child and teacher or caregiver is important because the social situation of development determines both the forms and the path along which further development proceeds (Vygotsky, 1982–1984/1998j, p. 198). Such documentation means going beyond determining that the social climate is positive or negative. Required are time-consuming observations that can capture the nature of teacher–child interactions. These observations should include the extent of emphasis on academic goals, the nature of teacher questions, and children's responses and reactions.

Documenting such information is important for two other reasons. For example, a typical math standard is that children can count to 20 (Stipek, 2006). First, this standard will be interpreted literally, and children will be taught by rote to count. However, they have no concept of the relationship of 7 to 6, for example (p. 457).

Recall from Chapter 3 the discussion of the young child's natural arithmetic in the description of learning to count. The child thinks at a concrete level. He determines quantity through form or shape (two sets of objects are equal in number if they form towers of equal height) or pluralities (a group of seven apples is greater than three apples because the total group is bigger). Development of "true" counting depends on the breakdown of this natural form and the replacement of this perspective by other processes. In other words, the development of counting that is not a rote process depends on the breakdown of the child's natural form and replacement by other processes (Vygotsky, 1982–1984/1997b, p. 151).

Second is the issue of the child's development in the broad capability of sign use. The experiments conducted by Vygotsky and his associates indicated that the young child had no conception of tasks that involved symbols. Some children, aged 4 to 6, were at the stage of naïve psychology. That is, they may have only some general awareness of the task but be unable to operationalize a strategy, or they do not understand the task at all. Either situation, in an environment in which a skill is important, leads to negative outcomes.

Middle School

Problems identified in middle-school classrooms include declines in student motivation and performance (e.g., Carnegie Council on Adolescent

Development, 1989; Anderman & Anderman, 1999) and student perceptions of their teachers as both impersonal and focused on social comparison (e.g., Feldlaufer, Midgley, & Eccles, 1988). Also, often activities were described as dominated by lecture and seat work at a time when students are capable of participating in more challenging exercises.

Some recommendations to address these problems focused on changing the social context of the classroom, which Maehr and Midgley (1991) referred to as the psychological environment. Included were organizational changes (teacher–student teams, creating schools within schools) and instructional changes that focus on developing meaning and promoting student engagement (Arhar, 1997; Maehr & Midgley, 1991). Subsequent research indicates the key role of the social environment of the classroom in the motivation and engagement of young adolescents (Ryan & Patrick, 2001). The primary dimension that predicted student engagement in eighth-grade mathematics was teacher caring and support (p. 454). This finding reflects the importance of Vygotsky's concept of the social situation of development, particularly the personal contact between learner and adult. It suggests that reform efforts at any level of schooling should begin with an analysis of the social reality that the learner must face, with particular attention to the nature of the personal contact between teacher and student.

Implications for Assessment

Vygotsky identified two constructs that can be useful in the assessment of children who are having academic problems. They are the child's interpretation of the environment and the unity of behavior that the child has mastered. Adults often are surprised at learning the views of children about the classroom. For example, some poor readers interpret the purpose of reading as pronouncing all the words correctly. They are unaware that the importance of reading is to develop meaning. Equally important is to develop an understanding of the social situation for the particular child. Specifically, is the child able to understand and make use of the resources in the classroom, such as teacher explanations, comments of other children, and so on.

Determining the unity of behavior that the child has mastered also is important. Naturally, the initial focus of an assessment of a child who is having problems, for example, in reading or arithmetic is to determine the cognitive operations with which the child is struggling. However, the root of the problem may be prior ideas or operations that the child has not mastered. In addition, the knowledge system and mental capabilities mastered by the child are important in her view of herself (personality) and her ways of adapting to the world (world view).

In summary, the social situation of development, the child's interpretation of the environment, and the unity of behavior the child has mastered are important in evaluating the fit between instruction and the learner and identifying the roots of current problems whether for the whole class or the individual child.

REFERENCES

Anderman, L. H., & Anderman, E. M. (1999). Social predictors of changes in students' achievement goal orientation. *Contemporary Educational Psychology, 25*, 21–37.

Arhar, I. (1997). The effects of interdisciplinary teaming on teachers and students. In J. L. Irvin (Ed.), *What current research says to the middle level practitioner.* Columbus, OH: National Middle School Association.

Bozhovich, L. I. (2004). Developmental phases of personality formation in childhood (I). *Journal of Russian and East European Psychology, 42*(4), 35–54.

Carnegie Council on Adolescent Development. (1989). *Turning points: Preparing American youth for the 21st century. Report of the Task Force on Education of Young Adolescents.* New York: Carnegie Corporation of New York.

Feldlaufer, H., Midgley, C., & Eccles, J. S. (1988). Student, teacher and observer perceptions of the classroom environment before and after the transition to junior high school. *Journal of Early Adolescence, 8*, 133–156.

Maehr, M., & Midgley, C. (1991). Enhancing student motivation: A schoolwide approach. *Educational Psychologist, 26*, 399–427.

National Institute of Child Health and Human Development, Early Child Care Research Network. (2002). The relation of global first-grade classroom environments to structural classroom features and teacher and student behavior. *Elementary School Journal, 10*(5), 367–387.

Pianta, R. C. (2003). *Experiences in p–3 classrooms: The implications of observational research for redesigning early education.* New York: Foundation for Child Development.

Rieber, R. W. (Ed.). (1998). Notes to the Russian edition. In *Collected works of L. S. Vygotsky: Vol. 5. Child psychology* (pp. 319–353). New York: Plenum.

Ryan, A. M., & Patrick, H. (2001). The classroom social environment and changes in adolescents' motivation and engagement during middle school. *American Educational Research Journal, 38*(2), 437–460.

Stipek, D. (2006). No Child Left Behind comes to preschool. *Elementary School Journal, 106*(5), 455–465.

van der Veer, R., & Valsiner, J. (1991). *Understanding Vygotsky: A quest for synthesis.* Cambridge, MA: Blackwell.

van der Veer, R., & Valsiner, J. (Eds.). (1994). *The Vygotsky reader.* Cambridge, MA: Blackwell.

Vygotsky, L. S. (1929). The problem of the cultural development of the child. *Journal of Genetic Psychology, 36*, 415–434.

Vygotsky, L. S. (1987a). The problem and the method of investigation. In R. W. Rieber & W. S. Carton (Eds.), *Collected works of L. S. Vygotsky: Vol. 1. Problems of general psychology* (pp. 43–51). New York: Plenum. (Original work published 1934)

Vygotsky, L. S. (1987b). Thinking and development in childhood: Lecture 4 in lectures on psychology. In R. W. Riebert & A. S. Carton (Eds.), *Collected works of L. S. Vygotsky: Vol. 1. Problems of general psychology* (pp. 311–324). New York: Plenum. (Original work published 1934)

Vygotsky, L. S. (1994). The problem of the environment. In R. van der Veer & J. Valsiner (Eds.), *The Vygotsky reader* (pp. 338–354). Cambridge, MA: Blackwell. (Original work published 1935)

Vygotsky, L. S. (1997a). Conclusion; further research; development of personality and world view in the child. In R. W. Rieber (Ed.), *Collected works of L. S. Vygotsky: Vol. 4. The history of development of the higher mental functions* (pp. 241–251). New York: Plenum. (Original work published 1982–1984)

Vygotsky, L. S. (1997b). Development of arithmetic operations. In R. W. Rieber (Ed.), *Collected works of L. S. Vygotsky: Vol. 4. The history of development of the higher mental functions* (pp. 149–152). New York: Plenum. (Original work published 1982–1984)

Vygotsky, L. S. (1997c). Mastering attention. In R. W. Rieber (Ed.), *Collected works of L. S. Vygotsky: Vol. 4. The history of development of the higher mental functions* (pp. 153–177). New York: Plenum. (Original work published 1982–1984)

Vygotsky, L. S. (1997d). On psychological systems. In R. Rieber & J. Wollock (Eds.), *Collected works of L. S. Vygotsky: Vol. 3. Problems of the theory and history of psychology* (pp. 91–107). New York: Plenum. (Original work published 1982–1984)

Vygotsky, L. S. (1998a). Development of higher mental functions during the transitional age. In R. W. Rieber (Ed.), *Collected works of L. S. Vygotsky: Vol. 5. Child psychology* (pp. 83–149). New York: Plenum. (Original work published 1930–1931)

Vygotsky, L. S. (1998b). Development of thinking and formation of concepts in the adolescent. In R. W. Rieber (Ed.), *Collected works of L. S. Vygotsky: Vol. 5. Child psychology* (pp. 29–81). New York: Plenum. (Original work published 1930–1931)

Vygotsky, L. S. (1998c). Dynamics and structure of the adolescent's personality. In R. W. Rieber (Ed.), *Collected works of L. S. Vygotsky: Vol. 5. Child psychology* (pp. 167–184). New York: Plenum. (Original work published 1930–1931)

Vygotsky, L. S. (1998d). Early childhood. In R. W. Rieber (Ed.), *Collected works of L. S. Vygotsky: Vol. 5. Child psychology* (pp. 261–281). New York: Plenum. (Original work published 1982–1984)

Vygotsky, L. S. (1998e). Imagination and creativity in the adolescent. In R. W. Rieber (Ed.), *Collected works of L. S. Vygotsky: Vol. 5. Child psychology* (pp. 151–166). New York: Plenum. (Original work published 1930–1931)

Vygotsky, L. S. (1998f). Infancy. In R. W. Rieber (Ed.), *Collected works of L. S.*

Vygotsky: Vol. 5. Child psychology (pp. 207–241). New York: Plenum. (Original work published 1982–1984)

Vygotsky, L. S. (1998g). The crisis at age seven. In R. W. Rieber (Ed.), *Collected works of L. S. Vygotsky: Vol. 5. Child psychology* (pp. 289–296). New York: Plenum. (Original work published 1982–1984)

Vygotsky, L. S. (1998h). The crisis at age three. In R. W. Rieber (Ed.), *Collected works of L. S. Vygotsky: Vol. 5. Child psychology* (pp. 283–288). New York: Plenum. (Original work published 1982–1984)

Vygotsky, L. S. (1998i). The crisis of the first year. In R. W. Rieber (Ed.), *Collected works of L. S. Vygotsky: Vol. 5. Child psychology* (pp. 243–259). New York: Plenum. (Original work published 1982–1984)

Vygotsky, L. S. (1998j). The problem of age. In R. W. Rieber (Ed.), *Collected works of L. S. Vygotsky: Vol. 5. Child psychology* (pp. 187–205). New York: Plenum. (Original work published 1982–1984)

Vygotsky, L. S. (1999). Analysis of sign operations in the child. In R. W. Rieber (Ed.), *Collected works of L. S. Vygotsky: Vol. 6. Scientific legacy* (pp. 45–56). New York: Plenum. (Original work published 1982–1984)

8

Development of World View
and Personality

The relation of the child to reality is from the very beginning
a social relation. . . . Every relation of the child to the outside
world, even the simplest, is always a relation refracted
through the relation to another person.
—VYGOTSKY (1982–1984/1998g, p. 216)

Only with the transition to thinking in concepts does the
definitive separation and development of the personality and
world view of the child occur.
—VYGOTSKY (1930–1931/1998a, p. 147)

In conceptualizing periods of cognitive development, Vygotsky (1982–
1984/1998k) identified a central determining factor. It is the nature of
the personal contact between the child and adults in the environment.
This contact, which itself changes, leads to changes in the child's consciousness. He described these changing situations for the child from
birth through age 3. His death prevented the same detailed analysis of
subsequent age-level periods. However, in other writings, he described
unique aspects of cognitive development in school-age children and adolescents.

175

THE DEVELOPMENT OF CONSCIOUSNESS:
BIRTH THROUGH PRESCHOOL

Vygotsky (1982–1984/1998k) defined consciousness as an integrated internal structure that includes affect, awareness, generalizations (content), and mental processes (functions). He noted that changes occur in the general structure of consciousness in the transition from one age level to another rather than changes in the separate processes or functions (p. 197). He also conceptualized cognitive development as a series of alternating critical and stable periods. Each critical period is so named because the central neoformation is a new form of personal contact between the child and the adult (a new social situation of development) that is a major change in development.

The lengthy period of development may be summarized as the development of the child's world view and personality, two mental syntheses that reflect the child's cultural development (Vygotsky, 1982–1984/1997a, p. 242). World view is the child's awareness of an external reality and her ways of relating to that reality (Vygotsky, 1930–1931/1998a, p. 147). World view, for example, ranges from simple adaptations to the environment, such as pulling a toy closer with a string, to complex activities, such as using a computer search engine to research a topic. In contrast, personality is the unity of behavior mastered by the child (Vygotsky, 1982–1984/1997a, p. 242) and his sense of "I" (Vygotsky, 1982–1984/1998e, p. 266). Discussed in this section are social relations and the development of consciousness, the preschool period, and implications for parents and teachers.

Social Relations and the Development of Consciousness

During the years from birth through preschool (to age 7), Vygotsky identified three critical periods. They are the newborn (0 to approximately 2 months), the emergence of autonomous speech (12 months), and the child's push for more independence from adults (approximately the third birthday). The central neoformation in each of those critical periods is a turning point in the child–parent relationship that makes possible further development in the following stable period.

The Beginning of Consciousness

Vygotsky's (1982–1984/1998k) theory is unique in that he acknowledged a role for personal contact early in development. This view contrasts with other perspectives that described the infant as aware of only his own experiences and states during the first year. Vygotsky (1982–

1984/1998g), however, maintained that the infant is a "maximally social being" from the first days of her life (p. 241).

Vygotsky (1982–1984/1998g) designated birth to approximately 2 months as a transitional period between birth and infancy. The social situation of development for the newborn is that, by virtue of birth, she becomes part of the social life of others (p. 211). The characteristics of the newborn's primitive mental life are (a) the dominance of nondifferentiated experiences that represent a sort of fusion of drive, affect, and sensation and (b) an inability to separate himself and his experiences from the perception of objective things (p. 213). The young baby at this age has no world view or personality.

The neoformation that represents a turning point in development occurs between 4 and 8 weeks. It is the social smile that appears in response to a human voice or a human face. It signals an awareness of other people and is the first social contact with adults. This acknowledgment of adults, which also expresses a need for communication, is the event that makes the newborn period a critical turning point in development.

The Emergence of the "Great-we"

Current discussions about infancy refer to the development of a particular relationship between the infant and the primary caregiver. This relationship is referred to as attachment, and it is described as an emotional bond between infant and adult.

Vygotsky (1982–1984/1998g) saw the child–caregiver relationship during this stable period of development somewhat differently. The newborn's first social response to an adult initiates a contradictory situation for the infant. It is the infant's increasing need for sociability and her inability to speak, coupled with her complete dependence on others for her every basic need. Objects appear and disappear from sight through the actions of adults, and the infant "moves through space always in the arms of others" (p. 215).

The central neoformation of infancy that emerges in the consciousness of the infant is the natural result of the fact that the only available path to the external world is through another person (p. 232). Vygotsky describes this new development as the infant's perceived "mental commonality," an indivisible mental communication with his mother or primary caregiver. Vygotsky selected the German term *Ur-wir*, or "Great-we," as best reflecting the nature of this relationship (p. 233). This perceived unity is similar to two children playing ball; the "I" and "you" merge in the single action of the internal "we" (p. 236). The infant prattles to get the attention of the caregiver, who responds by speaking to or playing with the infant. Also, the infant stretches out his arms to the caregiver, who, again, responds verbally and may also pick him up. The caregiver also may interact with the child by pointing out interesting objects and events in her visual field.

The infant's initial consciousness of a mental commonality, the "Great-we," with a primary caregiver precedes her consciousness of a sense of "I." Moreover, the young child's interactions with her world are not so much contact with "lifeless external stimuli" but are, instead, a primitive communication with the personalities around her (Vygotsky, 1982–1984/1998g, p. 236). Also, the child's prattling during the first year sets the stage for subsequent changes, such as speech, which are the foundation of further cultural development (Vygotsky, 1982–1984/1997a, p. 245).

The perceived "great-we" mental commonality also persists into early childhood. In particular, the young child believes that the people around him know his thoughts and his every wish (Vygotsky, 1982–1984/1998e, p. 266). The fact that adults interpret his actions and his efforts at speech contribute to this belief. In other words, the young child does not separate the thoughts and feelings in his consciousness from the thoughts and feelings of his caregivers (p. 266).

A Primitive World View

Another important event during infancy is the first use of tools. At approximately 9 to 10 months of age, the child can pull a rattle by its string and attempt to get an out-of-reach toy by throwing another one after it (Vygotsky, 1982–1984/1997a, p. 244; Vygotsky, 1982–1984/1997b, p. 201). These examples of adaptation to the external world demonstrate that the roots of thinking and speech are independent of each other.

During the first year, the infant also engages in other efforts to manipulate objects in the environment. Mentioned in an earlier chapter are the infant's rising up and dropping his body to move an out-of-reach object, and an older child screwing up his eyes in order to turn on a lamp (Vygotsky, 1982–1984/1997a, p. 245). Efforts to manipulate objects in the environment and the transition to socialized speech, which occurs in the second year, begin to separate adaptation to the natural world from adaptation to the social world (p. 247).

Early Speech and Consciousness

Following the stable developmental period of infancy, the second critical period occurs near the child's first birthday. Vygotsky (1982–1984/

1998j) noted that psychologists had identified the content of this period, but they had not emphasized its critical nature (p. 243). The three major events of this critical period are (a) the development and establishment of walking, (b) the emergence of affect and will, and (c) the emergence of autonomous speech (Vygotsky, 1982–1984/1998j, p. 243). The child is now not completely dependent on adults.

The changed nature of the personal contact between the young child and adults is the emergence of autonomous speech in the child. It is important because it is connected with the emergence of consciousness and also signals a changed social situation. Autonomous speech, therefore, is the central neoformation of this period. As noted in Chapter 5, autonomous speech is the child's effort to communicate in words, and it differs from prattling. Autonomous speech separates the prior period in which the infant can only act through others, but lacks speech, and the period when she begins to use adult words. Through autonomous speech, the young child can communicate in a rudimentary way about concrete objects in his visual field.

The Stable Period of Early Childhood

Vygotsky (1982–1984/1998e) designated the years from 1 to 3 as the stable period of early childhood. During this period, perception is the dominant mental function (Vygotsky, 1934/1987d, p. 198; Vygotsky, 1982–1984/1998e, p. 264; see also Vygotsky, 1934/1987c), reflecting the situation that mental functions do not develop evenly. At the beginning of early childhood, consciousness is not yet developed, acting "only on the basis of perception" (Vygotsky, 1982–1984/1998e, p. 264). That is, perception is linked to affect (e.g., a door beckons the child to open it), precipitating action, and memory consists of recognizing concrete situations. In other words, affectively colored perception is at the center of consciousness, with the other functions operating around it, "leading through affect to action" (p. 278). In the concept formation experiments, the young child's selection of objects is based on "subjective emotional connections among impressions" (Vygotsky, 1934/1987a, p. 139).

At about 18 to 24 months, the child begins to learn words in adult speech. These new words are a diversification of the syllabic construction of the child's autonomous speech. As described in Chapter 5, the child's speech develops in interactions with the "ideal form," the adult. The naming of objects begins to break up the affective-motor characteristic of perception by isolating objects from the background. In this way, attention begins to be separated from perception, and perception itself gradually transitions from nonverbal to verbal (Vygotsky, 1982–1984/1998e, p. 280). In other words, the development of speech during early childhood changes the relationship of the child to the environment around him (p. 268). Finally, the emergence of words in adult speech also contributes to the central neoformation of early childhood, the beginning of the systemic structure of consciousness (p. 281).

Near the end of early childhood, the child begins to develop a sense of "I myself" within the "Great-we" state (p. 266). He also, by age 3, can control affect, and "the old social situation of development is inadequate, the child enters the crisis of the third year and a new situation in personal contact is created" (p. 280).

The Critical Period at Age 3

Vygotsky (1982–1984/1998i) identified the months near the third birthday as a critical period. The child's social position relative to the adults around him, his relation to the authority of his parents, and the relationship of his personality to situations is changing (p. 288). The child begins to insist on her way of doing some things in which, formerly, she had cooperated with her caregiver. For example, she may protest the food her mother has prepared for her lunch. (However, in terms of understanding her perceptions and her belief that adults understand her thoughts, she continues to remain in the "Great-we" situation [Vygotsky, 1982–1984/1998e, p. 266].)

The central neoformation of this period is the child's resistance to adult suggestions that subsequently result in a different relationship with adults in his life. Negativism, for example, is the refusal to follow a request by the caregiver. It differs from disobedience because the request is often something the child likes to do. The refusal is directed toward the adult, not against the requested behavior. For example, the adult may ask the child if she would like to go get some ice cream, a favorite activity, but the child is likely to refuse.

Vygotsky pointed out that the issue for the child is not simply making his own decisions or becoming proficient at particular tasks. Instead, the issue is forging a new relationship with adult caregivers. Certain behaviors of the child appear perplexing because, to the adult, the child is simply being aggravating. For example, if asked whether she would like to wear the jacket or a sweater, the child is likely to reject both choices. However, Vygotsky (1982–1984/1998i) noted that the child's resistance is to the adult's role (making suggestions, in this case), not to the content of the request.

One outcome of this critical period is a reconstruction of the child's social relations to the people around him. The other is a more developed personality capable of managing some aspects of his daily life. In other words, the significance of this period is that new character traits appear in the child. Moreover, if this period is not concluded successfully, the result is a serious postponement of affective and decision-making aspects of the child's personality (Vygotsky, 1982–1984/1998k, p. 194).

Summary

Vygotsky defined consciousness as an integrated internal structure. Included are affect, awareness, generalizations, and mental processes. The development of consciousness begins at the end of the newborn period with the social smile, which signals an awareness of other people. During the subsequent stable period (infancy), the central neoformation is the emergence of the "Great-we," a perceived mental commonality with a primary caregiver. This perceived unity, which persists into early childhood, is similar to two children playing ball, in which the two merge into the single action of the internal "we." Another development during infancy is the first use of tools, a primitive world view.

The second critical period occurs near the child's first birthday. The three major developments of this period are (a) the establishment of walking, (b) the emergence of affect and will, and (c) the emergence of autonomous speech, which differs semantically and structurally from prattling. The importance of autonomous speech is that it is connected with the emergence of consciousness and it changes the nature of the personal contact between the young child and adults. It is the child's effort to communicate in words, and she is able to communicate in a primitive way about objects in his or her visual field.

During the subsequent stable period of early childhood, consciousness operates through perception, the dominant mental function. Initially linked to affect, perception of objects is linked to action, and memory consists of recognizing concrete situations. Words in adult speech begin to develop in the second half of early childhood, and the naming of objects changes the structure of perception and leads to the beginning of the systemic structure of consciousness.

Early childhood concludes with the critical period at age 3, which redefines the social relationship between the child and the adults around him. The child insists on her own way of doing things, even rejecting favorite activities when they are suggested by adult caregivers. These changed reactions differ from disobedience because they are in response to the caregiver, not the activity itself. In addition to a changed relationship with adults, the child emerges from this critical period with a more developed personality capable of managing some aspects of her personal life.

The Preschool Period

Vygotsky (1982–1984/1998k) identified the years from 3 to 7 as the preschool period. During this stable period, the child's thinking progresses from syncretic images to complexes, and speech continues to modify perception. In addition to analyzing perceptions, speech also synthesizes connections in perception. For example, the child says "The boy is running" on looking at a picture of this action (Vygotsky, 1930–1931/1998a, p. 88). However, the child is unable to use auxiliary stimuli to master her memory or her attention. In the area of practical activity, the 3-year-old is unable to act effectively on the particular situation. By about the age of 7, however, as discussed in Chapter 5, the child can verbally plan his actions related to the visual situation he faces. However, "in the true sense of the word, verbal thinking in the process of solving problems is rarely observed" (Vygotsky, 1930–1931/1998a, p. 118).

The major avenue of the child's cultural development in the preschool period is imaginary play, which is also the main source of the development of symbolic activity (Vygotsky & Luria, 1994, p. 151). Imaginary play is an important stage in the development of the child's world view because he is assigning new meanings to toys and other objects and imagines himself or herself in any of a variety of new roles (Vygotsky, 1982–1984/1997a, p. 250).

The Development of Imaginary Play

Vygotsky (1982–1984/1998e) noted that the traditional view of play included a wide variety of activities. Examples are opening or closing a door and riding a hobby horse. From the traditional perspective, both activities are undertaken for pleasure and, therefore, are play (p. 266). In contrast, Vygotsky defined play as "a unique relation to reality that is characterized by creating imaginary situations or transferring the properties of some objects to others" (p. 267).

The criterion of imagination, however, does not exist in consciousness at early childhood (Vygotsky, 1931/1966, p. 8; Vygotsky, 1982–1984/1998e, p. 267). Although the young child tends to a doll or a teddy bear, there is no thought of the doll being her daughter, for example, or of the teddy bear being anything other than a bear (Vygotsky, 1982–1984/1998e, pp. 267–268). Lacking is an extended imaginary situation in which the child (a) takes on a clearly defined role and (b) changes the property of a thing in noticeable ways (p. 268). Vygotsky referred to the activity of the young child as "quasi-play," because it lacks these characteristics.

In contrast, during the preschool period, the object in the situation, such as the stick that becomes a "horse," functions as the pivot for changing the child's perceptual structure. Vygotsky illustrates the transitions that occur in imaginary play with the inversion of two fractions. Initially, play is represented by the fractions (*object/meaning*) and (*action/meaning*). In these relations, the object, the stick, and the action of the child, such as galloping, determine the meaning. However, at the crucial moment when the stick actually becomes a horse for the child, when he stamps on the ground and imagines that he is riding a horse, the perceptual structure changes. The relationships are inverted and become (*meaning/object*) and (*meaning/action*) (p. 15). Meaning becomes the determinant of the role of the object and of the action. Meaning moves to the forefront with the object and the child's action takes a secondary role.

Two other characteristics of imaginary play are (a) the child does not confuse play activity with serious activity (Vygotsky, 1982–1984/1997a, p. 249) and (b) play is not symbolism (Vygotsky, 1931/1966, p. 13). For example, a postcard cannot be a horse. Instead, the child is operating with an object to which he or she can convey meaning in the context of a particular activity.

The Importance of Imaginary Play

The child's creation of an imaginary situation frees him from situational constraints. His actions are independent of the actual visual situation, and he begins to learn "to act in a cognitive rather than an externally visible realm" (Vygotsky, 1931/1966, p. 11). The child also is able to act above his average age. She establishes intentions and forms real-life plans and motives. Through imaginary play, the child can become a captain, a soldier, or anything else s/he wants to be (Vygotsky, 1982–1984/1997a, p. 249).

The creation of an imaginary situation is a way of establishing a new relationship between situations in thought and situations in real life (Vygotsky, 1931/1966, p. 17). It is a way of beginning to develop abstract thought. Later, during the school-age period, play "is converted to internal processes . . . internal speech, logical memory, and abstract thought" (p. 13).

In summary, the lengthy preschool period, from after the third birthday to about age 7, consists of several changes in the child's consciousness. Syncretic images are replaced by complexes, which are dominated by pseudoconcepts by school age. Also, the child relies on the characteristics of objects as a basis for explaining their names and other object features. Egocentric thinking also begins and develops during the preschool period. As described in Chapter 5, the child moves from syncretism of action to the phase in which the child can verbally plan his actions in visual situations.

An important development during the preschool period is the child's imaginary play. Initially, the object and the action in the situation are the child's source of meaning. Subsequently, the meaning constructed by the child determines the role of the object and the child's action. Imaginary play (a) allows the child to act above her average age, (b) frees him from situational constraints, and (c) initiates a new relationship between situations in thought and situations in real life.

Implications for Parents and Caregivers

The implications of Vygotsky's descriptions of the early years of development include the relationship with a primary caregiver and activities in preschool.

The Child–Caregiver Relationship

Chapter 5 discussed the importance of parents and other caregivers talking with infants and very young children. The functional use of speech (e.g., "Where is your teddy bear?") was emphasized. Vygotsky (1982–1984/1998g), in his description of the child's early years, identified another factor that is particularly important in cognitive development. It is the indivisible mental communication that the child perceives between herself and her primary caregiver. Referred to as the "Great-we," it differs from the current description of the relationship as a bond or an attachment. In contrast to attachment, which is emotional, Vygotsky's description includes a mental component. The child's perceived mental commonality between himself and his primary caregiver indicates a heightened sensitivity to the words and actions of his mother or other caregiver. It opens the door for the caregiver to engage in activities that can contribute to the child's understanding of adult speech. Understanding, which is passive, precedes the active use of speech. The child, in other words, understands more than he is able to produce in speech. Therefore, reading stories to the very young child and pointing out interesting objects and events are important activities, particularly when implemented by the primary caregiver.

Also important is that the influence of the perceived "Great-we" calls into question two practices observed in contemporary society. One is the use of individuals who are not proficient in the language of the parents as daily caregivers. The child lacks the rich orientation to her environment that the mental commonality of this age can provide. Second is the practice of "culture cramming" with CDs of Mozart and so-called educational computer games. They are not a substitute for the articulate caregiver–young child relationship, which opens up a new world before the child's eyes.

Preschool Activities

Chapter 7 discussed the pressure felt by preschool teachers to teach academic skills. Researchers in early childhood education have expressed the concern that an increasing emphasis on academic skills at a young age is also accompanied by a decline in understanding the role of play in cognitive development (e.g., Bergen, 2002; Church, 2005). Supporting Vygotsky's position, Church (2005) described the contribution to developing abstract thought when the "child uses objects to represent things, gestures to mime an object when no prop is available, or makes movements to represent a complex action, such as driving an ambulance" (p. 80).

Parents of preschoolers can support the child's imaginative play in several ways. One is reading and sharing stories, including stories with large, colorful pictures, using different voices for different characters, and making the sounds for different animals. In contrast, providing the child with authentic and detailed costumes that represent specific characters is not recommended. Instead, the best props are everyday objects that can take on a variety of meanings. A large bath towel can become Superman's cape or a magic carpet, and plastic bracelets can become expensive jewelry. Also, when the child wants to wear his Superman cape to day care or to meet his mother at the airport, this activity should be permitted. In addition, time should be available for the child's nondirected play, and encouragement for imaginative play is particularly important.

Finally, imaginative play should not become a structured activity in which the child, in advance, is required to inform the teacher of his or her plans for imaginative play. Such a requirement is far from conducive to encouraging imaginative play. Moreover, it upends the cognitive process. Imaginative play informs the child's intellect, not the reverse.

MATURATION OF WORLD VIEW AND PERSONALITY

The period referred to as the school age, from the critical period at age 7 to the critical period at age 13, is a time when the child experiences an increase, as well as an intensification and differentiation of social experience (Vygotsky, 1982–1984/1997a, p. 250). During the periods of development from the critical period at age 7 through adolescence, the individual's personality grows and matures (p. 250).

The School Years from Age 7 to 13

As indicated, the period referred to as the school age is bounded by two critical periods. Discussed in this section are the differentiation of external and internal aspects of personality (the critical period at age 7), cognitive development during the school age, and the critical period at age 13.

Differentiation of External and Internal Aspects of Personality

The crisis at age 7 was identified by psychologists prior to Vygotsky's work on developmental stages. This turning point was described in the literature as abrupt changes in the child in which he becomes difficult in the transition from preschool to school age (Vygotsky, 1982–1984/ 1998h, p. 289). However, Vygotsky noted that the critical period will occur differently in children who go from nursery school to kindergarten than in those who go directly to kindergarten from the family setting (p. 295). Nevertheless, in his view, age 7 will always be a turning point because a state occurs in which internal development concludes a cycle, and the transition to the next cycle is a turning point (p. 295).

Two aspects of the child's experience may appear to be a contradiction (Vygotsky, 1982–1984/1997a). They are that the child is becoming much more socialized as her experiences expand, and she also is becoming "a much more individualized being" (p. 250). In addition, the child's personality grows and matures as his social experiences intensify and become more diverse.

Vygotsky (1982–1984/1997a, 1982–1984/1998h) identified two major changes in the child during this critical period. The primary change is the separation of the internal and external aspects of his personality (Vygotsky, 1982–1984/1998h, p. 290). The observable indicator of this process is the loss of child-like directness. The naiveté and directness of the younger child indicates that he is the same inwardly as he is externally. A current example is the remarks of the young boy Dennis in the cartoon feature "Dennis the Menace." In the barbershop, for example, he asks his balding neighbor, Mr. Wilson, if he has to pay full price for a haircut.

Related to the loss of directness in the child is the development of a cognitive orientation to his own experiences (p. 291). Similar to the critical period at age 3, when the child develops a new relationship with adults, the critical period at age 7 consists of the child developing a new relationship to his own experiences. For example, the child develops an understanding of the meaning of his comments, such as " 'I'm angry,' " " 'I'm good,' " and so on (p. 291). In other words, feeling unhappy and knowing he is unhappy are two different experiences for the child.

A second aspect of the child's cognitive orientation to his experiences is that he begins to generalize from those experiences and feelings. In contrast, children who are severely mentally impaired, rejected at every attempt to join other children at play, do react to each instance but do not generalize; they do not develop a sense of worthlessness (p. 292). However, other children at the critical seventh year who are rejected a few times by a group of children begin to evaluate themselves, and their self-esteem may suffer. Such a self-evaluation differs from the view of the preschool child, who likes himself, but does not engage in self-evaluation. Vygotsky further concluded that the level of the demands we make of ourselves and for our success and our position begin specifically at this critical period (p. 290).

Cognitive Development during School Age

Vygotsky's detailed analyses of stable and critical periods end with his discussion of the critical period at age 7. However, he discussed aspects of the development of consciousness during school age and adolescence in other writings.

The nature of the learner's thinking in the years from 7 to adolescence differs in three major ways from the later years. They are the approach to addressing practical problem-solving activities, level of thinking (attention, perception, memory), and extent of concept formation.

In the realm of practical activity, the school-age child can plan his actions, execute them, and later provide an account of them. That is, he can execute strategies that depend on concrete thinking. Also, at about age 7, these strategies are beginning to turn inward as internal speech. However, internal speech does not become stable until about the age of 12. In addition, even when the learner relies on inner speech, he must check his planning with the actual visual situation (Vygotsky, 1930–1931/1998a, p. 119).

When the child reaches school age, memory and attention are relatively mature. During the school age, thinking is accomplished primarily through remembering (Vygotsky, 1930–1931/1998a, p. 91). That is, children address general questions through the recall of concrete operations. For example, in responding to the question "What is a bus?," children said such things as "Ladies ride in it," "It has a bell," and so on (p. 91).

The school-age child also lacks awareness and understanding of her thinking processes. S/he does not consider or respond to them and often does not control them (Vygotsky, 1982–1984/1997a, p. 250). The child's thought processes "flow with him" in the same way that his actions flowed when he was younger. The lack of awareness and volition (deliberate execution), previously present in the actions of the preschooler, appears in the thinking of the school child. However, the child does have the capacity for conscious awareness and self-directness of memory and attention.

As noted in chapters 4 and 6, the mechanism for developing control of one's thinking is instruction in subject matter (scientific) concepts. By age 7, the child's thinking has moved from syncretic images to complexes and then to the pseudoconcept, a higher form of complexes (Vygotsky, 1982–1984/1998c, p. 61). Through instruction, the school-age child can begin to identify a common trait of the examples of a concept, a first step toward developing conceptual thinking.

The Critical Period at Age 13

Vygotsky (1982–1984/1998b) referred to the critical period at age 13 as "the phase of a second negativism" because it is similar to the negative attitudes expressed in the critical period at or about the third year (p. 19). He noted that the various psychological discussions of adolescence, despite their differences, agreed on the presence of a negative phase at the beginning of that period (p. 19). Characteristics of this negativism are lapses in work capacity, lack of interest in formerly preferred activities, and a failure to complete school assignments (p. 21).

However, children do not exhibit the same degree of negativism. Vygotsky cited the research of Pavel Zagorovsky, a Soviet psychologist, who worked primarily in the area of adolescent psychology. His qualitative research indicated that some young adolescents exhibited stable negative attitudes, others had brief and short-lived negative reactions under certain conditions, such as family conflicts, and a third group exhibited no negativism (p. 22).

Vygotsky concluded that the critical period is heterogeneous and includes three types of processes described by Aron Zalkind, a Russian psychiatrist. They are (a) the stabilizing of former achievements, (b) processes that develop rapidly and are new, and (c) processes that set up emerging elements that become the basis for further creative activity in development (p. 24). In other words, regardless of the intensity of the negative attitudes, this stage "concludes and arrests childhood" and also creates something new that will develop further beyond the critical period (p. 24).

Vygotsky also noted that the basis for development in the adolescent period is the organic changes connected to sexual maturation (p. 16). Changes in the adolescent's interests typically coincide with this organic development, which also can precipitate negative reactions in the 13-year-old. However, Vygotsky emphasized the point that the adolescent's biological changes are not the sole factor operating during this period. The adolescent also is a "historical and social being" (p. 23). Specifically, the subsequent adolescent period is one in which the personality and world view mature (p. 23).

Summary

The developmental period referred to as the school age is preceded by the critical period at age 7 and is followed by the critical period at age 13. Psychologists identified age 7 as a critical period prior to Vygotsky's analyses of stable and critical developmental periods. Already noted in the transition from preschool to school was that the child abruptly becomes difficult. However, Vygotsky noted that the change may be experienced by children in different ways, given differences in the nature of their preschool experiences (nursery school to kindergarten or family setting to kindergarten). Nevertheless, at about the seventh year, internal and external aspects of the child's personality become differentiated. There is a loss of directness and naiveté in the child's behavior, and he develops a cognitive orientation to his own experiences. She develops an understanding of her affective states, such as happiness and anger. The child also begins to engage in self-evaluation.

Cognitive development during the subsequent school age includes the transition to inner speech, which is not complete until about age 12, developing a conscious awareness and some control of memory and attention, and beginning to move beyond thinking with pseudoconcepts. The mechanism for developing conscious awareness and some control of thinking is instruction in subject matter or academic concepts.

The critical period at age 13, although referred to as the second period of negativism, is not necessarily experienced strongly by children. Some adolescents may exhibit brief negative reactions to some situations, and others exhibit no negativism. Nevertheless, this critical period stabilizes the child's former achievements and initiates new processes and interests. Although changes in interests typically coincide with sexual maturation, biological factors are not the only factor occurring in this period.

The Nature of Development in Adolescence

Several important developments occur during adolescence, and they all emanate from a single center, which is the formation of "true" concepts (Vygotsky, 1930–1931/1998a, p. 121). Through forming concepts, memory and attention "transition from the system of perception to the system of thinking" (p. 108). That is, mastery of memory and attention is transformed from establishing patterns between external stimuli to the internal process of thinking with concepts. Perception, for example, means to think of visual images in terms of concepts and to synthesize the concrete and the general (p. 122). The adolescent also understands the meaning of a word as a concept. That is, the image of an object is complex in that it reflects its connections and relationships with other concept examples and other concepts.

In addition, "the imagination of the adolescent enters into a close connection with thinking in concepts" (Vygotsky, 1930–1931/1998f, p. 154), and it "begins to fulfill a completely new function in the new structure of the adolescent's personality" (p. 154). From a developmental perspective, the adolescent imagination is the successor to the child's imaginative play, which is linked to concrete objects. The path taken by the imagination in adolescence is a movement "from the concrete, visual image through a concept to the imagined picture" (pp. 163–164).

Two streams form the adolescent's creative imagination. One is a subjective activity that is closely connected to the adolescent's internal desires, incentives, and emotions, in which adolescent fantasy fulfills unsatisfied desire (p. 164). The other stream is objective creativity that leads to artistic works, scientific inventions, and technical constructions (p. 164).

In the area of practical thinking, the adolescent can solve problems without the visual situation. He can then transfer the solution to an action plan (Vygotsky, 1930–1931/1998a, p. 119). However, the real content of cognitive development in adolescence is the internal mastery of mental processes (functions), which consists of constructing new connections and interrelationships among the functions (processes). For example, categorical perception relies on concepts and ideas constructed through conceptual thinking and stored in logical memory in a network of related concepts. Formation of the new connections and relations among mental functions requires reflection on one's thinking, which Vygotsky described as "a substrate in the consciousness of the adolescent" (p. 182). This internal mastery of cognitive behavior through conceptual thinking is the highest level of sign use and is referred to as a process of revolution (Vygotsky, 1982–1984/1999, p. 55; Vygotsky, 1930–1931/1998a, p. 104).

In other words, personality and world view mature during adolescence. The broad distinction between childhood and adolescence that Vygotsky described is taken from the philosopher Hegel (Vygotsky, 1930–1931/1998a). Specifically, a thing initially is *in itself* and then turns into a thing *for itself* in the process of development. A human being in itself is the child. Then, through development, the child becomes an adolescent, a human being who is for him- or herself (p. 149).

Within Hegel's general designation, Vygotsky noted that the child assimilates higher forms of behavior through a social (external) mechanism. However, initially, the child is not conscious of these processes. Eventually, through a lengthy development, the individual becomes aware of the structure of particular capabilities and begins to control and direct them for himself (Vygotsky, 1930–1931/1998d, p. 171). This change is the "for himself" aspect of Hegel's description.

Development of the Self-Reflecting "I"

Vygotsky (1930–1931/1998d) noted that the development of personality in the adolescent had become an issue in paedology. Edward Spranger, a German philosopher and psychologist, maintained that a basic feature of adolescence was that the individual discovered his own "I" (p. 172). Vygotsky disagreed with the idea of discovery as the mechanism for this change. The problem was that Spranger treated the emergence of an awareness of oneself and self-reflection as a primary and independent development that precipitates all other changes in that period (p. 175). Instead, according to Vygotsky, this self-awareness and self-reflection is "one of the very last, perhaps even the last link" in the sequence of changes during adolescence (p. 175).

In other words, Vygotsky (1930–1931/1998d) described self-consciousness as "the last and highest of all the restructuring" of the adolescent personality (p. 176). It is the outcome of three types of conditions that contribute to the development of self-consciousness. The primary conditions are instincts and the capabilities inherited by the individual. Secondary conditions are the environment and acquired traits. The third type consists of reflection and self-shaping (p. 180). All are essential for the development of self-consciousness.

Vygotsky agreed, for the most part, with the research findings of A. Busemann, a German psychologist. In two studies, Busemann focused on the development of reflection and self-consciousness in the child and the adolescent (p. 173). The research subjects wrote compositions on such topics as "My Good and Bad Qualities" and "Am I Satisfied with Myself?" (p. 173). On the basis of his data, Busemann identified six stages in the development of consciousness of oneself. Vygotsky disagreed with

the stage concept; however, he agreed that the development of the consciousness of the self was not some type of "fixed and constant ability"
(p. 173).

The Role of Culture

Busemann attempted, from his data, to link the development of self-
awareness and understanding to the type of educational school attended
by the learner. Instead, Vygotsky maintained that the key was differences
in cultural environments, which influence the development of self-
consciousness. Specifically, the working class adolescent does not have a
deficient self-awareness but simply different kinds of capabilities that he
has mastered, accompanied by a "*different structure and dynamics of
self-consciousness*" (p. 178). For example, an upbringing in an atmosphere of physical labor and material want and no skill training contributes to a different type of self-awareness than an educated, economically
comfortable situation.

The Role of Reflection and Consciousness of the Self

Busemann's third point, which Vygotsky supported, was the depiction of
adolescence as a "qualitatively unique time" in development (p. 180).
During adolescence, reflection begins to play an important role. First, reflection contributes to self-shaping, and this process is significant for the
psychology of individual differences (p. 180). Second, mental acts attain
a personal character on the basis of the self-consciousness of personality
and on having been mastered by the individual (Vygotsky, 1930–1931/
1998d, p. 172).

Of course, one's mental life may be closed within itself and not
include self-reflection. Vygotsky noted that there is "a profound difference" between the nonreflecting personality and the personality that engages in self-reflection (p. 181). The adolescent who develops reflection
"is differentiated internally into the acting 'I' and into another 'I'—the
reflecting 'I' " (p. 181). Moreover, like the higher psychological functions, self-reflection is the result of the transfer of social relations inward. In other words, social consciousness becomes self-consciousness.

Culmination of Personality Development

Traditional views of the transitional age focused on descriptive representations of the adolescent's personality. These approaches used self-observation,
journals, and the poetry of adolescents to recreate the structure of the
personality on the basis of separate documented experiences.

In contrast, Vygotsky approached the study of the adolescent's personality from its structure and dynamics. He identified its distinguishing feature as consciousness of one's own mental operations and the possibility for internal control. In other words, the adolescent's actions acquire a personal character.

This revolution occurs only with the transition to thinking in concepts. Conceptual thinking becomes the basic means for (a) systematizing and recognizing the external world, (b) understanding others, and (c) understanding one's own experiences and oneself. The transition to thinking in concepts is the basis of the new personality structure that develops at adolescence (Vygotsky, 1930–1931/1998a, p. 148).

Vygotsky referred to the capacity to command one's own actions as the "will," which is another form of social relations applied to oneself (Vygotsky, 1930–1931/1998d, p. 181). Through "purposeful will," the adolescent manages his affect and can set goals and attain them (Vygotsky, 1930–1931/1998a, p. 126). According to Vygotsky, such mastery of behavior is a more distinguishing feature of humans than superior intellect.

In summary, several developments, all based on the formation of conceptual thinking, occur in adolescence. First is the development of self-directed attention, categorical perception, and logical memory. Second are the new connections and interrelations among those higher mental functions, a process that required reflection. Third is the development of self-consciousness, which is the highest level of the restructuring of the adolescent's capabilities and requires reflection and self-shaping. The adolescent who develops self-reflection is differentiated internally into the acting "I" and the reflecting "I." The culmination of personality development is the adolescent's management of affect and goal setting.

EDUCATIONAL IMPLICATIONS

Vygotsky identified several qualitative differences between the school-age child and the adolescent (see Table 8.1). The school age child can solve practical problems through verbal planning, has the capacity to develop self-organized attention and verbal memory, and thinks in pseudo-concepts. During adolescence, in contrast, practical problems can be solved verbally without reference to the concrete situation, and thinking in true concepts begins. The development of mature or true concepts, conceptual thinking, is responsible for the development of self-organized attention, categorical perception, and logical memory.

However Vygotsky (1934/1987a) cautioned that these higher levels of thinking are not simply the result of maturation. "Where the environ-

TABLE 8.1. Qualitative Cognitive Differences between the School-Age Child and the Adolescent

School-age child	Adolescent
1. Separation of the internal and external aspects of the child's personality. The child develops a cognitive orientation to his or her own experiences, which precipitates self-evaluation.	1. The learner develops an understanding of social reality through beginning to think in concepts. Social consciousness is transferred inward and becomes self-reflection, consciousness of oneself, and self-shaping.
2. Concept-related thinking is at the level of pseudoconcepts.	2. Thinking in true concepts begins.
3. The learner has the capability to develop self-organized attention and verbal memory. Required are transforming these elementary forms through the appropriation of cultural signs and symbols.	3. Self-organized attention and verbal memory are transformed into internal psychological functions through thinking in true concepts. Memory becomes logicalized through the systematic organization of content.
4. For schoolchild, "to think is to remember" (e.g., Vygotsky, 1930–1931/1998a, p. 98). The child recalls a concrete situation from his experience in response to a question intended to require thinking.	4. For the adolescent, "to remember is to think" (e.g., Vygotsky, 1930–1931/1998a, p. 92). The adolescent, in remembering, applies his judgment and makes decisions about the information he knows that relates to the idea, situation, or concept he is recalling.
5. Practical problems can be solved through verbal planning in the context of the situation.	5. Practical problems can be solved verbally without the need to rely on concrete actions or checking with the visual situation.

ment does not create the appropriate tasks, advance new demands, or stimulate the development of intellect through new goals, the adolescent's thinking does not develop all the potentials inherent in it" (p. 132). In other words, unless the curriculum and classroom instruction focus on learner development of *thinking in concepts*, cognitive development, as well as the individual's development of self-reflection, will be incomplete.

Thus, Vygotsky's theory poses a major challenge for educators and curriculum designers, particularly in situations in which many highly specific objectives form the curriculum framework. Implementing Vygotsky's perspective means that the guiding question for curriculum development should be, What are the acts of thinking that the learner should evidence in this subject? New tasks and demands in academic subjects establish the conditions for new steps in thinking. In addition to learning and understanding subject matter concepts, the adolescent must also be able to use the relationships between concepts when faced with new problems to solve.

At least two issues in assessment emerge in light of Vygotsky's theory. First is the extensive reliance on multiple-choice examinations, which are associated with student cramming of factual material. Second is the ubiquitous book report or term paper. The student can develop these products with little knowledge of key concepts or engagement in logical, abstract thinking. The school child, Vygotsky noted, typically answers a question intended to generate thinking by drawing on a remembered experience or other information. In other words, verbal facility (structural knowledge) is not synonymous with symbolic meaning. The ability to organize resources that address a particular topic does not require the level of thinking that reflects higher cognitive functioning.

In summary, school age and adolescence are important periods in the development of personality and world view. The types of ways that learners, particularly in middle and high school, adapt to the world cognitively (world view) constitute their strategies in the future. Similarly, the extent of conceptual thinking and logical memory that develops is a key factor in the extent of rationality in their views of themselves and the world.

REFERENCES

Bergen, D. (2002). The role of pretend play in children's cognitive development. *Early Childhood Research and Practice, 4*(2), 1–13.

Church, E. B. (2005). Great pretenders: Why imaginary play is the stepping stone to thinking abstractly. *Scholastic Parent and Child, 80.*

Vygotsky, L. S. (1966). [Imaginary] play and its role in the mental development of the child. *Soviet Psychology, 5*(3), 6–18. (Original work published 1931)

Vygotsky, L. S. (1987a). An experimental study of concept development. In R. W. Rieber & A. S. Carton (Eds.), *Collected works of L. S. Vygotsky: Vol. 1. Problems of general psychology* (pp. 121–166). New York: Plenum. (Original work published 1934)

Vygotsky, L. S. (1987b). Memory and its development on children. Lecture 2: Lectures on psychology. In R. W. Rieber & A. S. Carton (Eds.), *Collected works of L. S. Vygotsky: Vol. 1. Problems of general psychology* (pp. 301–310). New York: Plenum. (Original work published 1934)

Vygotsky, L. S. (1987c). Perception and its development in childhood. In R. W. Rieber & A. S. Carton (Eds.), *Collected works of L. S. Vygotsky: Vol. 1. Prob-*

lems of general psychology (pp. 289–300). New York: Plenum. (Original work published 1934)

Vygotsky, L. S. (1987d). The development of scientific concepts in childhood. In R. W. Rieber & A. S. Carton (Eds.), *Collected works of L. S. Vygotsky: Vol. 1. Problems of general psychology* (pp. 167–241). New York: Plenum. (Original work published 1934)

Vygotsky, L. S. (1987e). Thought and word. In R. W. Rieber & A. S. Carton (Eds.), *Collected works of L. S. Vygotsky: Vol. 1. Problems of general psychology* (pp. 243–285). New York: Plenum. (Original work published 1934)

Vygotsky, L. S. (1997a). Conclusion; further research; development of personality and world view in the child. In R. W. Rieber (Ed.), *Collected works of L. S. Vygotsky: Vol. 4. The history of development of higher mental functions* (pp. 241–251). New York: Plenum. (Original work published 1982–1984)

Vygotsky, L. S. (1997b). Development of speech and thinking. In R. W. Rieber (Ed.), *Collected works of L. S. Vygotsky: Vol. 4. The history of development of higher mental functions* (pp. 191–205). New York: Plenum. (Original work published 1982–1984)

Vygotsky, L. S. (1998a). Development of higher mental functions during the transitional age. In R. W. Rieber (Ed.), *Collected works of L. S. Vygotsky: Vol. 5. Child psychology* (pp. 83–149). New York: Plenum. (Original work published 1930–1931)

Vygotsky, L. S. (1998b). Development of interests at the transitional age. In R. W. Rieber (Ed.), *Collected works of L. S. Vygotsky: Vol. 5. Child psychology* (pp. 3–28). New York: Plenum. (Original work published 1982–1984)

Vygotsky, L. S. (1998c). Development of thinking and formation of concepts in adolescence. In R. W. Rieber (Ed.), *Collected works of L. S. Vygotsky: Vol. 5. Child psychology* (pp. 29–81). New York: Plenum. (Original work published 1930–1931)

Vygotsky, L. S. (1998d). Dynamics and structure of the adolescent's personality. In R. W. Rieber (Ed.), *Collected works of L. S. Vygotsky: Vol. 5. Child psychology* (pp. 167–184). New York: Plenum. (Original work published 1930–1931)

Vygotsky, L. S. (1998e). Early childhood. In R. W. Rieber (Ed.), *Collected works of L. S. Vygotsky: Vol. 5. Child psychology* (pp. 261–281). New York: Plenum. (Original work published 1982–1984)

Vygotsky, L. S. (1998f). Imagination and creativity in the adolescent. In R. W. Rieber (Ed.), *Collected works of L. S. Vygotsky: Vol. 5. Child psychology* (pp. 151–166). New York: Plenum. (Original work published 1930–1931)

Vygotsky, L. S. (1998g). Infancy. In R. W. Rieber (Ed.), *Collected works of L. S. Vygotsky: Vol. 5. Child psychology* (pp. 207–241). New York: Plenum. (Original work published 1982–1984)

Vygotsky, L. S. (1998h). The crisis at age seven. In R. W. Rieber (Ed.), *Collected works of L. S. Vygotsky: Vol. 5. Child psychology* (pp. 289–296). New York: Plenum. (Original work published 1982–1984)

Vygotsky, L. S. (1998i). The crisis at age three. In R. W. Rieber (Ed.), *Collected works of L. S. Vygotsky: Vol. 5. Child psychology* (pp. 283–288). New York: Plenum. (Original work published 1982–1984)

Vygotsky, L. S. (1998j). The crisis of the first year. In R. W. Rieber (Ed.), *Collected works of L. S. Vygotsky: Vol. 5. Child psychology* (pp. 243–259). New York: Plenum. (Original work published 1982–1984)

Vygotsky, L. S. (1998k). The problem of age. In R. W. Rieber (Ed.), *Child psychology. Vol. 5. Collected works of L. S. Vygotsky* (pp. 187–205). New York: Plenum. (Original work published 1982–1984)

Vygotsky, L. S. (1999). Analysis of sign operations of the child. In R. W. Rieber (Ed.), *Collected works of L. S. Vygotsky: Vol. 6. Scientific legacy* (pp. 45–56). New York: Plenum. (Original work published 1982–1984)

Vygotsky, L. S., & Luria, A. R. (1994). Tool and symbol in child development. In R. van der Veer & J. Valsiner (Eds.), *The Vygotsky reader* (pp. 99–174). Cambridge, MA: Blackwell.

Part IV

SOME IMPLICATIONS
OF VYGOTSKY'S THEORY

9

A New Way of Thinking

> It is easier to assimilate a thousand new facts in any field than to assimilate a new point of view of a few already known facts.
>
> —VYGOTSKY (1960/1997k, p. 1)

Vygotsky formally joined Russian psychology in the chaotic first decade after the Bolshevik revolution. He enthusiastically set about the task of building a psychology that would address the nature of human consciousness and the complexity of the development of human cognition, beginning with its early roots. He also advocated an objective, comprehensive, causal–dynamic psychology.

He did not succeed in constructing a complete psychological system. However, he did create a framework for understanding the complexity of cognitive development, and his penetrating analyses of issues include insights relevant to current theory and practice. Yaroskevsky (1999) noted that Vygotsky searched for new ways to solve problems, and that the uniqueness of his quest is reflected in his individual style of thinking (p. 245).

The overall implication of his work is not unlike the patterns in a kaleidoscope. A kaleidoscope is a tube that contains loose bits of colored plastic reflected by small mirrors. The result is a particular geometric pattern of the colored plastic bits. When the individual puts the tube up to one eye and rotates it slightly, the bits of plastic shift and form an entirely new pattern. Vygotsky's cultural–historical theory, in one sense, represents such a shift imposed on the research and thinking about cognitive development and the processes of schooling and education. Discussed in this chapter are issues in Vygotsky's thinking, suggestions for psychology and educational psychology, and implications for society.

ISSUES IN VYGOTSKY'S THINKING

Vygotsky's goal was to determine the psychological principles responsible for the highest levels of cognitive development. Discussed in this section are the dialectical nature of cognitive development, the concept of unity, and pervasive threads in his work.

The Dialectical Nature of Cognitive Development

Vygotsky (1960/1997a, 1960/1997d, 1930/1997f) agreed with the philosopher G. W. F. Hegel that (a) reality consists of the processes of change, (b) humans create a number of worlds referred to as cultures, and (c) historical development includes both detours and reversals.

Basic Principles Applied to Cognitive Development

Two types of change described by Hegel are found in Vygotsky's depiction of cognitive development. One is that developments, ideas, and processes may be countered by an opposing development, idea, or process. A resolution of the contradiction or polarity between the two is transcended by a third position. According to Hegel, the continual struggle between old and new results in a superior development often referred to as *synthesis* (Graham, 1987, p. 53).[1]

Characteristics of dialectical processes in cognitive development include the "qualitative transformations of certain forms into others, a complex merging of the process of evolution and revolution, a complex crossing of external and internal factors" (Vygotsky, 1960/1997d, p. 99). In other words, forms of thinking are not static categories. Manifestations of this form of change include the initial development of perception

---

[1]Graham (1987) noted that, despite popular opinion, Hegel did not use the neat formulation of "thesis–antithesis–synthesis" often attributed to him. He rarely used the term *synthesis* to indicate the moment when opposite views are transcended (p. 47). Also, he opposed the reduction of his analysis to "a triadic formula, and warned that such a scheme was 'a mere pedagogical device,' a 'formula for memory and reason' " (Hegel, 1959, p. 77, in Graham, 1987, p. 47).

ahead of the other mental functions, followed by the movement of memory and attention to the forefront, and so on. The essence of the development of the mental functions is not an increase in the number of connections among them but that the connections change (Vygotsky, 1982–1984/1997g).

Also, the critical periods identified by Vygotsky are examples of "qualitative leaps" from the prior stable periods. The child's autonomous speech is an example; it is qualitatively different from the young child's prattling.

A second type of dialectical change is a sequence of small changes that accumulate gradually and then precipitate a qualitative change. Vygotsky's (1930–1931/1998c) designation of stable periods is an example of this type of change. For example, the child begins to learn adult words during the period referred to as early childhood. New words contribute to the semantic and syntactic structure of the child's consciousness. At the end of early childhood, the mental framework in the child's consciousness is qualitatively different than it was at the beginning.

Also important is that the dialectical perspective has no problem in dealing with opposites that are related to each other. An example is the mind–body debate that was ongoing at the time Vygotsky entered psychology. He pointed out that dialectical thinking viewed the mind and the brain as two components of the same entity (Vygotsky, 1930/1997f). In his discussions of the newborn, infancy, and the young child, he related early cognitive developments to emerging components of the brain as they were known at that time.

The Issue of Continuity and Change

Every learning theorist (e.g., Bandura, Gagné, Skinner) and cognitive development theorist (e.g., Piaget, Vygotsky) is faced with the issue of explaining continuity and change. Basically, the question is how to account for continuity in learning or development while also addressing the fact that human beings change from child to adulthood (development) or novice to expert (learning). Specifically, how do the elements identified by the theorist to account for basic learning or development function to bring about major changes without destroying the continuity of development or learning? Typically, learning theories identify the basic mechanism of learning and then say "more of the same." That is, the same mechanisms account for both basic learning and the changes that bring about complex learning. Skinner's operant conditioning, for example, designated the stimulus–response–reinforcement mechanism as the agent of behavioral change. Complex behaviors are produced or shaped by chains of this basic mechanism. In other words, the acquisition of complex behaviors basically requires the repetition of the same mechanism that produces simple behaviors.

Vygotsky, however, maintained that such approaches were in error because the process itself undergoes change. He described the problem associated with relying on the same mechanism to explain both initial and subsequent complex behaviors in his discussion of the form versus content issue. Specifically, theorists were describing the acquisition of complex behaviors (new content) through prior forms (basic mechanisms of learning or development). He compared this approach to the situation in which new substances are poured into existing containers. This approach is faulty, in his view, because form and content are inseparable; therefore, the continual process of development is characterized by change in that very process. Development reorganizes itself as it proceeds (Vygotsky, 1930–1931/1998c), and psychology must determine the events in this process. Dialectical logic is uniquely suited to this task because explaining change while preserving continuity is the essence of this philosophy. A key example is Vygotsky's identification of critical and stable periods in development in which the nature of the change (smooth or disjointed) is the basis for identifying the different periods.

The Concept of Unity

Vygotsky (1934/1987, 1935/1994) noted that psychologists frequently began their work by partitioning a particular mental whole into its constituent elements. He identified two problems that are associated with this practice. One problem, mentioned in Chapter 2, is that these subdivisions do not reflect the characteristics of the whole. Vygotsky's illustrative example is the decomposition of water into its elements, hydrogen and oxygen. Second, the partitioning leads to inaccurate research questions and answers.

Vygotsky (1934/1987) also identified two advantages of studying a unit of the whole. One is that it facilitates the study of processes that undergo change during development. An example in biology is the living cell because it includes the basic features of life that are essential in the living organism (p. 46).

An example in Vygotsky's work is the term *experience* ("perezhivanie"), which represents the unity of environmental and personal features (Vygotsky, 1935/1994, p. 343). This designation avoids the problem of casting the environment in terms of a static set of characteristics and then attempting to identify connections to the development of the child.

Second, identification of such units in cognitive psychology focuses on the meaning of a particular entity for the developing child. The unit referred to as experience, for example, captures the meaning of the environment for the child beyond its concrete, observable characteristics.

The issue of the appropriate unit of study is particularly important, in Vygotsky's view, in the analysis of verbal thinking. Psychologists had partitioned verbal thinking into the separate elements of thought and word. They then were faced with the task of constructing some external mechanical connection between them (Vygotsky, 1934/1987, p. 46).

Vygotsky's solution was to identify the "inner aspect of the word," word meaning, as the appropriate unit of study for verbal thinking[2] (p. 47). Vygotsky's rationale for selecting word meaning was that a word does not simply refer to a particular object. Instead, each word is a "concealed *generalization*;" it relates to "an *entire group or class of objects*" (p. 47). As a generalization, therefore, it is an act of thinking. In addition, it belongs to the domain of speech (p. 47). Social interaction, which requires speech, depends on meaning, just as thinking does. Moreover, the social interactions that involve the higher mental functions are possible only because, through thinking, humans reflect on reality through generalizations (p. 49). In other words, communicating any experience to another person presupposes that the individual can relate his experience to a specific class or category of experiences that the recipient understands. Moreover, Vygotsky noted that this requirement applies to the simplest of social exchanges, such as communicating to someone that the speaker is cold (p. 49).

Vygotsky further pointed out that children who do not know the generalization represented by a word often cannot communicate their experiences to others. Recall, from Chapter 5, that true communication (not autonomous speech) is possible between child and adult if the child has grasped a few of the aspects of the meaning of a word. The importance of at least partially understanding the meaning of a word in order to communicate with others led to Vygotsky's conclusion that word meaning is "*a unity of thinking and speech* [and] *a unity of generalization and social interaction, a unity of thinking and communication*" (p. 49).

Vygotsky concluded that, in addition to clarifying the internal unity of thinking and speech, word meaning made possible "more effective research on the relationship of verbal thinking to the whole life of consciousness" (p. 50). Also important, he noted, is that it contributed to

---

[2]Minick (1987) described Vygotsky's use of the terms *instrumental act, psychological systems,* and *word meaning* as denoting three different periods in Vygotsky's work. He does acknowledge, however, that Vygotsky did not abandon concepts that were central in his work and that the new terms were simple expansions of basic principles.

the major focus on his research, which was *"the idea of development"* (p. 51).

Pervasive Threads

Three pervasive threads may be distinguished in Vygotsky's work. They are his focus on changes in human consciousness, his focus on the learner, and his identification of theoretical flaws in existing theory and research.

Changes in Human Consciousness

As early as 1925, Vygotsky (1925/1997b) began to criticize psychology for failing to engage in the study of consciousness (p. 63). For Vygotsky, human consciousness includes the objective information/content in the mind, the individual's cognitive capabilities (psychological functions in Vygotsky's terminology), the mental apparatus associated with sensory and motor functions, awareness of one's own thinking, interpretations of events in the world, and intentions, interests, motives, and other affects or attitudes. Also important is that Vygotsky agreed with the perspective of Engels and Marx that consciousness is a social product (Rieber, 1998, endnote 6, p. 332).

Vygotsky identified changes in human consciousness through the stages of sign use, the development of speech, and the formation of concepts. In describing each of these developments, he traced the progression of thinking from a lack of awareness to learner mastery and control of cognitive operations. In the stages of sign use, the child first progresses from the direct execution of a psychological function (e.g., attention and memory) to an awareness but incomplete understanding of the role of signs in the cognitive operation. Then the child learns to construct connections in his thinking between the object of the task and a selected external sign or symbol. The fourth stage of sign use constitutes another change in the learner's consciousness. Management through external signs is replaced by internal signs and symbols.

Similarly, in the emergence of speech, the child's autonomous speech is his first effort to attach combinations of consonants and vowels to various objects in her visual field. This development reflects a change in the child's consciousness from the infant's prattling. Then the beginning of the use of adult speech represents the first semantic organization of the child's consciousness. However, initially the child is unaware of the arbitrariness of language and treats the name of an object as simply one of its characteristics.

The development of so-called egocentric speech is essential to the child's mastery of practical problems and influences the child's consciousness in another way. As the child progresses from syncretism of action to verbal accompaniment and then to verbal planning, he is able to bring past information to bear on the situation. He also is able to look forward and identify the needed end result, such as getting the candy from the top of the cupboard. During school age, the child's verbal planning becomes internal speech, another major change in the child's consciousness.

The lengthy development of concepts, which is not completed until adolescence, is also referred to as the development of word meaning. Initially, perception and the joining of objects on the basis of subjective criteria (syncretic images) dominate. Then the child begins to think in complexes; she joins objects together on the basis of concrete, yet accidental, connections.

Beginning with complexes, the child's concept-related thinking is important for the development of consciousness in two ways. First, the levels of concept-related thinking (complexes, pseudoconcepts, and "true" concepts) reflect the information about the world that the child has acquired. Second, each level consists of both a concept-related structure (e.g., complexes) and a particular way of thinking about the world. Pseudoconcepts, for example, involve the formation of categories or object groupings with the defining characteristics of a concept. However, the cognitive operations associated with pseudoconcepts are very different from thinking in true concepts. At the higher level, the learner can compare and contrast concepts, place them in superordinate and coordinate relations with each other, and apply them in various ways. These and other acts of judgments are the basis for Vygotsky's designation of thinking in true concepts as logical thinking.

Also important is that the elementary functions of attention, perception, and simple memory are restructured through thinking in concepts. Logical memory, for example, consists of the connections and relationships among concepts, categorical perception includes complex relationships among events and objects, and self-directed attention is controlled internally through thinking.

Then, during adolescence, the individual's world view and personality take shape, and self-consciousness and self-reflection also develop. These developments, in Vygotsky's view, are based on the individual's attainment of conceptual thinking.

Identifying Theoretical Flaws

Throughout his brief career, Vygotsky worked to develop a scientific psychology that would end the fragmented nature of the discipline. In that effort, he analyzed and critiqued contemporary views, synthesizing some into an emerging broad view of psychology. In his critiques, he had the ability to go directly to the heart of the issue under discussion, exposing the fallacies and methodological flaws in the thinking of others. This circumstance of Vygotsky's thinking was first evident in his presentation on research methods at the 1924 Second All-Russian Congress of Psychoneurology. At that time, studying the mind rather than the material world was suspect in the eyes of Lenin. However, Vygotsky (1926/1997j, p. 44) pointed out that psychology had only three choices: Researchers had to deny the very existence of the mind, accept the biological absurdity that the mind is completely unnecessary in the behavioral system, or find a way to research it.

Then, in reviewing Gestalt theory, Vygotsky noted that these theorists claimed their explanation of learning (reorganization of one's perception) was universal. However, Vygotsky pointed out that any principle that applied equally to chickens and mathematicians could not explain development. Also, as noted in Chapter 5, those psychologists who maintained that speech is independent of thinking throughout life were in error. To support that view, Vygotsky noted, meant that speech could never influence thinking, which is not true. Similarly, Stern, instead of investigating the ways in which children develop speech, maintained that children discover the names of objects. However, Vygotsky pointed out that children lack the intellectual capability to discover the symbolic role of words. They begin to use words when designating objects because other family members do.

Vygotsky's analyses sometimes upended the assumptions and theories of others. Most notable was Piaget's views of speech. In his view, the infant was self-absorbed, was unaware of an external reality, and only became socialized into an adult world at about the age of 7. Not so, according to Vygotsky. The infant from birth is a social being with a need to communicate with others. Also, so-called egocentric speech becomes a tool to assist the child in solving concrete problems, and it is an example of the child beginning to gain control over his thinking.

Disagreements among psychologists, anthropologists, and others sometimes precipitated a resolution by Vygotsky. For example, some supported the view that the processes of thinking were universal across cultures, and others maintained that levels of thinking in primitive and advanced cultures varied. Vygotsky's resolution of this issue stated that the primitive or elementary psychological functions, which are biological in origin, are universal. In contrast, the nature of higher psychological functions, which are the result of cultural development, vary across societies.

SUGGESTIONS FOR PSYCHOLOGY AND EDUCATIONAL PSYCHOLOGY

At the time that Vygotsky formally entered psychology, the discipline was quite young. The physical sciences were almost 400 years old, but barely 50 years had passed since Wilhelm Wundt and Franz Brentano had written their texts on their views of the new discipline. These events mark the beginning of the separation of psychology from philosophy. However, the new discipline had yet to develop an identity. Psychology at that time was both chaotic and underdeveloped, yet the intellectual caliber of the profession was high (Rieber & Wollock, 1997, p. x). In the lengthy paper, "The Historical Meaning of the Crisis in Psychology," Vygotsky (1982–1984/1997i) addressed the issues threatening progress in the discipline as he saw them. Three of the topics he discussed are relevant for contemporary psychology, described by some as overdeveloped and chaotic (Rieber & Wollock, 1997, p. xi). One is his suggestions for psychological research (Vygotsky, 1960/1997h, 1982–1984/1997i). These suggestions were discussed in Chapter 2. The others are the life cycle of an idea and the issue of language.

The Life Cycle of New Ideas

The rationale for Vygotsky's (1982–1984/1997i, pp. 241–246) analysis of the development of important discoveries was twofold. First, such discoveries tend to become explanatory principles for psychological phenomena. Second, they also take psychology "beyond its proper boundaries" (p. 241).

An example of an important psychological discovery taken beyond its area is the conditional reflex. Initially identified in the physiological research of Ivan Pavlov, the conditional reflex was predicted by John Watson to be the key to controlling behavior in daily life. Watson (1924) proclaimed that, given a dozen healthy infants, he would be able to train any of them into any specialty he selected—"doctor, lawyer, artist, merchant-chief—regardless of his talents, penchants, tendencies, abilities, vocations, and race of his ancestors" (p. 82).

As illustrated in Table 9.1, any important discovery that becomes a general theoretical concept undergoes five stages in its development (Vygotsky, 1982–1984/1997i, pp. 241–246). First is a factual discovery of some significance. Next, the idea spreads to other areas, its link with the situation that brought it about is weakened, and it is changed somewhat. In the third stage, the idea becomes "a more or less abstractly formulated principle" (p. 242). It is altered by new material, and it also alters the discipline where it began.

The identification of the conditional reflex, as indicated in Table

TABLE 9.1. An Application of Vygotsky's Life Cycle of New Ideas to Early Behaviorism in American Psychology

Stage in the cycle	Early behaviorism
1. A factual discovery that alters the accepted conception of some area.	1. Ivan Pavlov identified the conditional reflex. A reflex, specifically salivation, was conditioned to respond to some neutral stimulus, such as footsteps. (Vladimir Bekheterev also conditioned the finger retractions reflex, which responds to pain, to a flash of light, and other events.)
2. The influence of the discovery spreads to adjacent areas and, in the process, becomes more abstract. The idea is stretched to material that is broader than the original research focus.	2. The idea of the conditional reflex becomes classical conditioning in American psychology. John Watson (1916) extended the application from salivary and motor reflexes to the area of emotions that are not reflexes. He conditioned a toddler's fear reaction to the appearance of a white rat. He also maintained that conditioning accounted for the adult's complex repertory of emotional reactions.
3. The idea takes control of much of the discipline where it began. It changes as it incorporates new material and changes the areas it enters. The outcome for the idea is linked to the outcome of the discipline it represents.	3. Behaviorism, initiated by classical conditioning, became the dominant movement in American psychology (Boring, 1950). Researchers attempted to discover the factors that caused a particular stimulus (condition or event) to trigger complex response. This research is referred to as stimulus–response (S-R) theory.
4. The idea separates from the basic concept and links psychology with other disciplines. The idea may become part of a philosophical system and may be constructed as "a universal principle or even as a whole world view" (Vygotsky, 1982–1984/1997i, p. 242).	4. John Watson (1924) believed that the focus on behavior initiated by classical conditioning would place psychology in the ranks of the true sciences, such as zoology. He also believed that any healthy infant could be trained into any specialty regardless of individual characteristics.
5. The idea now enters a major struggle for its existence. The typical outcome at this stage is rejection as a world view. It may wither away or become a part of another world view. It no longer exists as an idea that would revolutionize science.	5. Both the classical model and the S-R position that identified cues or drive stimuli as behavioral triggers were unable to account for the establishment of complex behaviors such as reading. Classical conditioning became simply a special case of behaviorism in which the dominant paradigm is operant conditioning.

Note. Summarized from Vygotsky (1982–1984/1997i).

9.1, demonstrated that salivation, a physiological reaction to the sight or smell of meat powder, could be trained (conditioned) to respond to other events (stage 1). Watson then applied this concept to emotional reactions, which are not reflexes (stage 2). Then researchers who identified themselves as behaviorists began to apply the idea that a certain stimulus "triggers" a particular reaction to a new area: complex voluntary behaviors. They searched for the factors that would cause a particular stimulus to trigger complex responses, such as reading and singing. They were known as S-R theorists.

The fourth stage in the life of a new idea is one in which the conquest by the idea pushes it to continue developing. The conquest may be in the form of a project supported by one school of thought, the entire domain of psychological thought, or all disciplines (Vygotsky, 1982–1984/1997i, p. 242). It separates from the basic concept and links psychology with other disciplines, such as biology and physics. For example, in addition to assisting psychology to become a "true" science, classical conditioning was forecast to have a major role in daily life. Watson (1924) predicted he would be able to train any healthy infant into any vocation he chose.

The fifth stage in the life of a new idea is the most dangerous (Vygotsky, 1982–1984/1997i). The original discovery has "inflated into a world view like a frog that has swollen to the size of an ox," and it could easily "burst like a soap bubble" (p. 242). Separated from the facts that led to the idea and generalized as far as possible, the idea reveals its true face and the social tendencies that led to it (p. 243).

Typically, in this stage, the idea "is forced to go through its development backwards" (p. 243). It is accepted as a new discovery but no longer is treated as a world view. Although it may "participate in the general, open struggle of ideas . . . as a small item in an enormous sum, it vanishes like a drop of rain in the ocean, and ceases to exist independently" (p. 243).

Examples discussed briefly by Vygotsky included psychoanalysis, the conditional reflex, and Gestalt psychology. His comments also reveal the biting nature of some of his critiques. In psychoanalysis, "sexuality became a metaphysical principle . . . and psychoanalysis became a world view" (p. 245). In other words, "communism, the church, and Dostoyevsky's creative work . . . myth and Leonardo de Vinci's inventions— it is all disguised and masked sex and sexuality" (p. 245).

Similarly, the conditional reflex, which began in Pavlov's salivation studies of dogs, was soon used in all domains of psychology. In an earlier essay, Vygotsky (1925/1997b) cautioned that "before drawing very grand and crucial conclusions," psychologists should be aware that the research on reflexes was just beginning (p. 67). Then, in his discussion of the crisis in psychology, Vygotsky (1982–1984/1997i) noted that, "just as with psychoanalysis, it turned out that everything in the world is a reflex. Anna Karenina [a tragic heroine in Russian literature] and klepto-mania, the class struggle and a landscape, language and dream are all re-flexes" (p. 245).

Gestalt psychology also had traversed the same path. It began with concrete investigations into the processes of perception. Then, not only did it conquer animal psychology, but the thinking processes of apes turn out to be a Gestalt process (p. 245). Subsequently, after becoming a world view, the Gestalt was discovered in physics, chemistry, physiology, and biology: It "appeared to be the basis of the world. When God cre-ated the world he said: let there be Gestalt - and there was Gestalt every-where" (p. 245).

The major difficulty with making a principle broader and more em-bracing is that it is then easier to stretch it to cover almost any fact (Vygotsky, 1925/1997b, p. 64). The problem is that "the extension and content of a concept are always inversely proportional" (p. 64). Further, "because the extension of universal principles rushes to infinity, their psychological content decreases to zero with the same speed" (p. 64).

Nevertheless, each of the ideas in the theories discussed by Vygotsky "is extremely rich, full of meaning and sense, full of value and fruitful in its own place" (Vygotsky, 1982–1984/1997i, p. 246). The problem, as indicated, is in their elevation to the position of universal laws. There they are "equal to each other, like round and empty zeros" (p. 246). The perceptual structure of Gestalt psychology is the reflex reaction of Pav-lov and is accounted for by the sexuality of Freud. The importance of the tendency to elevate each new idea to the status of a universal law is that it indicated the need in psychology for general explanatory princi-ples. In the absence of such principles, psychology "grabs for any idea, albeit an unreliable one" (p. 246).

Vygotsky's proposed solution to this problem was that the discipline must develop a general psychology. In his view, this general psychology would describe broad concepts and essential philosophical principles, whereas the special disciplines address specific issues. The relationship between a general psychology and the special disciplines would be anal-ogous to that between algebra and arithmetic. Specifically, each arith-metical operation is a special case of some algebraic formula (p. 256).

Vygotsky envisioned his proposed general psychology as investigat-ing the facts associated with theories being debated by the specific subdisciplines. Such an investigation ultimately establishes "objective laws and facts" (p. 257). In this way, the general psychology would func-tion as a type of clearinghouse for new facts in the discipline.

Needless to say, the general psychology described by Vygotsky

(1982–1984/1997i) has yet to be developed. Thus, new ideas have continued to emerge and undergo the life cycle identified by Vygotsky. An example is the structural model of information processing introduced by Donald Broadbent (1958). Using the computer as a metaphor, it portrays the individual's processing of physical signals from the environment through a series of bins or boxes to long-term memory. It is an example of the influence of the input–processing–output nature of the computer on both the formulations of cognitive psychology and research and practice in educational psychology.

The Issue of Language

As stated in Chapter 2, Vygotsky (1982–1984/1997i) did not agree with the view that the development of science consisted primarily of the registration of facts. Instead, science consists of natural material that (a) has been selected according to a particular feature and (b) is framed in a concept. Identifying a fact with a word (concept) is a step toward understanding that fact. The reason is that the name places the fact into a group of events that has been studied empirically (p. 249). An example in psychology is the conditional reflex. This term refers to a reaction that (a) is automatically triggered by a particular stimulus and (b) has been trained to respond to a previously neutral stimulus.

The importance of concepts is that they are tools of thinking, and the state of a science can be determined by examining the language used to characterize its operations. For example, physics, chemistry, and mathematics have highly developed and exact languages.

In contrast, the language of psychology is "terminologically insufficient" (p. 281). In the "dictionary" of psychology, Vygotsky (1982–1984/1997i) identified three different kinds of words. They are everyday words and philosophical language, which are vague and ambiguous, and terms taken from natural science. The problem with appropriating natural science terms is that a scientific term then represents a nonscientific concept. Examples are intensity and excitation (p. 281). A related problem is the indeterminate use of terms. For example, according to Vygotsky (1982–1984/1997i), Edward Thorndike applied the term *reaction* to such phenomena as temper, dexterity, and action (p. 283).

Vygotsky's concern with the language used in psychology was that "the troubled condition of the language reflects a troubled condition of the science" (p. 282). An example is the various terms applied to the relationship between the mind and the body. Included are dualism and parallelism (mind and body are two separate developments), monism (the development of mind and body are two sides of a broad developmental process), and identity (the development of mind and body cannot be separated). The contradictory terminology reflects problems with the theory: "What is true of the word is true of the theory" (p. 291).

The problem of weaknesses in terminology identified by Vygotsky also exists in contemporary psychology and educational psychology. The current problem is that of several terms that each address a different nuance of a particular concept. An example in the area of motivation is the various terms that address a student's academic goal orientation. Included are learning, mastery, task-focused, ego-involved, performance-approach, and performance-avoid goals as well as work avoidance and failure avoidance. Similarly, aspects of personal belief in oneself are variously labeled self-confidence, self-concept, self-efficacy, and self-esteem. In the area of cognition, for example, the terms for the types of memory/information storage include short-term store, episodic, semantic, working and long-term memory, schema, verbal networks (base strings, propositions, condition–action pairs), visual codes, the state concept (active, inactive), and connectionist networks.

The proliferation of terms in these and other areas of psychology indicates the need for unambiguous concepts that can serve as tools for thinking in the development of the discipline. However, accomplishing this task, according to Vygotsky (1982–1984/1997i, p. 291), requires that word choice become part of the research process. Word choice and experiment must be worked out simultaneously (p. 291). In this way, the word "occupies the territory that was conquered by the investigation" (p. 291) and is consistent with the general requirements of objectivity.

SOME IMPLICATIONS FOR SOCIETY

Vygotsky's discussions of cultural signs and symbols included differences in cognitive development across cultures (Vygotsky, 1929; Vygotsky & Luria, 1930/1993). Cultural diversity in symbols leads to differences in the level of mental functions. Implicit in his discussions is that societies would continue to progress in terms of creating signs and symbols that promote abstract, logical thinking. New inventions and new technologies are accompanied by enriched language and mathematical systems that address those developments. He did not envision a period in which regression to earlier forms of thinking might occur in a society.

He also viewed societies as constructed in such a way that the knowledgeable adult, the representation of the ideal form of cognitive behavior to be attained, is the major influence on the emerging generation. Examination of the emergence of new symbol systems, changing adult roles, and the management of new technologies in contemporary society raises questions about future cognitive development.

The Changing Form of Cultural Signs

Vygotsky (1960/1997a, 1960/1997d, 1960/1997h, l960/1997k, 1982–1984/1998a) identified the symbol systems of a culture as the means whereby members of the culture learn to think and grow in their cognitive development. Included are language, mathematical systems, and other symbols linked to thinking. He also maintained that the basic unit of communication and thinking is the same: the word (Vygotsky, 1934/1987).

However, the late 20th and early 21st centuries have seen the rapid growth of another form of cultural communication: the visual image. In the form of television (available 24 hours a day), film, and computer games, the visual image is becoming both the prevalent form of entertainment and a primary means whereby individuals obtain information about the world. Newspaper readership has declined and cities that formerly produced morning and evening editions of their newspapers have discontinued the later edition. Paradoxically, television is becoming the common currency of the culture as a source of information while, through its various messages, it serves as a means of dividing the viewers.

The visual image also has found a home in the educational setting. The term *visual literacy* is referred to as a skill that is variously described as the interpretation and critique of images, the ability to understand images, and the ability to produce images and use them to express oneself. One rationale for the use of visual images in instruction is that children learn to read pictures before they learn to read words. Moreover, a rationale for the use of graphic books in the classroom (translation: comic books) is that children are more actively involved in the reading process! Also, recently, the term *visual rhetoric* has emerged to reflect a focus on images as rational expressions of cultural meanings.

These views of images as language have profound implications for society. From Vygotsky's perspective, images reflect concrete graphic thinking, in which perception and attention are inextricably linked. Moreover, the processing of ongoing visual images, in which the sequence and pace are controlled by another, does not enhance reflection. In addition, the hallmarks of thinking are self-organized attention, categorical perception, conceptual thinking, and logical memory, and their development is not facilitated by the processing of concrete images. In Vygotsky's view, the teacher's responsibility is to move the student from concrete, graphic memory to verbal memory and then to logical memory. Although graphic books may be holding students' attention, the issue for Vygotsky is for the student to develop the internal mechanisms to direct and control his or her attention.

The major question for the future is the effects on a culture when the predominant symbols for communication and information are visual images. The recognition of co-occurring images, from Vygotsky's perspective, is the definition of signalization. It is an elementary cognitive process in which judgment is based on the recall of similar images and their observed consequences. In other words, the question for society is to examine the levels of thinking that are occurring as the symbol system of the culture shifts from the printed word to visual images.

Changing Roles

Vygotsky (1935/1994) identified the environment as the source of the child's cognitive development. The social situation of development, the personal contact between child and adult at a particular point in time, initiates the child's cognitive development in each period of development (Vygotsky, 1982–1984/1998c).

In these relationships, the adult is the "ideal form" of cognitive behavior. Through interactions with the child, the adult initiates and guides the process of cognitive development. This process begins in the particular relationship between the infant and the caregiver and continues in the school setting in the relationship between teacher and student.

In identifying the environment as the source of development, Vygotsky (1935/1994) commented on the uniqueness of the young child's situation. Unlike the development of primitive humans, the child has before her the end result of the developmental process (pp. 347–348). Further, although the child cannot make use of many aspects of the adult's thinking, this situation changes as she grows and develops.

However, the social environment, the source of the child's cognition, can change in unexpected ways. Such changes also can alter the child–environment relationship. Vygotsky (1935/1994) himself expressed concern about differences in the environment of the child who goes to nursery school and the one who remains at home.

Moreover, since Vygotsky developed his theory, the social environment in Western societies has changed even more. The extended family (parents, children, and grandparents) under one roof is a rarity. Thus, the number of adults who can interact with the child on a one-to-one basis has decreased.

Another major change is the emergence of the teenage years as a distinct developmental period in which peer values and customs can have a major influence on the individual. Particular music, certain movies, and product marketing are targeted toward teenagers. Many members of this group, either as a result of part-time employment or parental generosity, also have disposable income that they control.

In addition, personal computers, the Internet, and related technologies did not exist when the teenager's parents entered the world of work. New technologies and accompanying social changes have marginalized the adult as a primary source of contact and information.

This situation is in sharp contrast to adolescence as Vygotsky described it. The conditions for developing rational, mature levels of logical thinking that lead to self-reflecting individuals are not dominant in the present culture. In other words, a subculture, as yet somewhat amorphous and poorly defined, is developing in the adolescent years. To the extent that the developing individual's behaviors are interdependent with the context of his or her social environment, the conditions for developing the higher mental functions are absent. Although many adolescents pursue a postsecondary education, a question is whether those years compensate for the earlier years in developing mature logical thinking.

Managing New Technologies

Vygotsky (1930–1931/1997c) identified three laws essential for the development of higher mental functions. They are the use of external signs and symbols in the culture to alter one's thinking, the transformation involved from a reliance on external stimuli to internal stimuli, and one-on-one interactions with an adult who serves as the source of ways of thinking. He also identified two prerequisites to the development of those higher functions: conscious awareness of one's thinking and some capability to control those processes.

In the development of abstract thinking, Vygotsky described a major role for writing. The consciousness of words and sentences that it requires, as well as learning to translate oral speech into written words that communicate ideas, serves to identify writing as a technology.

Evaluation of new technologies for the capability to enhance thinking must be done in terms of the ways that they relate to the requirements just mentioned and the ways that they require new thinking by the user. For example, a key development of early childhood is that the young child begins to separate attention from perception (Vygotsky, 1982–1984/1998b). This development is essential to the development of self-organized attention, which itself is essential for the development of the other higher functions (Vygotsky, 1982–1984/1997e). Extensive television watching by young children is discouraged because it is detrimental to the key separation of these two processes.

Vygotsky also differentiated between symbol use for communication and symbol use for thinking. Therefore, evaluation of computer technologies for classroom use must address the question of the thinking processes that the technology requires and fosters. For example, simulations that illustrate chemical or physical processes can develop student responses to particular elements of situations that are difficult to grasp. However, the simulation only can serve as the starting point for developing conceptual thinking about those processes. In the simulation, the student is responding to concrete graphic stimuli, which the classroom teacher can use as a foundation for further instruction.

One advantage stated for computer use is the contribution to student research. Material on a vast array of topics can be accessed, compiled, and summarized. This use, however, can foster superficial familiarity with the particular topic. Also, some information on the Internet is inaccurate, which is not surprising, given the lack of review of information. Also required for thinking are developing conceptual thinking and logical memory, both of which require in-depth examination and study of particular topics. To the extent that the result of search methods is not subjected to this type of analysis, those higher functions are not developed.

Summary

Beginning with the premise that rational thinking is the ultimate human development, Vygotsky's thinking encompassed a range of topics that have the potential to inform contemporary psychology. Paramount among them is the qualitative nature of the development of thinking and the role of culture in that process.

Topics that Vygotsky studied in detail are the development of speech, stages in the development of higher mental functions or capabilities, the primacy of language, the pivotal role of concept development in the development of cognition, the important relationship between structure and content in thinking, and the age-level periods in the development of higher psychological functions. He analyzed these developments through the prism of mastery of one's own thinking and the personal–environmental interaction captured in the social situation of development. Implications for society include evaluating the changing forms of symbols, the changing role of adults, and issues in managing new technologies.

In general, the contributions of Vygotsky's work to the present may be expressed in the lines from his favorite poet, Tyntchev (Robbins, 1999, p. xi).

> Not everything that flowered must wilt,
> Not everything that was must pass.

REFERENCES

Boring, E. G. (1950). *A history of experimental psychology* (2nd ed.). New York: Appleton-Century-Crofts.

Broadbent, D. (1958). *Perception and communication*. London: Pergamon.

Graham, L. R. (1987). *Science, philosophy and human behavior in the Soviet Union*. New York: Columbia University Press.

Minick, N. (1987). The development of Vygotsky's thought: An introduction. In R. W. Rieber (Ed.), *Collected works of L. S. Vygotsky: Vol. 1. Problems of general psychology* (pp. 17–36). New York: Plenum.

Rieber, R. W.(Ed.). (1998). Notes to the Russian edition. In *Collected works of L. W. Vygotsky: Vol. 5. Child psychology* (pp. 319–353). New York: Plenum.

Rieber, R. W., & Wollock, J. (1997). Prologue. In R. W. Rieber & J. Wollock (Eds.), *Collected works of L. W. Vygotsky: Vol. 3. Problems of the theory and history of psychology* (pp. vii–xiii). New York: Plenum.

Robbins, D. (1999). Prologue In R. W. Rieber (Ed.), *Collected works of L. S. Vygotsky: Vol. 6. Child psychology* (pp. v–xii). New York: Plenum.

Vygotsky, L. S. (1929). The problem of the cultural development of the child. *Journal of Genetic Psychology, 36*, 415–434.

Vygotsky, L. S. (1987). The problem and the method of investigation. In R. W. Rieber & A. S. Carton (Eds.), *Collected works of L. S. Vygotsky: Vol. 1. Problems of general psychology* (pp. 43–51). New York: Plenum. (Original work published 1934)

Vygotsky, L. S. (1994). The problem of the environment. In R. van der Veer & J. Valsiner (Eds.), *The Vygotsky reader* (pp. 338–354). Cambridge, MA: Blackwell. (Original work published 1935)

Vygotsky, L. S. (1997a). Analysis of higher mental functions. In R. W. Rieber (Ed.), *Collected works of L. S. Vygotsky: Vol. 4. The history of the development of higher mental functions* (pp. 65–82). New York: Plenum. (Original work published 1960)

Vygotsky, L. S. (1997b). Consciousness as a problem for the psychology of behavior. In R. W. Rieber & J. Wollock (Eds.), *Collected works of L. S. Vygotsky: Vol. 3. Problems of the theory and history of psychology* (pp. 63–79). New York: Plenum. (Original work published 1925)

Vygotsky, L. S. (1997c). Dynamics and structure of the adolescent's personality. In R. W. Rieber (Ed.), *Collected works of L. S. Vygotsky: Vol. 5. Child psychology* (pp. 167–184). New York: Plenum. (Original work published 1930–1931)

Vygotsky, L. S. (1997d). Genesis of higher mental functions. In R. W. Rieber (Ed.), *Collected works of L. S. Vygotsky: Vol. 4. The history of the development of higher mental functions* (pp. 97–119). New York: Plenum. (Original work published 1960)

Vygotsky, L. S. (1997e). Mastering attention. In R. W. Rieber (Ed.), *Collected works of L. S. Vygotsky: Vol. 4. The history of the development of higher mental functions* (pp. 153–177). New York: Plenum. (Original work published 1982–1984)

Vygotsky, L. S. (1997f). Mind, consciousness, the unconscious. In R. W. Rieber & J. Wollock (Eds.), *Collected works of L. S. Vygotsky: Vol. 3. Problems of the theory and history of psychology* (pp. 109–121). New York: Plenum. (Original work published 1930)

Vygotsky, L. S. (1997g). On psychological systems. In R. W. Rieber & J. Wollock (Eds.), *Collected works of L. S. Vygotsky: Vol. 3. Problems of the theory and history of psychology* (pp. 91–107). New York: Plenum. (Original work published 1982–1984)

Vygotsky, L. S. (1997h). Research method. In R. W. Rieber (Ed.), *Collected works of L. S. Vygotsky: Vol. 4. The history of the development of higher mental functions* (pp. 27–63). New York: Plenum. (Original work published 1960)

Vygotsky, L. S. (1997i). The historical meaning of the crisis in psychology. In R. W. Rieber & J. Wollock (Eds.), *Collected works of L. S. Vygotsky: Vol. 3. Problems of the theory and history of psychology* (pp. 233–343). New York: Plenum. (Original work published 1982–1984)

Vygotsky, L. S. (1997j). The methods of reflexological and psychological investigation. In R. W. Rieber & J. Wollock (Eds.), *Collected works of L. S. Vygotsky: Vol. 3. Problems of the theory and history of psychology* (pp. 35–49). New York: Plenum. (Original work published 1926)

Vygotsky, L. S. (1997k). The problem of the development of the higher psychological functions. In R. W. Rieber (Ed.), *Collected works of L. S. Vygotsky: Vol. 4. The history of the development of higher mental functions* (pp. 1–26). New York: Plenum. (Original work published 1960)

Vygotsky, L. S. (1998a). Development of higher mental functions during the transitional age. In R. W. Rieber (Ed.), *Collected works of L. S. Vygotsky: Vol. 5. Child psychology* (pp. 83–149). New York: Plenum. (Original work published 1982–1984)

Vygotsky, L. S. (1998b). Early childhood. In R. W. Rieber (Ed.), *Collected works of L. S. Vygotsky: Vol. 5. Child psychology* (pp. 261–281). New York: Plenum. (Original work published 1982–1984)

Vygotsky, L. S. (1998c). The problem of age. In R. W. Rieber (Ed.), *Collected works of L. S. Vygotsky: Vol. 5. Child psychology* (pp. 187–205). New York: Plenum. (Original work published 1982–1984)

Vygotsky, L. S., & Luria, A. R. (1993). *Studies in the history of behavior: Ape, primitive, and child.* (Original work published 1930)

Watson, J. B. (1916). The place of the conditioned reflex in psychology. *Psychological Review, 23*, 89–108.

Watson, J. B. (1924). *Behaviorism.* New York: Norton.

Yaroshevsky, M. G. (1999). Epilogue. In R. W. Rieber (Ed.) *Collected works of L. S. Vygotsky: Vol. 6. Scientific legacy* (pp. 245–266). New York: Plenum. (Original work published 1982–1984)

Glossary

Conditional–genetic analysis. The process of determining the hidden real connections that represent the essential nature of a process. It differs from both descriptions of external characteristics and analyses that break down a process or phenomenon into its component parts (Vygotsky, 1960/1997a, pp. 67–70).

Cultural development. Mastering methods of behavior that are based on the use of signs as a means to accomplish a particular psychological operation (Vygotsky, 1929).

Development of higher psychological functions. "A complex combination of elementary functions, in a perfecting of forms and methods of thinking, [and] the development of new methods of thinking based mainly on speech or some other system of signs" (Vygotsky, 1930–1931/1998b, p. 168).

Dynamics of development. All of the laws that govern the appearance, changes, and connections of the new structure in each period of development (Vygotsky, 1982–1984/1998d).

Education. "The artificial development of the child; the artificial mastery of the natural processes of development" (Vygotsky, 1982–1984/1997e, p. 88). In addition to influencing certain processes of development, education restructures cognitive functions.

Egocentric speech. The child's speech that is for himself and fulfills a cognitive function very different from the function of communicative speech (Vygotsky, 1930–1931/1998b, p. 170; Vygotsky, 1934/1987c, p. 74).

Genetic (developmental) analysis. Begins with the initial point of a psychological function and re-establishes all processes of development.

Imitation. Mental activity that the child can do with direction, cooperation, or the aid of leading questions (Vygotsky, 1982–1984/1998d).

Instrumental act. Any situation that includes the simultaneous presence of both an object stimulus and a means stimulus (psychological tool). The components are (a) the problem to be solved, (b) one's mental processes directed toward solving the problem, and (c) the psychological tool that dictates the coordination and course of the mental processes (Vygotsky, 1982–1984/1997e).

Instrumental method. "A means of investigating behavior and its development that discloses the psychological tools in behavior and the structure of the instrumental acts created by them" (Vygotsky, 1982–1984/1997e, p. 88). The instrumental method may utilize any methodology, such as experiment or observation. It can be successfully applied in social–historical and ethnic psychology, the area of higher forms of memory, attention, verbal or mathematical thinking, and so on and child and educational psychology (p. 88).

Intellectualization of mental functions. The time when the learner begins to relate rationally to his or her own thinking (Vygotsky, 1934/1987d, p. 324).

Law of concept equivalence. Any concept can be described in terms of other concepts. Also, these interrelationships are unique for the child at each level of his or her development of concepts (syncretic, complexes, and potential concepts; Vygotsky, 1934/1987b).

Law of revolution. The process of the transition of a cognitive function or capability from an external operation to an internal operation where it primarily is governed by internal symbols and concepts (Vygotsky, 1930–1931/1998a, p. 104; Vygotsky, 1930–1931/1998b, p. 170; Vygotsky, 1982–1984/1999, pp. 53–55).

Measure of generality. The positioning of a child's view of a concept in terms of (a) the nature of the child's thinking about it (graphic to abstract) and (b) the relationship of the concept to the child's other concepts (subordinate, superordinate, or parallel; Vygotsky, 1934/1987b).

"Naïve" psychology. A stage in the development of sign use and speech. In sign use, the child attempts to use auxiliary stimuli to manage memory and attention but is unsuccessful. In speech, the child is able to use words in communication but is unaware of the internal (symbolic) structure (Vygotsky, 1929; Vygotsky & Luria, 1994).

Neoformation. The mental and social changes occurring during a particular age period that reconstruct the consciousness of the child (Vygotsky, 1982–1984/1998d, p. 190).

Participation. A characteristic of the child's complexive thinking in which the child places objects in two or more concepts (Vygotsky, 1934/1987a).

Personality. A social concept; arises as a result of cultural development; encompasses the unity of behavior that the child or adolescent has mastered (Vygotsky, 1982–1984/1997b). Personality is constructed on the fact that the child applies to himself the devices of adaptation that he applies with respect to others.

Pseudoconcept. The capability of matching concept examples to a model on concrete, observable characteristics (Vygotsky, 1931/1994, 1934/1987a).

Psychological system. Organization of the developing higher mental functions in which different functions are dominant at different ages (Vygotsky, 1982–1984/1997c).

Psychological tool. Any sign or symbol that is used to master one's thinking (Vygotsky, 1960/1997d, p. 60).

Rearmament. The discarding of one means stimulus for managing one's thinking for another that is more effective and efficient (Vygotsky, 1960/1997d; Vygotsky & Luria, 1930/1993).

Sign. Every conditioned stimulus, artificially created by humans, that functions as a means of mastering behavior (Vygotsky, 1960/1997d, p. 54).

Signalization. The recognition of co-occurring stimuli in the environment, a characteristic of the primitive or elementary mental functions (Vygotsky, 1960/1997d, p. 55).

Signification. The process of creating and using artificial signs to master one's thinking (Vygotsky, 1960/1997d, p. 55).

Social situation of development. The relation between the child and social reality at a particular point in time (Vygotsky, 1982–1984/1998d). Reconstructions of the child's social situation of development are the changes that signify critical stages of development.

Syncretism. A combination or coalescence of often mutually opposed beliefs, principles, or practices into a new conglomerate whole typically marked by internal inconsistencies (Vygotsky, 1934/1987a, p. 135).

Voluntary action. "Manifest where we find the mastering of one's own behavior with the assistance of symbolic stimuli" (Vygotsky & Luria, 1994, p. 135).

World view. That which characterizes a person's behavior as a whole; the child's method of relating to the world (Vygotsky, 1982–1984/1997b).

Zone of proximal development (ZPD). A ZPD is "the domain of transitions that are accessible by the child" (Vygotsky, 1934/1987b, p. 211); "the area of immature, but maturing processes" (1982–1984/1998d, p. 202).

REFERENCES

Vygotsky, L. S. (1929). The problem of the cultural development of the child. *Journal of Genetic Psychology, 36*, 415–434.

Vygotsky, L. S. (1987a). An experimental study of concept development. In R. W. Rieber & A. S. Carton (Eds.), *Collected works of L. S. Vygotsky: Vol. 1. Problems of general psychology* (pp. 121–166). New York: Plenum. (Original work published 1934)

Vygotsky, L. S. (1987b). The development of scientific concepts in childhood. In R. W. Rieber & A. S. Carton (Eds.), *Collected works of L. S. Vygotsky: Vol. 1. Problems of general psychology* (pp. 167–241). New York: Plenum. (Original work published 1934)

Vygotsky, L. S. (1987c). The problem of speech and thinking in Piaget's theory. In R. W. Rieber & A. S. Carton (Eds.), *Collected works of L. S. Vygotsky: Vol. 1. Problems of general psychology* (pp. 53–91). New York: Plenum. (Original work published 1934)

Vygotsky, L. S. (1987d). Thinking and its development in childhood. In R. W. Rieber & A. S. Carton (Eds.), *Collected works of L. S. Vygotsky: Vol. 1. Problems of general psychology* (pp. 311–324). New York: Plenum. (Original work published 1934)

Vygotsky, L. S. (1994). The development of thinking and concept formation in adolescence. In R. van der Veer & J. Valsiner (Eds.), *The Vygotsky reader* (pp. 185–265). Cambridge, MA: Blackwell. (Original work published 1931)

Vygotsky, L. S. (1997a). Analysis of higher mental functions. In R. W. Rieber (Ed.), *Collected works of L. S. Vygotsky: Vol. 4. The history of the development of higher mental functions* (pp. 65–82). New York: Plenum. (Original work published 1960)

Vygotsky, L. S. (1997b). Conclusion; further research; development of personality and world view in the child. In R. Rieber (Ed.), *Collected works of L. S. Vygotsky: Vol. 4. The history of the development of higher mental functions* (pp. 241–251). New York: Plenum. (Original work published in 1982–1984)

Vygotsky, L. S. (1997c). On psychological systems. In R. W. Rieber & J. Wollock (Eds.), *Collected works of L. S. Vygotsky: Vol. 3. Problems of the theory and history of psychology* (pp. 91–107). (Original work published 1982–1984)

Vygotsky, L. S. (1997d). Research method. In R. W. Rieber (Ed.), *Collected works of L. S. Vygotsky: Vol. 4. The history of the development of higher mental functions* (pp. 27–63). New York: Plenum. (Original work published 1960)

Vygotsky, L. S. (1997e). The instrumental method in psychology. In R. W. Rieber & J. Wollock (Eds.), *Collected works of L. S. Vygotsky: Vol. 3. Problems of the theory and history of psychology* (pp. 85–89). New York: Plenum. (Original work published 1982–1984)

Vygotsky, L. S. (1998a). Development of the higher mental functions during the transitional age. In R. W. Rieber (Ed.), *Collected works of L. S. Vygotsky: Vol. 5. Child psychology* (pp. 83–149). New York: Plenum. (Original work published 1930–1931)

Vygotsky, L. S. (1998b). Dynamics and structure of the adolescent's personality. In R. W. Rieber (Ed.), *Collected works of L. S. Vygotsky: Vol. 5. Child psychology* (pp. 167–184). New York: Plenum. (Original work published 1930–1931)

Vygotsky, L. S. (1998c). Early childhood. In R. W. Rieber (Ed.), *Collected works of L. S. Vygotsky: Vol. 5. Child psychology* (pp. 261–281). New York: Plenum. (Original work published 1982–1984)

Vygotsky, L. S. (1998d). The problem of age. In R. W. Rieber (Ed.), *Collected works of L. S.*

Vygotsky: Vol. 5. Child psychology (pp. 184–205). New York: Plenum. (Original work published 1982–1984)

Vygotsky, L. S. (1999). Analysis of sign operations of the child. In R. W. Rieber (Ed.), *Scientific legacy* (pp. 45–56). New York: Plenum. (Original work published 1982–1984)

Vygotsky, L. S., & Luria, A. R. (1993). *Studies in the history of behavior: Ape, primitive, and child*. Hillsdale, NJ: Erlbaum. (Original work published 1930)

Vygotsky, L. S., & Luria, A. R. (1994). Tool and symbol in child development. In R. van der Veer & J. Valsiner (Eds.), *The Vygotsky reader* (pp. 99–174). Cambridge, MA: Blackwell.

APPENDIX A

The Cross-Cultural Study

In the late 19th century, Wilhem Wundt proposed the idea that culture influences thinking. Wundt, often referred to as the father of psychology for his experiments on reaction times, advocated a "second psychology." The purpose would be to address higher cognitive capabilities such as deliberate remembering, reasoning, and language. He maintained that these capabilities are created by a community of individuals (Cole, 1996). Wundt used the term *Kultur* (culture) to designate art, science, and sophistication, the products of advanced civilizations (Jahoda, 1993). He also identified higher psychological processes as learning, thought, memory, volition, and so on (van der Veer & IJzendoorn, 1985, p. 2). However, this aspect of Wundt's work did not become well known at that time.

Anthropologists and sociologists who were Vygotsky's contemporaries proposed various relationships between culture and thinking, and Vygotsky was familiar with their work. Emile Durkheim, leader of the French sociological school, maintained that each society transmits a set of "collective representations," "clever instruments of thought," to each individual (van der Veer, 1991). Other views were as follows: Complex forms of memory originate in the concrete history of society (Janet); primitive people generalize information differently from those in technological societies (Rivers; Luria, 1979, p. 58); and human societies differ in the extent of their higher mental processes (Lévy-Bruhl; Vygotsky & Luria, 1930/1993).

Vygotsky and Luria (1930/1993), in their discussion of cultural development, argued for the existence of historical differences in cognitive development between primitive humans and contemporary societies (Knox, 1993). Their com-

227

parisons drew on the writings of Richard Thurnwald and, particularly, Lucien Lévy-Bruhl. Differences between the languages of primitive cultures, which were concrete and situation specific, and the language of European societies, which included generic categories and abstract concepts, seemed to be a factor in cognitive development.

Vygotsky and Luria were interested in obtaining experimental data that higher levels of cognition were culturally determined. Luria (1976) noted that psychology had barely begun to address the specific sociohistorical shaping of cognitive processes (p. 12). A problem for research on this issue was the difficulty in finding situations in which the restructuring of social systems had rapidly changed social life and, possibly, individuals' ways of thinking.

Such a situation presented itself with the implementation of Stalin's First Five-Year Plan. Under this plan, collective farms were replacing individual farms. Also, those identified as "Kulaks" (prosperous farmers who were, therefore, capitalists) were to be liquidated by deportation, imprisonment, or execution (Hosking, 2001).

In 1930, the remote Central Asian provinces of the USSR were experiencing the beginning of collectivization and other socioeconomic changes. Vygotsky and Luria chose the remote villages of Uzbekistan and a few villages in the mountainous areas of Kinghizia for their research (Luria, 1976, p. 14). Five groups participated in the study. They were (1) illiterate women, who, under Islam, had to remain within the *ichkari* (women's quarters); (2) peasants in remote villages, who continued to maintain individual farms; (3) women who attended short-term courses in teaching kindergarten, who had practically no literacy training; (4) collective farm workers involved in running the farms who had completed some short courses; and (5) female students in a teachers' school who had completed 2 to 3 years of study (p. 15). In other words, the research project included two isolated and illiterate groups and three groups with varying literacy levels and some exposure to technological change.

The hypothesis investigated in the study was whether "the structure of psychological processes changes as a function of history" (Luria, 1971, p. 160). Specifically, the researchers "hypothesized that people with a primarily graphic–functional reflection of reality would show a different mental process from people with a system of predominantly abstract, verbal, and logical approach to reality" (Luria, 1976, p. 18). The study, led by Alexander Luria, was conducted in two summer expeditions in 1931 and 1932. Vygotsky did not participate because his tuberculosis had worsened.

Areas of thinking addressed in the study were perception, generalization and abstraction, inferences from syllogisms, problem solving, imagination, and self-analysis and self-awareness. The research is an example of a qualitative fieldwork study. Sessions with the researchers began with long conversations with the subjects in natural settings. Many were conducted in the relaxed atmosphere of a tea house, where the villagers spent most of their free time (p. 16).

Others were conducted in the fields and mountain pastures in the evenings around the campfires.

Discussions frequently involved groups in which participants exchanged opinions, and two or three individuals might simultaneously solve a problem, each with a different answer (p. 16). The researchers gradually introduced the particular tasks, which were similar to riddles, a custom familiar to the subjects. The researchers followed up the answers with related questions, and an assistant recorded extensive notes. The study yielded some 600 protocols that indicated the subjects' thinking (van der Veer & Valsiner, 1991).

Tasks and questions for the six stages of the study are illustrated in Table A.1. The data indicated that responses to even simple perceptual tasks depended largely on the subjects' experience and their cultural milieu (Luria, 1976, p. 45). For example, when asked to name the colors in the skeins of wool, the collective farm workers and women students used categorical names (red, blue, yellow) with occasional descriptive designations, such as dark blue. In contrast, the ichkari women used only graphic names, such as fruit-drop iris and spoiled cotton (p. 26).

In addition, the collective farm workers and students usually arranged all the colors in seven or eight groups. In contrast, the ichkari women insisted that the task could not be done. Others arranged the skeins into groups of increasing brightness. For example, one series included pale pink, pale yellow, pale blue, and so on.

In the generalization and abstraction tasks, the uneducated subjects used concrete "situational" thinking; they did not interpret words as symbols of abstract classification categories (p. 54). For example, they indicated that no object could be removed from the group hammer–saw–log–hatchet. One rationale was that the saw, hammer, and hatchet all had to work together, but we still need wood, because we cannot build without it (p. 56). When told that another person had grouped the tools together, omitting the log, one subject responded, "Probably he's got a lot of firewood" (p. 56). In response to the travel problem (see Table A.1), some subjects guessed 1 minute and another suggested that if he knew the distance, he could answer (p. 123). Uneducated subjects also had difficulty with the other tasks. One elderly man from a remote mountain camp, given the question about what he would like to see in other cities or countries, responded quite poignantly:

> Probably there are interesting cities, as you say, but I don't know what's interesting about them. I know that I won't get to see them. . . . They took my horse away, and the road is long; I can't even imagine how I would get there. (p. 139)

Luria (1976) concluded from the study that the prevalent belief that the basic structures of perception, representation, reasoning, and so on remain

TABLE A.1. The Six Stages of the Cross-Cultural Study

Stage	Focus	Tasks and questions
1	Basic perceptual processes	Naming and classifying 27 colors in skeins of wool; naming and classifying geometric figures
2	Generalization and abstraction	Given four objects, which three are similar and can be placed in one group?
3	Deduction and inference	Completing syllogisms in which the premises were not always drawn from graphic–functional experience
4	Reasoning and discursive processes	"It takes 30 minutes to walk to village X, and it is five times faster on a bicycle.
	As applied to solving problems	How long will it take on a bicycle?" (Luria, 1976, p. 121)
5	Imagination	"Ask me three questions. What would you like to know?" (p. 137)
6	Self-analysis and self-consciousness	"What sort of person are you? What are your good qualities and shortcomings?" (p. 150)

Note. Summarized from Luria (1976).

unchanged in different cultural conditions was not supported (p. 164). Instead, major shifts occur in cognitive activity when cultural situations change. Cognitive activity goes beyond the purely concrete and situational to abstract categorical thought and drawing inferences using verbal and logical processes (p. 163).

REFERENCES

Cole, M. (1996). *Cultural psychology.* Cambridge, MA: Belknap Press.

Hosking, G. (2001). *Russia and the Russians: A history.* Cambridge, MA: Harvard University Press.

Jahoda, G. (1993). *Crossroads between culture and mind.* Cambridge, MA: Harvard University Press.

Knox, J. E. (1993). Translator's introduction. In L. S. Vygotsky & A. R. Luria (Eds.), *Studies on the history of behavior: Ape, primitive, and child* (pp. 1–35). Hillsdale, NJ: Erlbaum.

Luria, A. R. (1971). Towards the problem of the historical nature of psychological processes. *International Journal of Psychology, 6*(4), 259–272.

Luria, A. R. (1976). *Cognitive development: Its cultural and social foundations*. Cambridge, MA: Harvard University Press.

Luria, A. R. (1979). *The making of mind*. Cambridge, MA: Harvard University Press.

van der Veer, R. (1991). The anthropological underpinnings of Vygotsky's thinking. *Studies in Soviet Thought, 42,* 73–91.

van der Veer, R., & IJzendoorn, M. H. (1985). Vygotsky's theory of the higher psychological processes: Some criticisms. *Human Development, 28,* 1–9.

van der Veer, R., & Valsiner, J. (1991). *Understanding Vygotsky: A quest for synthesis*. Cambridge, MA: Blackwell.

Vygotsky, L. S., & Luria, A. R. (1993). *Studies in the history of behavior: Ape, primate, and child*. Hillsdale, NJ: Erlbaum. (Original work published 1930)

APPENDIX B

Shif's Research

Shozefina I. Shif, a student of Vygotsky, conducted a study of everyday and academic concepts in school children. The stated purpose was to test Vygotsky's hypothesis that everyday and academic concepts develop in different ways (Vygotsky, 1934/1987, p. 167). As indicated in Table B.1, Shif used social science concepts. Of interest is that 1 year before Shif's study, the Communist Party had warned educators not to introduce an antiproletarian world view in their training (van der Veer & Valsiner, 1991, p. 271). When Shif began her study in 1932, she tried to merge a theoretical goal with current societal demands. The concepts she selected were from a course on the history of the communist movement in the Soviet Union (p. 271).

As indicated in Table B.1, the children's knowledge of everyday and academic concepts was compared by their completion of sentences that ended in "because" (causal relationship) or "although" (implication). The use of these relationships replicated the question format used by Piaget in some of his studies on children's thinking.

The results reported by Shif indicated a higher percentage of sentence completions with academic concepts for second graders in both conditions (causal, implication) and for fourth graders with the sentences involving implication. However, van der Veer and Valsiner (1991) reported that Shif analyzed the correct answers to the questions that involved academic concepts. She found that many of the second-grade children simply repeated stereotypical phrases taught in class. These answers were low in semantic content (p. 272). In contrast, the

233

TABLE B.1. Summary of Shif's Research with Everyday and Academic Concepts

1. *Sample*: second graders (ages 8–9) and fourth graders (ages 11–12).

2. The academic concepts included "exploitation," "serfdom" (Vygotsky, 1934/ 1987, p. 181), "bourgeois," "capitalist," and "landowner" (p. 228).

3. Materials were sequences of pictures that illustrated a particular relationship involving either everyday or academic concepts (p. 167).

4. The experimenter told a brief story about each picture. The story concluded with an incomplete sentence that ended in either "because" or "although."

   Examples related to everyday life:
   " 'Kayla went to the movie theater because. . . . '
   'The train left the tracks because. . . . '
   'Olya reads poorly although. . . . ' " (p. 168).

5. *Results (percentage of correct completions)*:
   Second graders:

	"Although"	"Because"
Everyday concepts	59%	16.2%
Academic concepts	79%	21.3%

   Fourth graders:

	"Although"	"Because"
Everyday concepts	81.3%	65.5%
Academic concepts	81.8%	79.5%

6. *Analysis*: Results indicated a higher percentage of completions for academic concepts in three of the four comparisons. However, van der Veer and Valsiner (1991) reported that Shif's analysis of responses indicated that many second graders simply repeated stereotypical phrases learned in class. The answers were low in semantic content (p. 272). In contrast, the answers of the older children reflected understanding of causal and implicative relations.

Note. Summarized from Vygotsky (1934/1987).

answers of the fourth graders did not simply repeat material they had memorized; their answers reflected an understanding of causal and implicative relations.

Vygotsky also identified three limitations of the research. First, the research only addressed general features of the child's social science concepts, not the specific characteristics. Second, the research did not differentiate among different types of causal relationships; therefore, phases of development within the school age were not identified (p. 240). Third, additional research was needed to address the issue of the relationship between the basic features of everyday concepts and the development of conscious awareness and deliberate use in the emerging system of academic concepts (p. 240).

REFERENCES

van der Veer, R., & Valsiner, J. (1991). *Understanding Vygotsky: A quest for synthesis*. Cambridge, MA: Blackwell.

Vygotsky, L. S. (1987). The development of scientific concepts in childhood. In R. W. Rieber & A. S. Carton (Eds.), *Collected works of L. S. Vygotsky: Vol. 1. Problems of general psychology* (pp. 167–241). New York: Plenum. (Original work published 1934)

Index

Page numbers followed by an *f* or *t* indicate figures or tables.